# TEN-THIRTY-THREE

*Dead Man Running*
*Elizabeth: Behind Palace Doors*

# TEN-THIRTY THREE

## The Inside Story of Britain's Secret Killing Machine in Northern Ireland

### Nicholas Davies

MAINSTREAM
PUBLISHING

EDINBURGH AND LONDON

Reprinted, 2007

First published in Great Britain in 1999 by
MAINSTREAM PUBLISHING COMPANY (EDINBURGH) LTD
7 Albany Street
Edinburgh EH1 3UG

ISBN 9781840183436

A catalogue record for this book is available from the British Library

Typeset in Garamond.
Printed and bound in Great Britain by
Cox & Wyman Ltd. Reading

# Contents

# List of Abbreviations

| | |
|---|---|
| 14th Int | 14th Intelligence Company |
| ASU | active service unit |
| COPs | close observation platoons |
| DUP | Democratic Unionist Party |
| FRU | Force Research Unit |
| HMSU | headquarters mobile support unit |
| INLA | Irish National Liberation Army |
| IRA | Irish Republican Army |
| JIC | Joint Intelligence Committee |
| JIS | Joint Irish Section |
| MISR | Military Intelligence Source Report |
| MIU | Military Intelligence Unit |
| MRF | mobile reaction force |
| NICRA | Northern Ireland Civil Rights Association |
| QRF | quick reaction force |
| RPG | rocket-propelled grenade |
| SDLP | Social and Democratic Labour Party |
| TCG | Tasking Co-ordination Group |
| RUC | Royal Ulster Constabulary |
| UDA | Ulster Defence Association |
| UDR | Ulster Defence Regiment |
| UFF | Ulster Freedom Fighters |
| UPVF | Ulster Protestant Volunteer Force |
| UVF | Ulster Volunteer Force |
| UCBT | under-car booby-trap |
| E4A | the RUC's covert surveillance unit |

# *Author's Note*

This book has taken five years to research and write. I heard the basic outline from a member of the security services several years ago but needed to verify and substantiate the facts and the details surrounding each and every killing and attack which allegedly involved Brian Nelson. After much research and many meetings, three former members of the British security and intelligence services, with intimate knowledge of the Force Research Unit, agreed to talk to me of their experiences with that organisation. They did so only in the strictest confidence, after I had given assurances that their names would never be revealed. Even so, two of those officers have since been threatened with 'executive action' – the customary expression for murder.

After I had completed eight chapters, the British government discovered I was writing a book about the work of the Force Research Unit. They brought a High Court action against me, forbidding me from carrying out any further work on the manuscript. After ten months of legal argument, the High Court gave me permission to continue. Ten-Thirty-Three is the result.

*Nicholas Davies*
July 1999

## Chapter One

# The Conspiracy

The rain lashed down on the Belfast rush hour that September evening in 1987, making driving conditions hazardous and drenching the men and women making their way as quickly as possible across the rain-soaked streets to the partial protection of the bus shelters. The wind made it worse, whipping across sheets of gusting rain from the west, tearing at their raincoats, causing all to turn their backs, shielding their faces in a useless effort to avoid the deluge.

From the secure safety of his warm car the man laughed to himself as he sat in comfort, the heater clearing the windscreen inside while the wipers tried to keep pace with the water cascading down outside. He took surreptitious glee watching the women wrestling with their umbrellas, only to see them blown inside out by the force of the gale. Slouched in the driving seat, puffing on his cigarette, he inhaled the smoke deep into his lungs, but kept his eyes peeled for the 'Q' cars expected at any moment. Though he had the good fortune to be out of the bad weather, the man was far from happy, fucked off with having to sit and wait every time your man had to be escorted from the pick-up to the safe-house in the suburbs of Belfast.

'Fuckin' little waster,' he mumbled to himself with venom in his voice as he saw no sign of the two vehicles he was waiting to escort, 'fucking my life up for that cunt.'

He didn't mince his words, never did; and he knew that was probably one of the reasons he was still on escort duty, following 'touts' around Belfast after seven years with the Force. He never even got to drive the touts around the city, always working as tail-end Charlie, out of sight and out of mind. But he kept hoping that one day, just one day, something would go wrong and he would be there with his .38 ready to blast some fucker to pieces. He hoped that man would be a tout because he despised them, always had, always would, no matter which side they were on. The vague thought that one day he might use his .38 in vengeance brought a smile to his lips and he patted his shoulder holster. The only consolation in his desolate, lonely, boring life was the thought of gunning someone down and, of course, the monthly pay-cheque and the overtime that came with the job each and every moment he sat in his Ford on escort duty. To him, overtime meant drinking money and the occasional tart, because he never told the wife about those extra earnings. He believed his overtime was his reward for sticking the fucking awful job day in, day out. He loved a drink. He never went straight home but would always stop for a couple of pints, or more, of Murphy's before walking home for the inevitable ear-bashing from the wife. He knew he wasn't a good husband, wasn't a good NCO either; but he had found himself a cushy number with long hours working for the best security squad in Northern Ireland – the Force Research Unit (FRU).

Well-built, in his forties, and with a bulging waist-line, the man, born and bred in Northern Ireland, appeared to be paying little or no attention to the nose-to-tail line of traffic passing his stationary vehicle. But while watching the world go by, he was listening for the loudspeaker concealed under the dashboard, waiting for the signal that Ten-Thirty-Three was on his way.

He knew that this Ten-Thirty-Three was some important tout, being picked up two or three times a week and treated like fucking royalty. He had seen him a few times and he didn't like what he saw. Ten-Thirty-Three appeared shifty, shabby and sharp, a man not to be trusted. Some of the touts he had seen he had quite liked, especially the ones who enjoyed a drink, the occasional plausible rogue, but not Ten-Thirty-Three. When he was around, the man felt uneasy but didn't really know why.

'We'll be with you in a couple of minutes,' a voice said quietly and concisely from the loudspeaker.

The driver made no reply but sat up, adjusted his position and threw the half-smoked cigarette out of the window. Time for him to wake up, pay attention to what was going on and concentrate on the job in hand; his hour of day-dreaming was over.

Three minutes later he saw the two vehicles he had been waiting for, approaching in convoy. He put the car in gear and moved out into the line of traffic immediately behind the second vehicle. The three cars were now in line as they moved away towards Ballynahinch in north Belfast.

Fifteen minutes later the two front cars pulled into the drive of a suburban house and the escort driver drove past and away to his favourite pub. His day was done.

The occupants stepped smartly out of their cars and into the protective cover of the porch before greeting each other in muted tones. One used his key to the front door and once inside one of them went immediately to the kitchen to put on the kettle. 'Tea or coffee?' he shouted.

Both men opted for tea with sugar.

When they were all comfortable in their armchairs, Ten-Thirty-Three, the small, lean man with straight black hair and dark-rimmed glasses, was the first to speak. 'Fuckin' weather,' he said in his broad Belfast accent, 'no fuckin' good for my lads.'

'It'll pass,' came the measured reply from the well-built man in his forties who seemed to be in charge. 'Don't worry about it.'

'Have you got any photos for me?' said Ten-Thirty-Three, trying to sound calm but giving away some impatience in the tone of his voice, as though wanting to get on with the job. Sometimes he would speak as if he were in charge of proceedings, the important person who gave the orders to his bosses, the contact men who were his constant handlers.

'Yes, one,' replied the well-built man.

'Only one?' complained Ten-Thirty-Three, sounding somewhat irritated, 'Who the fuck is that?'

'The man you asked for, Patrick Hamill,' came the reply, and the photograph of Hamill was handed over. The mugshot showed a man in his late thirties. He was looking straight at the camera and it was obvious the photo had been taken officially, either for a passport or for police files.

'Any address?' asked the little man.

'Yes, he lives in a council house not far from Beechmount off the Springfield Road in west Belfast. He has a wife and two kids, but although he has lived here for some years he is originally from Leicester in England.'

'Anything else? Any job, any precise address, any haunts?'

'Yes,' replied the man in charge, 'He spends a lot of time at the Felon's Club, the Republican club on the edge of Milltown cemetery in Andersonstown. Do you know the place?'

'Not exactly,' replied Ten-Thirty-Three, 'it's not the sort of place I'd be invited,' and he laughed at his own joke.

'Suppose so,' came the reply, 'but you have heard of it?'

'You mean the cemetery where the IRA bury their dead? Aye. What else can you tell me?' he asked.

'Well, not much, actually. Hamill was an active member of the Belfast Brigade of the Provos some years ago,' replied the well-built man, speaking in a matter-of-fact, unemotional voice. 'He's someone we would describe as a political activist, nothing more. He was jailed in the Maze for conspiracy to murder, possession of weapons and membership of the IRA. He was released a few years ago. We don't think he's very active in the Provos any more, a man of little or no significance as far as we're concerned. What are your plans for him?'

'We just want to check him out, see if he's active any more,' replied Ten-Thirty-Three, picking up his black briefcase and tucking the photograph inside. 'Have you got a P-card on the man? They're always useful.'

P-cards were an invaluable ID used by Military Intelligence as a quick reference guide to suspects. These cards – the P stood for 'personality' – would state the suspect's name, address, telephone number, family details, car make, colour and registration number, and if the suspect had a job the card would carry his work details, his tax reference and national insurance number. More importantly, the P-card would also include details of his immediate and extended family, alleged friends and acquaintances, even people he visited, the places he was seen drinking or visiting and the people he talked to and drank with. Everything that was known of a suspect, his life and his friends, was filed on the cards so that relatives, friends and acquaintances could be checked and cross-checked.

'You'll get it next time,' he was told. 'Until then, work on what we've given you. See if any of your fellas can find out anything more about this Hamill guy – it could be useful.'

'Okay, have it your way,' replied the little man, 'but those P-cards save a whole lot of time, you know.'

'We know,' said the man in charge with a chuckle, the first time he had shown any emotion during the conversation. 'Remember, we put them together.'

'Aye,' the other man replied. 'Is that it, then?'

'That's it; what else would you be wanting? That's a target for you to check. Remember, though, keep us informed. Don't leave us in the lurch, okay?'

'Okay,' replied Ten-Thirty-Three, 'understood.'

And, after downing their cups of tea, the three left the room, flicked off the lights, double locked the front door with a Chubb and a latch key, and drove away. Two miles away Ten-Thirty-Three was dropped off near his home and the two 'Q' cars went their separate ways.

Ten-Thirty-Three, the thin, unattractive little man with the slicked-back dark hair was Brian Nelson, the chief intelligence officer of the Ulster Defence Association, the principal Protestant paramilitary organisation which, in August 1992, would be proscribed by the British government. The other three men were officers of the Force Research Unit, a secret wing of British Army Intelligence, the 180-strong organisation set up in 1979 specifically to collate intelligence-gathering in Northern Ireland on behalf of the army. The Force Research Unit was not the usual military intelligence-gathering organisation, however, but designed rather to be hard and aggressive, to carry the undercover war raging on the streets of Belfast to the enemy within, the Provos.

For ten years, Britain's Ministry of Defence never admitted the existence of the Force Research Unit. The FRU was never included in any Defence Ministry reports or pamphlets; never included in any British Army listings, never included in any Ministry budgets. Officially, the FRU did not exist and the officers, handlers and back-up staff who worked in the secret organisation were allegedly attached to the 14th Intelligence Company (14th Int), known to the security services in Northern Ireland as an undercover unit working with the British Army. But the FRU also had its own budget and was represented on the Tasking Co-ordination Group (TCG) – the group including MI5, the SAS, the RUC Special Branch and the army – which co-ordinated all the security and intelligence services in Northern Ireland.

Nelson and his two handlers would meet perhaps twice or three times a week to discuss intelligence-gathering between the army and the UDA, and they would keep each other informed of what was going on. The escort back-up driver was never seen by Nelson; in fact, Nelson didn't even know there was a back-up vehicle. That was straight-forward army practice, in case someone had tailed Nelson and discovered his secret meetings with British Intelligence in one of the numerous safe-houses dotted around Belfast.

Two months later, at another safe-house outside the city, the three would meet again at Nelson's request because on this occasion he wanted exact details of Hamill's home, his whereabouts, and a copy of the army's P-card. At that meeting the FRU handlers were left in no doubt that Nelson's UDA bosses intended to take out Hamill and they had asked Nelson to find out every possible detail about the man's life, his work place, his favourite pubs and clubs and any other haunts.

As they sat and talked, Nelson checked the P-card he had been given. 'Is that everything?' he asked petulantly. 'Nothing else?'

The two FRU handlers looked at each other but only one replied: 'That's your lot, okay?' he said with not a little impatience in his voice.

'Okay then, if that's all you've got,' said Nelson rather cockily, 'I'll be on my way.'

'Any plans for Hamill?' he was asked.

'That's not up to me,' replied Nelson, 'I just supply the intelligence and others make the decisions.'

'But you will hear something? You will hear what's going down?'

'I don't usually,' he replied, 'but if I hear anything I'll let you know.'

'Good, make sure you do. Okay?'

'Don't get shirty with me,' said Nelson, somewhat belligerently. 'If I hear anything I'll let you know. In the meantime, can you take me for a drive? Show me Hamill's house, the Felon's Club and anything else which might help us identify the man?'

'Well, you've got his photo, it's up to date,' he was told, 'so you shouldn't make any mistakes.'

'It's not me,' he repeated, 'I just supply the information. It's down to others. You know that.'

'Aye, we know that,' said the officer with heavy sarcasm in his voice, 'we know that.'

'Let's go then,' said the man in charge, 'we'll show you everything we know.'

With no back-up car for fear of attracting unwanted attention, Nelson and the two FRU men took off to west Belfast, the heart of Republican territory. They had already shown Nelson the exact location of Hamill's home in Forfar Street on the large, detailed Belfast street map issued by the Director of Military Survey. The handlers also pointed out the Felon's Club which was several hundred yards from the Andersonstown Leisure Centre and they drove down Beechmount Avenue, nicknamed 'RPG7 Avenue' because of the number of rocket-propelled grenade (RPG) attacks against army and RUC vehicles travelling along that road. Being the Protestant UDA's intelligence officer, Ten-Thirty-Three had no intention of venturing into Republican areas on his own, asking questions which might get him 'arrested' and cross-questioned by the Provisionals in their inimitable fashion. He knew that would end with a bullet in the back of the head, for this was no game.

The FRU handlers were happy to help their UDA colleague. Nelson was the most important Loyalist agent that the Force Research Unit had ever handled in the ten years of the organisation's secret existence. The two FRU officers, sitting in the front seats, took the UDA man on a reconnaissance drive throughout the area, pointing out to him various landmarks – the Republican clubs and pubs, the Milltown cemetery and other places which they thought might be of importance to Nelson. They also took the risk of driving around the staunch Provo neighbourhood and showed him the house in Forfar Street where Hamill lived with his wife and two young children. On the return journey they pointed out the Felon's Club where Hamill spent a few evenings most weeks drinking and chatting to his Republican mates. But not for one minute did they contemplate stopping for even a few seconds, or even think of questioning any passers-by, for they knew they would have instantly realised these three men in the unmarked car were either inquisitive Protestant troublemakers, members of a Prod paramilitary force or attached to the security services.

At a further meeting in January 1988, Nelson nonchalantly informed his handlers that UDA gunmen were planning attacks on the homes of known Provo targets. The handlers looked at each other, worried at this sudden and serious turn of events. They simply noted the statement and passed it to high authority for evaluation.

'Do you intend to hit their homes or the Provos?' he was asked.

'The Provos, of course,' came Nelson's reply. 'We're not interested in the wives and kids.'

'Whom do you intend to hit?' one FRU officer asked.

'No idea,' Nelson replied, 'they don't give me that sort of information. That's the ops side; I'm intelligence, remember?'

'You will tell us if you hear the names of any targets, won't you?' one asked.

'Of course I will,' he said.

After that meeting the two FRU officers, believing that a Loyalist paramilitary attack was now imminent, wrote out a Military Intelligence Source Report (MISR) warning of probable UDA attacks on known Provos and this, in turn, was passed by their senior officers to the Joint Irish Section (JIS), the name given to MI5 headquarters in Northern Ireland.This was passed in a secret encrypted report to the Joint Intelligence Committee (JIC) in London, the committee chaired by the Prime Minister, Margaret Thatcher. The source report would, automatically, also be distributed to army chiefs in Lisburn, senior Special Branch officers and senior RUC officers who had clearance to receive such top-secret intelligence.

Over the next few days, however, nothing came back from DowningStreet or the JIS to the Force Research Unit officers; no advice, no instructions and no orders. There was no suggestion from any political, military or security service sources suggesting that anything must be done to stop such attacks taking place. With no advice, guidance, instructions or orders, the Force Research officers also decided to take no action.

Three weeks later, at about 3 p.m. on 8 September 1987, a dark saloon Vauxhall car was stolen from outside a Protestant pub off the Shankill Road, north Belfast. Ten minutes later the driver pulled up at a prearranged spot and two men clambered into the back. Both were armed, one with a revolver, the other with a sub-machine-gun. The car was driven to a roadside parking lot near the Felon's Club and, while the two men in the back ducked down out of sight, the driver slipped down in his seat so that he could just see over the facia. Anyone glancing at the vehicle would have thought there was no one was inside.

Not long before six o'clock Patrick Hamill walked out
of the Felon's Club a happy man having spent the afternoon drinking with his Republican mates. Without
bothering to check under his vehicle for any suspicious
packages, he got into his car and drove off. A few minutes
later he pulled up outside his house, not even noticing the
dark saloon car slowly coming to a halt on the other side
of the road. He got out, locked the car door and walked
across the footpath towards his home.

He let himself in, closed the door and walked into the
kitchen. Within minutes there was a knock at the front
door and his wife, Laura, opened it. Two men, wearing
masks and carrying handguns, brushed her aside and
strode in.

'We're from the IRA,' one said. 'Who lives here?'

Patrick Hamill replied, 'I do, with my wife and the
kids. What do you want?'

'What's your name?' the gunman asked, confused that
the man in front of them was speaking with an English
accent and was certainly not from Northern Ireland.

'Patrick Hamill,' he replied, 'and this is my wife Laura.'

The two gunmen looked at each other for a second and
then one of them aimed at Hamill and pulled the trigger,
shooting him in the chest at point-blank range. His wife
screamed in horror as she saw her husband crumple to the
floor. His two-year-old daughter, Kelly, who was also in
the room, moved towards her father and, as she did so, the
gunman with the revolver bent over the man's body and
fired one more shot into the victim's head, splitting the
skull. Hamill's body shook for a second and the two
gunmen turned on their heels and walked swiftly out of
the door without saying another word. Behind them they
could hear the harrowing screams of the dying man's wife
and the pitiful cries of his daughter. They took no notice.

A neighbour, George Crilly, spoke later of the shooting,
saying, 'We heard the two shots at about 5.45 in the
evening. My wife and I ran out and we saw Laura Hamill
on her knees on the footpath screaming, "They shot my
Paddy, they shot my Paddy."

'I ran into their house and saw Patrick Hamill lying on the floor with a pool of blood around his head. I knew he was a goner. His wee daughter Kelly was running around in circles screaming and crying for her daddy. It was pitiful.'

Mr Crilly said the fleeing gunmen fired another shot at a man in nearby Colinward Street as they were making their escape but the man was not injured. There was also severe criticism from many neighbours in Forfar Street that the RUC took an astonishing fifty minutes to arrive after the 999 call had been made. In comparison, the ambulance which was called at the same time took only three or four minutes to arrive at the scene. Patrick Hamill died in hospital some hours later. He never regained consciousness.

'When the RUC didn't arrive I phoned Springfield Road barracks and told them of the shooting,' said Mr Crilly. 'They told me that they had been made aware of the shooting and were taking appropriate measures.'

It was not surprising that there had been no RUC or army patrols in the area at that time, nor was it a surprise that the RUC and the army took so long to respond to the 999 distress call. That afternoon the Force Research Unit had put out a 'restriction order' on the immediate area around Forfar Street, making certain that all RUC and army patrols would be out of that area for a few hours around 5 p.m. Such restriction orders were frequently enforced whenever the RUC, the British Army or any one of the security services wanted to operate in a certain area at a specific time on a specific date, for they would not want their operations accidentally or inadvertently interrupted by one of the other security services.

Such requests, which were nearly always granted, were made to the Tasking Co-ordination Group – a committee, as mentioned earlier, made up of officers from MI5, the British Army, the SAS, the Special Branch and Military Intelligence, whose job it was to ensure that there were no overlapping operations happening in the same place at the same time. That could lead to disaster. On this occasion a

senior FRU officer had made such a request to the TCG
hours beforehand and it had, as expected, been granted.
Every member of the TCG, every organisation involved in
the security services in Northern Ireland, had therefore
been fully aware that something was about to occur in or
around Forfar Street and Beechmount at that time on that
day. But the area was empty of any troops, police or
undercover agents, providing easy access and easy escape
routes to anyone taking part in clandestine operations in
the immediate area. Such extraordinary freedom was
always provided by the Force Research Unit, after consultation with the TCG, on many occasions during those
years when Brian Nelson worked hand in glove with
British Military Intelligence. And, as a result, many
people, including Provo hit-men and activists, Sinn Fein
politicians and members and Republican supporters and
sympathisers were targeted and killed. So were a number
of ordinary, decent Catholics killed for no reason at all
apart from the fact that they were members of the
Province's religious minority.

The following morning a FRU handler, operating
under orders from a senior officer, put in a telephone call
to Nelson's home in Belfast but the UDA man wasn't
there. He left a message to be called urgently and a meeting was set up for later that day.

This time, however, when the three men walked into
the safe-house they didn't bother to sit down. There were
no pleasantries between Nelson and his handlers.

'What do you know about this Hamill killing?' Nelson
was asked.

'I know nothing about it,' he replied. 'I knew nothing
about it until after it happened.'

'Who did it?' demanded the FRU officer in charge in a
tone of voice which would brook no excuses.

'I've no idea who carried it out,' Nelson replied, 'but I
do know exactly how it was done.'

'How?'

'I was told,' Nelson said, 'that the guy had been clocked
over a period of time so that his identity was confirmed.

Yesterday afternoon he was followed home from the club. He parked his car outside his house about fifteen yards from his front door. I understand that once he was inside his house he was approached and asked to identify himself. When he did so he was shot. That's all I know.'

'Why didn't you phone here to let us know?' he was asked.

'Because I had no idea until I heard about it on the radio last night.'

'You'll be hearing from us,' said the senior FRU handler, indicating from his brusque manner that the meeting was at an end. Without saying a word, the two officers escorted Nelson to the door and he was taken away by car to his destination. Inside the safe-house one officer turned off the tape-recorder and noted the exact time and date so that there would always be a record of that interview with Nelson. They returned to their headquarters and a meeting was held with the officer commanding the unit. The full facts of the killing were given to him, as well as Nelson's explanation. An MISR was written out detailing what had occurred.

But of course no action whatsoever was taken against Nelson. Nor was it ever intended that it should be. Nelson was working for the Force Research Unit and, in a very short space of time, he would become the most important person in the chain that began inside Military Intelligence and ended with the UDA gunmen who carried out the random sectarian killings.

Hamill's murder was not just one isolated killing. It was part of a series of sectarian shootings carried out over a period of two years in Northern Ireland, from 1987 to 1989, when Brian Nelson was the UDA's intelligence officer. British Army Intelligence was directly involved in many of those killings, providing photographs, up-to-date information, addresses, phone numbers and car registrations of Provisional IRA activists, as well as advice as to the most efficient way the UDA gunmen could track and target suspects. Some of those Provo targets were subsequently murdered, others would survive the attempts to kill them and many more were targeted but never actually attacked.

On nearly every occasion, prior to the killings and murder attempts, intelligence was passed from the FRU officers to the Joint Irish Section headquarters in Northern Ireland and then distributed to the Joint Intelligence Committee. On no occasion were instructions received by the FRU in Belfast telling them to halt the sectarian targeting and killings. And yet the Prime Minister, MI5 officers, senior security officers and all members of the Joint Intelligence Committee, who usually met once a week in London, were aware that a man named Brian Nelson, the intelligence officer of the UDA, was involved in many of the murders and dozens of conspiracies to murder during that period. It was further known that officers of the Force Research Unit were 'handling' Nelson during that time. And yet nothing was done to stop the killings. The battle against the Provisional IRA had entered a new phase about which Prime Minister Thatcher appeared fully aware.

## Chapter Two

# The Recruit

The guard on night duty at the joint army/RUC base in Belfast slowly shook his head from side to side as he watched the slim man in black winkle-pickers, black trousers and a three-quarter-length grey-and-black check coat make his solitary way along the deserted, rain-splashed streets that Boxing Day morning in 1985. It was 5 a.m. and still dark as night and the guard presumed the lone figure was a drunken late-night reveller making his way home, not caring that he was soaked to the skin. But the guard took more notice when the man stopped outside the imposing, well-protected army and police base at New Barnsley as though trying to find the way in. There was no way the guard would let anyone walk off the streets into the base without permission from a senior officer.

As the man stood under the glare of security lights in front of the large metal gates he seemed unsure as to whether to proceed further, looking around him and then casting his eyes over the fortress-type building which seemed strangely quiet, as though deserted. But the guard, secure inside the sanger by the entrance, could see the man perfectly well, silhouetted against the powerful arc lamps. With dark, almost black, swept-back hair, the visitor's pale unshaven face bore the marks of a recent brawl, with bruising and marks around the eyes, and his rumpled, dishevelled clothes gave the appearance of a man who had slept rough that night or not at all.

At that early hour on Boxing Day hardly a car could be seen or heard in the city and the guard wondered what on earth the man was doing standing there as if waiting for someone. He thought it odd that the scruffy visitor wore only a white shirt, a light coat and thin trousers, for the weather was bitterly cold and the rain had added to the misery of the morning. The dawn was barely rolling back the night and the rain clouds that had brought the downpour to Northern Ireland that Christmas night were still overhead.

'Anyone at home?' the visitor shouted at the gates in a broad Belfast accent, but there was no reply.

Minutes passed and the man looked annoyed as he scanned the building. Suddenly, his attention was drawn to a side gate as it opened.

A young soldier, armed and wearing a flak jacket, called to him: 'In here.'

As the man walked through the gate, the soldier asked, 'What do you want?' speaking brusquely as if annoyed at being interrupted during his long, cold vigil of guard duty that night.

'I want to see someone from British Intelligence,' the man said.

'I see,' said the officer, sounding sceptical, 'What about?'

'I only want to see someone from British Intelligence,' the visitor repeated, 'I'll explain everything to him.'

'Come with me,' said the soldier and led him inside.

The man certainly looked the worse for wear, as though he had been drinking heavily and had not slept for a couple of days. But he did not appear drunk or disorderly, instead speaking quietly, weighing each word.

A British Army sergeant told the visitor he would have to be searched and the man raised his arms and spread his legs as though carrying out an order which he had obeyed a thousand times before. But so had many a man in Belfast those past fifteen years.

'He's clean,' said the soldier a minute later having checked the visitor's pockets, his trouser-legs and even the inside of his black socks which covered his thin, hairy calves.

The sergeant returned and told him that as it was so

early in the morning he would have to wait for a couple of hours before someone could see him.

'That's all right,' said the visitor, nodding his head, 'I'll wait.'

'Before anyone will see you,' continued the sergeant, 'we'll need some details – name, address, that sort of thing – so we can check you out on the computer.'

The visitor gave them his name and his former regimental number when he was serving in the British Army with the Black Watch. He also told them that he was now employed as an intelligence officer with the Ulster Defence Association. The sergeant immediately reacted to that statement, glancing up at the soldier, and both looked somewhat confused that this apology for a man standing shivering in front of them could possibly be a UDA intelligence officer. But they decided to make their un-welcome early visitor feel at home. After taking down the details they asked the man if he would like a cup of tea and a bacon sandwich.

'Aye, I would that,' he said, but there was little enthusiasm in his voice.

An hour or so later he was asked if he really did want to wait or whether he would prefer to return at some other more convenient time.

'No,' he replied, 'I need to see someone this morning. I'll wait.'

The clouds and the rain had disappeared, leaving a bright, clear morning and the sun had broken through, shafts of sunlight penetrating the guard-room where the visitor sat waiting patiently for his promised interview.

At 9.30 a.m. he was shown into a small, bare room about ten feet by eight feet with a single radiator which gave out remarkable heat. The man had dried off in the warmth of the base and his tea and bacon sandwich had made him feel better but he still relished the heat coming from the radiator. Sitting behind a small table were two stoutly built men in their early forties, both wearing civilian clothes, with no suggestion that they represented the army, the police or any of the security services. They appeared somewhat brusque, even annoyed, as though they had been woken too early on a morning when they would have expected a lie-in, a little time to recover from the Christmas festivities. These men were from the Force Research Unit who had responsibility for dealing with all Loyalist paramilitary-related activities.

They had already been briefed by the duty sergeant and been handed computer files on their early-morning visitor revealing his name was probably Brian Nelson, aged thirty-six, a former member of the Ulster Volunteer Force (UVF), a hardline Protestant terrorist organisation whose members were fiercely Loyalist. From a quick reading of the bare facts before them, the intelligence officers could see that Nelson's army record with the Black Watch had been abysmal. He had not only refused to obey orders but had appeared regularly on company orders for minor misdemeanours, resulting in many weeks in the glass house. He had continually gone absent without leave until the army decided, in 1969, that they no longer required his services. In 1975 Nelson had been jailed for five years for possession of arms and explosives. On his release after serving three years in prison he had immediately rejoined the UDA and, by 1980, had been appointed one of the organisation's intelligence officers.

'What can we do for you?' asked one of the thick-set officers.

'Do you want to know who I am?' Nelson asked.

'No,' he replied, 'we already have your details on this print-out. You're Brian Nelson, right?'

'Correct,' he said. 'I'm an intelligence officer with the UDA'.

'Yes, we know,' said the officer. 'Now, how can we help?'

'I might be able to help you,' said Nelson. But before he continued, he wanted to check he really was speaking to British Intelligence. 'You are with Army Intelligence?' he said.

'Yes. Why do you ask?'

'Because I don't trust the RUC or Special Branch,' he

said. 'That's why I've walked here this morning, to this place in New Barnsley, a Catholic area, although I was born in the Protestant Shankill Road and I live on the Silverstream estate. It must have taken me an hour and a half to get here and most of the time it was pissing with rain. But I hoped there would not be many people about at this hour on Boxing Day so I took the risk. I knew I was stupid walking through a Catholic area but I was determined to see someone from Army Intelligence because if I had spoken to the peelers or the Special Branch it would have gone straight back to the UDA and I didn't want that.'

'We're both from British Military Intelligence,' said the first officer, 'We were both army, like you.'

'How do you know I was in the army?' he asked, a little belligerence creeping into his voice. Nelson's reaction revealed he was not thinking straight – either through exhaustion or too much alcohol. He had forgotten he had given the sergeant his army details only hours before.

'Black Watch. You were stationed in Scotland,' replied the officer. 'Does that satisfy you?'

'All right,' Nelson replied.

'So what's up then?' the officer enquired.

'I want to get even,' replied Nelson.

'With whom?'

'With the UDA and the UVF, of course,' Nelson said.

'Why? What's the problem?'

'It happened this morning at a party,' he told them in a matter-of-fact voice with little or no passion or emphasis. 'I was at this UDA party on the Silverstream estate with my wife. There were about forty people there. We had a few drinks and everyone was laughing and some were dancing, while others were getting pissed. This particular man kept dancing with my wife, Jean, flirting with her, trying to smooch her, feeling her up – you know the sort of thing.

'I didn't mind at first and continued to drink until I began to feel a bit pissed and suggested we should go home as she too was feeling the worse for wear. This man volunteered to walk both of us back home and it seemed a good idea for I was feeling legless. When we arrived home we felt better – the walk in the fresh air must have helped – and I offered him a drink. I had been in the kitchen mixing drinks for a few minutes when I heard Jean scream. At first I took no notice, thinking they were just larking about. Then I heard her shouting, "No, no, no, get off!" and knew there was trouble.

'This bloke was lying on top of her, trying to screw her. Her dress was halfway up her body and he was trying to force himself on top of her, pulling at her knickers, while she was trying to push him away. I exploded, yelling at him, asking what the fuck he thought he was doing, trying to screw my wife.

'"Fuck off back to the kitchen," he said, "we're just having some fun."

'"Just having fun," I shouted, "you're trying to rape my wife."'

Nelson continued, still speaking without passion. 'Jean had managed to extricate herself from beneath the man, and was pulling down her dress, trying to make herself respectable while the fucker kept trying to pull down her knickers.

'"Get the hell out of here now," I shouted at him. "Fuck off and don't come back."

'"Don't talk to me like that," said the man as he climbed to his feet. "I'm UVF and no one talks to me like that."'

Nelson explained that as soon as the UVF officer got to his feet the man lashed out at him with his fists, sending him sprawling across the room. Nelson got to his feet and tried to hit the other man who was stronger, taller and heavier. Within seconds he had hit Nelson a number of times around the head and he had gone down again, his head reeling from the effects of the drink and the punches. Jean had rushed to help her husband but had been brushed aside by the man who announced that he was fucking off.

But Nelson wasn't finished. He was determined to get his own back. His pride wounded, and his attempts at

teaching the man a lesson having failed, he had stormed
back to the party, the blood from his encounter spattered
on his shirt. He had demanded from the senior UDA
officers attending the party that they should discipline the
man or arrange for the UVF to discipline him. They
refused, saying the matter was personal and private and
nothing whatsoever to do with the UDA.

'I had just told senior UDA officers that a man had
tried to rape my wife, the wife of one of their intelligence
officers, and they didn't want to know,' he said. 'They
simply did not give a damn. And that's why I'm here. If
there is any way I can get back at either the UDA or the
UVF then I will gladly do so. Tell me what you want, what
information you require, and I will supply it. I hate them
for dismissing the attempted rape of the wife of one of
their officers as something of no interest, no concern to the
organisation. Well, if they want to play the game that way,
I'll make sure I get my own back. Whatever you want me
to do, I'll do it.'

'If the UDA wouldn't help,' the officer inquired, 'why
didn't you go to the police?'

'The peelers?' Nelson said, his voice raising an octave
with surprise. 'Fuck off! A man with my record go to the
police and complain? You must be fuckin' nuts. They
would have just kicked me out of the station. Don't you
realise the RUC are up to the hilt with the UDA and the
UVF? They provide the Loyalists with all their
information.'

'You did five years for possession; is that correct?'

'Yes,' Nelson replied, 'I thought you might know that.'

The two officers asked Nelson questions concerning the
hierarchy of the UDA and the UVF and of recent changes.
His answers were impressive, suggesting that he knew the
facts, answering all the questions quickly and accurately.
They weren't yet certain that Nelson was a UDA
intelligence officer, as he claimed, but he certainly knew
details of both the UDA and the UVF leadership.

The two officers asked Nelson if he would like another
cup of tea as they needed to check some facts.

'Yes,' he replied, 'I'm thirsty.' Then, in a somewhat more aggressive vein, he asked, 'What are you going to check? Don't you believe me or something?'

'Of course we believe you,' the officer said, 'why wouldn't we?'

'I don't know,' he said, 'but you're acting suspiciously. I thought I could trust the army.'

'You can trust the army,' the officer replied, 'but of course we have to check facts.'

'All right,' he replied, sounding as though he wasn't too happy with the way things were going.

Within ten minutes the officers returned and told Nelson that everything he had told them had checked out.

'We'll have to work something out,' one told Nelson. 'Can you give us a call in about a week and perhaps come back and have another chat? When you phone just ask for Mick and wait on the line. It might take a minute or two to get the call put through but please just wait. Here's the phone number; keep it to to yourself, okay?'

'Okay,' Nelson replied, 'but you won't forget?'

'We won't forget'.

Brian Nelson was an Ulsterman born and bred. Born in 1950, he had two brothers and a sister. He attended primary and secondary schools in Belfast and in 1965, at the age of fifteen, left school without a single qualification. His father, a shipyard worker, arranged for the young Brian to begin four years' training as a joiner but within eighteen months Nelson became bored with the job and quit.

He fancied becoming a soldier and joined the Black Watch, the Scottish infantry regiment, but it seems he wasn't cut out for the discipline and rigorous training of such a regiment. Brian Nelson had a problem – he couldn't and wouldn't take orders. He was constantly going absent without leave and would be picked up by the police or military police and returned to his regiment for disciplinary action. Constantly on company orders for minor misdemeanours, Nelson would spend many months paying for his crimes, peeling potatoes, scrubbing floors, sweeping the parade ground, weeding gardens and painting coal white. Fed up with such a recalcitrant recruit, the Black Watch gave him his marching orders in 1969. He was just nineteen.

Back in Belfast, Brian Nelson found himself attracted to the Protestant cause as the Northern Ireland Civil Rights Association, a mainly Catholic-supported organisation, was about to be forced into the background by the IRA who had belatedly realised that the civil-rights rebellion of the Northern Ireland Catholic minority had provided an extraordinary opportunity to push the Republican cause. These were the days of civil-rights marches, peaceful demonstrations and justified demands from Catholics for greater equality – in jobs, housing and, more importantly, the democratic process.

Brian Nelson joined the Ulster Protestant Volunteer Force (UPVF), which had been founded by the Revd Ian Paisley in 1969. Paisley's idea was to establish sections of the force on every Protestant housing estate in Belfast to act as a defence unit in case of attack from Catholics. Everyone who joined signed a form stating their name, address, age, occupation and, more importantly, whether they had any experience in the police, army, fire brigade or medical services. Brian Nelson, allegedly a veteran private in the British Army, was exactly the sort of experienced young man Paisley's UPVF wanted. Later, most of the young men who had registered with the UPVF would join the Ulster Defence Association.

About this time, Brian Nelson met and fell in love with a pretty teenage Belfast girl named Jean from a sound Protestant family. Jean, only seventeen, was described as bright, personable, impetuous, sexy and fun. They seemed to hit it off and within a few months of meeting, the rather nondescript Brian Nelson, with no qualifications, no training, no job, little future, zero prospects and with an uncharismatic personality, proposed to the vibrant young girl. Only a few months later they were married. In time, Brian and Jean Nelson would have four children and would live on the all-Protestant Silverstream estate in the Shankill area of Belfast. They rented their small, unpretentious home from the Northern Ireland Housing Executive.

Nelson's induction into the UPVF gave him the much-needed credibility he yearned for. Now, finally, he was a man of some importance. He had spent time in the British Army, had undergone basic weapons training using rifles and Bren-guns, knew how to drill and march, survive forced marches and the basics of field training and camouflage. He had, of course, never actually been involved in active service but, in the ranks of the Ian Paisley's volunteer force, Nelson was someone to whom the rest of the raw recruits looked up to with respect. Within months, he was promoted to street defence leader, a sort of NCO, in charge of the street in which he lived, organising meetings, exercises, drills and weapons training and in charge of discipline. He revelled in his new-found status and during the next few years he would become far more confident, even arrogant. In the UDA he would become authoritarian, not wishing to have his views challenged by others in the organisation whom he believed did not have his experience or his military background.

When patrolling the streets of Protestant north Belfast, Nelson and his defence unit would wear masks and carry pickaxe handles. They would carry out nightly street patrols, cordoning off the area, organising look-outs, watching for any sign of an attack from Catholic areas. Whenever rumours spread that the Catholics were about to launch an attack, Nelson would organise the distribution of Molotov cocktails, iron bars and wooden staves.

Most of the time he carried with him a .22 starting pistol, not that such a weapon would have been much use in a gun battle, but to Nelson the pistol showed that he had power and, if necessary, could always be used to scare people. Because of his slight build he knew that in a straight fight he wouldn't stand much of a chance; but a pistol to hand, even a .22 starting pistol, gave him a weapon he would not hesitate to use.

In 1975 Nelson's fascination with handguns and his apparent addiction to the Protestant military cause went too far and he found himself in court charged with poss-ession of both arms and explosives. He had been caught with three handguns and three sub-machine-guns, as well as a small amount of explosives. It was suggested that he might have been acting as the quartermaster for the UDA. He was sentenced to five years in jail but, with good behaviour, he was out again in 1978 when the sectarian war was at its height.

He returned to the UDA and asked to become involved once again with the Loyalist cause. By then, Nelson was seen by senior UDA officers as a man to be trusted; a man with a military background, who had organised his street defence force in the 1970s with efficiency, and who had been prepared to risk his freedom and go to jail carrying out operations on behalf of the Loyalist cause.

In the meantime, Nelson took jobs laying floors, mainly in industrial buildings, and earned good money, but the work wasn't regular and he would often be short of cash. The Nelson family, like tens of thousands of other Northern Ireland families, survived on state benefits.

As promised, seven days after that first Boxing Day meeting Brian Nelson phoned the New Barnsley special number and, as instructed, asked to speak to Mick. He was asked to wait and two minutes later found himself talking to one of the same handlers he had met previously.

'Would you like to drop by some time for another chat?' Nelson was asked.

'No,' he replied, 'I don't fancy visiting the Catholic area again; it's too risky. Can't you meet me around the Shankill or somewhere?'

'Yes, of course,' came the reply, 'I was going to suggest that in any case. There's no point in taking unnecessary risks.'

A meeting was arranged. Nelson was told to stay in the Shankill area and walk down a particular road alone at a given time on a given date. If his two handlers had not picked him up before a particular crossroads he was to understand that the meeting had been aborted and return home, and phone the New Barnsley special number the

following day. It was explained to him that the meeting
would only be aborted if something untoward occurred. He
was told to take no notice of anyone and not to get into any
car unless one or both of the handlers he knew were in the
vehicle. In the event, Nelson was on time and picked up by
his handlers, Sean and John. He was then driven to a safe-
house and, over tea and biscuits, the three chatted for more
than two hours.As usual, after that meeting, as after every
meeting he attended, the Nelson file was updated. After
consultation with senior officers, the decision was taken to
go along with Nelson. It was obvious to FRU senior officers
and the handlers who had interviewed him that Nelson was
knowledgeable about the UDA hierarchy, including the
most recent events. They weren't sure at that stage if Nelson
genuinely wanted to help the security forces or whether he
was playing some game. FRU officers always worked on the
assumption that any stranger who walked in off the street
with an offer to help had to be watched most carefully. It
wouldn't have been the first time that someone had offered
to work as an informer when they were really operating as
a double agent. They all thought it most bizarre that
Nelson had turned up alone, dishevelled and the worse for
wear, so early on Boxing Day morning. But it made the
officers think that maybe he was genuine. They decided to
give him as much rope as necessary in the hope of bringing
him on side.

By January 1986 the army was desperate for good
contacts inside the Loyalist paramilitary organisations.
Before the decision to form the Force Research Unit, all
intelligence on the Loyalist organisations had been
collected and disseminated by the RUC Special Branch.
Some army officers believed that vital intelligence
concerning the Loyalists was not always passed on to the
army, making them feel as though they were trying to keep
an eye on the terrorists wearing blindfolds. Some officers
even wondered whether parts of the RUC's intelligence
about the IRA were in fact not being supplied by agents
and informants inside the Republican movement but by
the Loyalists.

Throughout the mid-1980s concern was growing among officers of the Joint Irish Section – in reality MI5 operating in Northern Ireland – that the Loyalist paramilitaries were building up their forces, recruiting volunteers, training members and trying to purchase substantial shipments of arms and explosives from right-wing organisations in Europe and South Africa. They had no proof of this, but reports from MI6 officers working overseas suggested the Loyalists were becoming more active and more high-profile. At the same time, MI5 officers in Belfast were made aware that Protestant Loyalists were involved in streamlining their organisation into a fighting force capable of tackling and defeating the IRA if it ever became necessary. The recruitment and training of members and the attempt to acquire arms, ammunition and explosives from overseas made the JIS anxious to infiltrate the UDA and find out exactly how serious the threat had become.

And that was the reason that every couple of weeks the two FRU handlers would meet the lacklustre Nelson who always appeared down at heel, dressed in flash but out-of-date clothes, his famous winkle-pickers and a car-coat that had seen better days. At every meeting he would ask for money. Usually the handlers gave him twenty pounds, enough to buy some food for the family and maybe a beer or two for himself. They had heard that he liked a drink, usually whisky chasers after pints of lager. And he had a reputation for getting rip-roaring drunk, at which point he would become melancholy and miserable.

The operational information Nelson supplied at that time was pathetic, low-grade and useless. But the handlers persisted because they knew the little titbits he did give were all accurate. He obviously did have inside knowledge of the UDA, and he obviously knew details of the personalities and the command structure which were very useful to the FRU in building up their knowledge of the principal Loyalist outfit. He also provided detailed information on the training of UDA gunmen, their weapons, firearms and bomb-making facilities as well as the number of recruits coming forward. Importantly, Nelson knew about the organisation's financing and, on occasion, where the money was coming from. He gave his handlers the names of those UDA people putting together dossiers on Provisional IRA gunmen and bomb-makers as well as Sinn Fein politicians. The Force Research Unit found much of that extremely useful and decided Nelson could potentially be a great recruit. He was given the source number '1033' – Ten-Thirty-Three. It would become the most infamous number ever given to a Military Intelligence agent.

# Chapter Three

## *The Force Research Unit*

Ever since the modern-day troubles erupted in Northern Ireland in the late 1960s, the security services, including the RUC, had only been reacting, sometimes using desperate measures, to the torrent of extraordinary events that was to lead to a virtual civil war on the streets of Belfast. They had found it all but impossible to form policies which would allow them to take the initiative from the hardline Republicans who seized every opportunity to press forward with their cause, the establishment of a united Ireland.

NICRA (the Northern Ireland Civil Rights Association), an innocent middle-class pressure group, supported by both Catholics and a number of Protestants, followed the lead of American civil-rights leaders demanding equality for the black minority during the 1960s. NICRA demanded social justice for the downtrodden Catholic minority of Northern Ireland, better housing, equal job opportunities, fair voting in local elections, an end to gerrymandering and the establishment of government machinery to handle people's complaints. At that time there were no calls for a united Ireland – in fact, no fundamental Republican issues were even raised. Given the conditions and the circumstances in which Northern Ireland's Catholics lived, the agenda was hardly radical.

In August 1968, the first civil-rights march was organised, and two and a half thousand people turned out on a rainy Saturday afternoon to walk from Coalisland to Dungannon. Protestors from both sides of the sectarian divide took part but they were met at their destination by jeering, cat-calling supporters of the Revd Ian Paisley's Protestant Volunteers. Two months later another NICRA march took place in Derry, this time demanding one person/one vote, in which two thousand people took part. Within minutes of the NICRA organisers ending the peaceful demonstration and the marchers walking away singing the famous song 'We Shall Overcome', RUC police trapped the demonstrators in a narrow street and attacked them with batons and their fists, ferociously beating the hapless marchers. Rioting broke out that night in the Catholic area of Bogside, heralding thirty years of strife, the death of three thousand people, mass destruction and a burning hatred between the two communities. That thoughtless decision by the RUC began a series of fateful, loose-thinking judgements which would have the most profound repercussions throughout the three decades of troubles that followed. Politicians in Westminster and Belfast were also guilty of some crass errors of judgement which helped to prolong the agony and the suffering of both communities.

It also appeared that the powers of law and order on both sides of the Irish Sea, including Home Office ministers and their advisers, MI5, the Special Branch, the RUC and the many security services brought in to counteract the Provisional IRA and the Irish National Liberation Army (INLA), failed for most of the time to infiltrate the Republican terrorist groups or track down the gunmen and bombers. Planners in London and Belfast often seemed to be at their wits' end deciding how to tackle the problems confronting them.

Good, reliable intelligence appeared to be lacking for the great majority of those thirty years but, although this was recognised, the steps taken to correct the situation only infrequently achieved the necessary results. Too often, it seemed, policies came into force which had not been properly thought through and, as a result, actions undertaken by the RUC and the security forces sometimes resulted in overzealous enthusiasm, transgression of orders and even revenge, with some officers taking the role of Nemesis.

Throughout most of the 1970s the security forces were starved of intelligence material. When the troubles erupted the RUC's entire complement of Special Branch officers (then called Crime Special) amounted to just twenty people. And their experience in keeping a watching brief on the IRA had been directed solely at the old, Official IRA, with no knowledge whatsoever of the new young breed of hardline Republicans who became the Provisional IRA. Indeed, during the period of internment without trial in 1971, many of those arrested on advice from the Special Branch had to be released because it had been decades since they had been involved in any Republican activity, if ever.

As a result of that débâcle a team of MI5 agents was dispatched to the Province in 1972 with the express purpose of reorganising the Special Branch operation of the RUC and setting up a workable, intelligence-gathering network, including the use of agents who could infiltrate the Republican organisation and provide really useful, high-grade intelligence on which senior army and RUC officers could reliably plan operations.

The MI5 team discovered that Special Branch had not a single address of any of the known high-ranking Republicans, Sinn Fein leaders or IRA officers. In many cases they had no names or identities either. Electoral registers were worthless, particularly in urban areas, as thousands of people, mainly Catholics, were moving house to avoid persecution. And the situation was not improving: RUC patrols had all but ceased in Catholic areas and the British Army, with no local knowledge whatsoever, was given the impossible task of providing information of possible IRA suspects during their street patrols. As a result, the intelligence dripping slowly into RUC and army headquarters was negligible and the information that did come in was usually false or useless. So, the army was ordered to adopt a new, likeable image in a bid to win the hearts and minds of those Catholics who were not hardline Republicans or members of Sinn Fein or the Provisionals and who wanted an end to the violence. A policy of 'tea and sympathy' was encouraged whereby squaddies would be told to stop and chat with the locals during their patrols in an effort to gain their confidence and, maybe, some useful information. When anyone did pass on information, a follow-up patrol would contain an intelligence officer who would try to elicit more details and gain the person's confidence. These people would be recorded as 'casual contacts' and their information would be cross-referenced so that a general picture of Republican activity could painstakingly be put together.

But this process was both slow and uncertain and the rapid escalation of killings and bombings by the IRA called for more drastic measures. As a result the army was empowered to 'screen' suspects, picking people at random off the streets and arresting and detaining them for up to four hours during which time they were allowed to cross-question them about any subject they wished.

At the same time MI5 suggested – and the Home Office agreed – that the army should take a more proactive role in intelligence-gathering; an entirely new unit, the Mobile Reaction Force (MRF), was set up, tasked with following up intelligence leads by the covert surveillance of suspects.

Within twelve months MRF boasted a squad of 120 men, mostly volunteers who were then trained by the SAS. Unfortunately, the SAS personnel were more used to jungle, desert or arctic warfare than the wet, crowded streets of Belfast. They had, however, been trained to kill and this was also passed on to the MRF volunteers. Within a matter of months, though, it became increasingly obvious that the MRF squad, which was controlled by HQ Northern Ireland, was targeting innocent Catholics, and the decision was taken to disband the unit before questions could be asked as to why the squad appeared to have a licence to kill. Their surveillance work was taken over by J-Troop, in reality the SAS, and Close Observation Platoons (COPs), as well as a new unit, E4A, the crack covert surveillance squad set up inside the RUC.

Once again, RUC personnel were encouraged, during

their 'screening' of pliable Catholics, to try and persuade them to act as informants in an effort to keep a close watch on IRA gunmen and bombers. But, because of the historical antagonism towards the RUC, Catholics were more prepared to chat to army personnel rather than RUC officers. The screening technique had revealed that many young, cash-strapped Catholics from deprived back-grounds, who were on the fringes of Republican organ-isations, were prepared to assist the security forces, especially if it meant earning some much-needed pocket money. So, volunteers from the British Army were recruited to act as handlers and sent on short courses called Unit Intelligence and Acquisition Training. So successful was the targeting of these young Catholics that within a few years a number of them had been promoted to positions of importance inside the IRA and the INLA, providing 80 per cent of operational intelligence on a daily basis.

By the 1980s it was decided that the handling of these reliable and valuable young agents should be taken out of the hands of officers who were usually from infantry regiments working under the direction of HQNI, and set up in a completely new unit which was to be called the Force Research Unit. The FRU personnel, all volunteers, were withdrawn from mainstream barracks and housed separately in their own secure offices and compounds, or quartered in safe-houses. The FRU was also set up with its own administration section, motor transport depot and clerks. And the personnel were given good salary increases as well as generous expense accounts. Overnight, the FRU became an élite organisation.

Recruitment had always been a major problem for Army Intelligence. The major problem which they faced from the outset was in persuading bright, sensible strangers from both communities to work for the British Army. In the previous ten years of the troubles anyone who was prepared to work undercover for either side of the sectarian divide had already been recruited.

It had been easier for the mainly Protestant Special Branch to recruit informants because they were generally

kith and kin. But it had been significantly more difficult
for the Branch to recruit Catholics as they were much
more likely to be supporters of the Republican gunmen,
bombers and hardline activists. Many had been led to
believe the terrorists were fighting on their behalf to gain
better housing, schools, jobs and opportunities for the
Catholic minority, who had been given a rough deal by the
Protestant majority for decades. Indeed, many Catholics
did view the Provisional IRA as their defenders, the only
people with the courage and the capability of protecting
them from their Protestant masters and the power of the
British Army.

Even before the FRU was set up, it was admitted that
the new force would stand or fall on the quality of the
informants they were able to recruit from the Catholic
community. Although many Catholics might have been
sickened by the violence of the Provisionals, they could not
bring themselves to cross the divide and help the RUC, an
organisation most of the community looked upon with
deep suspicion. Perhaps, the security services thought,
there was an avenue open to them. Maybe those wavering
Catholics might be prepared to provide the army with
information. It was recalled that when the army first arrived in Northern Ireland in the early 1970s the soldiers
were cheered and welcomed by the Catholic minority, who
hailed them as protectors against the hated 'B Specials' and
the Protestant RUC.

Following in the footsteps of both the Special Branch
and MI5, Army Intelligence quickly discovered that
recruiting reliable touts from within the Catholic
community was all but impossible – not only did they not
wish to betray their leaders or their 'gallant' activists but they
did not wish to risk torture and almost certain death if ever
their relationship with Army Intelligence became known to
the Provisional IRA. Any man or woman joining Oglaigh na
hEireann (Gaelic for the Irish Republican Army) had to
promise to promote the aims of the organisation and obey
all orders and regulations issued by the army and its officers.
And every recruit had to agree to three pledges:

1. No volunteer should succumb to approaches or overtures, blackmail or bribery attempts, made by the enemy and should report such approaches as soon as possible.
2. Volunteers who engage in loose talk shall be dismissed.
3. Volunteers found guilty of treason face the death penalty.

However, though these were the pledges every Provo recruit would make, the reality was far more all-encompassing. Any Catholic found working undercover for the Special Branch, Military Intelligence or any intelligence service was likely to face questioning, knee-capping, torture or even death if it was believed vital information had been handed over.

Despite the fear that knowing all this must have generated, there was one great bait to encourage people to work undercover or even just supply low-grade information – money. Jobs were hard to come by in Northern Ireland, and the unemployment rate in the 1970s, '80s and '90s was often in excess of 20 per cent. Every Catholic was aware that most job opportunities were usually offered to Protestants first. Catholic families, entire streets and housing estates of them in Belfast, had to survive on the dole and any other government hand-outs to which they were entitled. Work was always at a premium for any household and it is not surprising that the offer of good money for a little information proved irresistible for a number of men and women.

As well as the rather hit-and-miss technique of stopping people at check-points and inviting them for a cup of tea or a pint of beer, FRU handlers were urged to try and persuade members or former members of the Provisional IRA, the INLA or the Irish People's Liberation Organisation (IPLO) to work with them. Such people, under-standably, would be of tremendous use to Army Intelligence – if they could be persuaded, or bribed, to do so. It was believed that a number of former Provos had left the organisation under a cloud or after major disagreements with senior IRA officers. These were the kind of people Army Intelligence were keen to recruit. And these disenchanted people were often short of money, some in fact desperate to find ways of supporting their families. Tracking them down, of course, was another matter. It was also difficult to find the right time and place to make the all-important first approach; if that went wrong, it could easily end up with the FRU handler looking down the barrel of a gun. All such approaches were fraught with danger, even though powerful, armed back-up teams were provided to ensure the safety of the officer making contact.

The Force Research Unit was partly made up of soldiers and Royal Marines who had been hand-picked from their regiments. All were checked out before being asked whether they would be interested in joining such an outfit which would entail working exclusively in Northern Ireland, operating undercover and dealing with high-grade intelligence, sometimes having to work for extensive periods without a break – and all with the ever-present risk that if they were ever tracked down and captured by the IRA they would, without a doubt, face torture and almost certainly be executed.

There were compensations, however. Anyone who joined the FRU would be considered the 'pick of the bunch', and, as a result, given instant promotion with a higher salary, generous allowances, greater freedom within the confines of the job, good housing and extended leave.

Training to become a handler (but not a member of the back-room staff) was rigorous and demanding. Volunteers would first undergo a series of tough interviews and, if they were then invited to join the training scheme, would be sent to the mainland for an intensive seven-week course mapped out by the SAS. (Many of the instructors, in fact, were drafted in from the SAS headquarters in Hereford.) Those six weeks were no holiday camp. Those in command of the new Force Research Unit needed a team of men with the same diligence and determination, the same strength and stamina as the young soldiers for whom being 'badged' in the SAS was the high point of their military career. Training included firearms instruction and frequent visits to the small-arms firing-range to practise shooting pistols, revolvers and automatic weapons. They were also trained on the SAS's sophisticated firing-range, a model town constructed like a Belfast street with pop-up cut-outs of men and women. Some of these represented innocent members of the public while others were paramilitary gunmen. An officer had to be able to locate the 'person' and make an instant assessment about whether to shoot or not.

The FRU recruits were also trained in car drill and instructed how to use their car as a weapon if ambushed on the open road. Recruits were taught how to react, usually by accelerating and driving straight towards the gunmen, forcing them to scatter or risk serious injury. They were also shown how to avoid being trapped in a car and how to make an escape in such circumstances. In addition, the SAS instructors taught the FRU recruits the basic rudiments of unarmed combat, how to react if caught in close-quarter battles and how to conduct a fighting retreat in the face of overwhelming odds.

By the time the recruits had completed their course they would be far fitter than when they began. They tackled tough assault courses; endured long-distance forced marches with heavy packs; practised endurance running and faced long, hard PE lessons. To encourage team spirit, aggression and quick thinking, they also took part in five-a-side rugby matches using a heavyweight medicine ball.

Intelligence instructors taught them how to handle touts, how to talk to them, encourage them, persuade them to become informants for Military Intelligence. And they were shown briefing techniques to make sure they not only received all the material their tout brought in but also how to persuade him or her how to go about their under-cover work. They were also taught how to pick-up and drop-off their informants in busy streets or main roads without any passers-by being suspicious.

It was not surprising that the fall-out rate during their SAS training was about twenty per cent, and anyone who failed the course was returned to their unit. By the time the new FRU handlers returned to Belfast to begin their thankless and demanding task, though, they had been trained to a high degree of professionalism. Nearly every one of them had an army background, some even came from the SAS itself, so practically all the handlers had some uniformed army background, ensuring that discipline would never be a problem.

One undesirable side-effect of setting up this élite organisation was that jealousies were created in the close working relationships of Northern Ireland. Special Branch officers, undercover specialists, 14th Int personnel and others drafted in to combat the IRA's terrorist activities soon came to realise that anyone working for the FRU got special treatment: paid the same as those working undercover in dangerous areas, given more privileges, promoted more quickly, allocated better accommodation and flashier cars. Not surprisingly, that didn't go down too well with the rest, who believed they should be given the same privileges considering they were carrying out similar jobs and were exposed to the same risks.

Until 1979 the army had relied on the RUC and the RUC Special Branch to provide all the information covering both the Loyalist and Catholic areas of the Province. But the army had become increasingly concerned throughout the late 1970s that they were not receiving enough good intelligence about IRA activities, especially about the Provo gunmen and bombers. Army chiefs believed that as the hatred between the Catholic and Protestant communities intensified, the RUC, a police force manned 95 per cent by Protestants, was receiving very little intelligence from the Catholic community which, understandably, had never trusted the RUC. Throughout the 1970s the Catholic community had looked increasingly towards the Provisional IRA for protection, believing that both the RUC and the British Army had turned against the Catholic community and were simply engaged in preserving the status quo with all power resting in the hands of the Protestants.

FRU headquarters was located at Lisburn, the army's headquarters in Northern Ireland, and comprised eighty officers and a hundred support staff. There was also a high-grade information section situated in the basement at Lisburn staffed by five people. They were responsible for processing and checking top-secret highly sensitive intelligence material which was brought in to the handlers by their agents in the field.

Much thought had gone into setting up the Force Research Unit. The politicos and senior army officers believed the army needed a hard, top-flight group of men, as tough as the SAS, who would be trained to deal with the Provos with dynamic aggression. The FRU would be the army's eyes and ears, recruiting informants, and, if possible, keeping abreast of the latest Provo plans. What they hoped for was to infiltrate not only the Provo infrastructure but also to track down members of Provo active service units which were making life such hell for the people of Northern Ireland.

FRU handlers had to undergo a strict training programme before being admitted to the secret intelligence unit. Initially the recruits were trained by 14th Intelligence Company, the aggressive army surveillance unit set up in 1978 to succeed the unpopular Mobile Reaction Force. The 14th Int were based outside Belfast, and had a staff of fifty. They were under the direct control of the Director, SAS, a brigadier stationed in Hereford. Many SAS NCOs were seconded to the unit for periods of up to two years. The 14th Int also had the authority to react in certain circumstances, arresting, detaining and even shooting suspects if necessary. Although many SAS men did not look forward to working with 14th Int for a two-year tour of duty, they did lead privileged lives during their stay in Northern Ireland, with top pay, great food, good living accommodation, extra leave and special pubs where they could drink with no fear of meeting paramilitary terrorists from either side of the sectarian divide. One of the reasons many SAS men did not want to work in Northern Ireland was not the danger involved but the fact that they might have been losing out on more exotic postings like Belize which, to many, was like a great holiday adventure with wild parties, cheap booze and beautiful women on hand.

From the outset FRU had a severe problem recruiting reliable informants who could be persuaded to volunteer to act as intelligence agents in the Catholic community. As a result, a screening process was introduced whereby likely candidates could be picked up and held. At that time, the British Army had the legal authority to arrest anyone on suspicion and detain them for four hours, questioning them about their job, their family, their interests and their involvement in politics, including membership of any political parties. Both before and after such interviews the suspect was always examined by a doctor to ensure that no 'roughing-up' or 'intimidation' had taken place.

In fact, the FRU handlers treated the suspects with kid gloves, for their only intention was to instil confidence in those they 'arrested' so that at a future date they might be able to recruit them as agents or informants in the field. They would offer them cakes, biscuits and tea, make them feel at ease, crack a few jokes and try to reach a judgement as to whether the suspect might one day be susceptible to persuasion, even prepared to provide information to the army. Before the suspect was allowed to go free, the handler would have tried to arrange a drink, a pint in a pub with no suggestion of recruiting them for intelligence work. And FRU handlers would wear civilian clothes for 90 per cent of their working day to help potential recruits and agents feel more comfortable, less threatened.

But after twelve months of adopting the FRU screening technique, the RUC complained that FRU handlers were taking their undercover agents, ruining years of working with the Catholic community. Whether that was true or not, a decision was taken among the senior British commanders at Lisburn that screening would have to stop and a new recruitment method introduced.

A new, rather desperate, recruiting process was introduced in which FRU handlers would take part in vehicle check points, chatting to motorists when they were stopped, wondering as they talked to each driver whether he or she could perhaps be a potential recruit. If there was the vaguest possibility of a motorist showing signs of being amenable then the handler would invite the stranger for a drink and a chat, sometimes even for a cup of tea, not to answer questions or face an interrogation, of course, but simply as a friendly gesture. The handler might invite this total stranger for a further chat, and when the opportunity arose would suddenly ask him, 'Do you fancy earning a few quid?'

The stranger would usually look askance at the FRU handler but, living in the cauldron of Northern Ireland's dirty games, would quickly realise he was being asked to work for one or other of the paramilitary organisations or, more than likely, the RUC Special Branch. It was at this point that most people simply got up and left. If they didn't, the handler believed he might have a chance of recruiting a new tout. But the success rate was less than one in ten. The scheme did bring in some much-needed recruits but the great majority proved useless.

There were other recruiting techniques practised by the FRU at that time, some quite bizarre. Handlers would find the name of a Republican or Loyalist sympathiser who may have been interviewed by the RUC for some innocuous offence and the FRU would send him, anonymously in brown envelopes, a hundred pounds cash, in ten-pound notes. If the sympathiser failed to hand in the money to a police station or nothing was heard of the hundred pounds from any other source, the FRU handlers would send the man another mysterious hundred pounds. Handlers might send as much as five hundred pounds spread over five or six weeks. And then the handlers would visit the man – they were nearly all men – who was usually out of work and short of money, and have a quiet, pleasant, friendly chat with the man who, by then, had started to rather enjoy his unexpected weekly cash bonus. It would be explained to the sympathiser that, if he so wished, it could be arranged that the hundred pounds bonus would become a regular weekly payment but, for that to happen, he would have to start supplying sound information to the army. Occasionally, the ruse worked and the success ratio was 20 per cent, one in five agreeing to work for army intelligence.

It was, of course, most unusual – virtually unheard of, in fact – for someone to walk into an army base in Northern Ireland offering to provide information to Army Intelligence. That was the reason why two FRU handlers were bundled from their beds at such an ungodly hour on Boxing Day to come to the base and listen to a man who refused to talk to anyone unless the officer was from Military Intelligence.

The arrival of ex-soldier Brian Nelson at New Barnsley army base at the end of 1985 would provide the FRU, British Intelligence, MI5, the Tasking Co-ordination Group, Joint Irish Section as well as the Joint Intelligence Committee in London with a remarkable, unbelievable opportunity. At that time, the intelligence services knew a surprising amount about the Provisional IRA's activities, both north and south of the border, but very little about the Loyalist paramilitary organisations which were then flexing their muscles as never before. The intelligence services desperately needed good, sound information from someone inside the heart of the UDA. Nelson would be that man.

## Chapter Four

## Enter MI5

By the beginning of March 1986 Force Research Unit handlers began to believe that they had wasted too much time and energy on Nelson, a man who, for no good reason, seemed to have a high opinion of himself. The intelligence he brought in, on a weekly or fortnightly basis, sounded more like gossip the local chippy would know rather than the UDA's principal intelligence officer. At each meeting, his two handlers, Sean and John, would wait for his promised pearls of wisdom, only to be informed of irrelevant nonsense such as a Loyalist club which had decided to instal two fruit-machines rather than one; and even, on one occasion, that the UDA had decided to buy petrol from a particular garage to save 2p a gallon! Indeed, in those first few months, Agent Ten-Thirty-Three brought in not one piece of intelligence upon which the British Army could mount a single operation.

Back at headquarters, Nelson's handlers decided to discuss the matter with senior officers. They felt certain there were other, more lucrative sources of information which should be followed, rather than wasting the time of highly trained officers talking to a man who believed the cost of a gallon of petrol was of vital importance in the fight against terrorism.

Then, much to the relief of Sean and John, their new recruit announced without warning that he was leaving the Province for a job overseas. One of his friends had found a firm in West Germany that needed competent floor layers to work in factories around the Bavarian town of Regensberg, north of Munich. It was a job Nelson could do well and, at the same time, earn good, regular money. A flat in Regensberg had been found where the Nelson family could live together. It would mean a respite from the bombs and bullets of Belfast. In April 1986 Brian, Jean and their children headed for a new life in West Germany, handing over the keys to their rented house in the Shankill. Sean and John would celebrate Nelson's departure with a couple of pints of beer, happy to be rid of the UDA's useless chief intelligence officer.

On the Northern Irish political scene, however, changes were occurring at a rapid rate and the security services were worried. In November 1985, Prime Minister Margaret Thatcher and the Taoiseach, Garrett Fitzgerald, urged on by President Ronald Reagan, had signed the Anglo-Irish Agreement, which broke new political ground in two major areas. Firstly, Britain handed the Irish government a role to play in Northern Ireland, inviting them to establish a secretariat at Maryfield, Co. Down, staffed by Irish government officials, and permitting those officials to oversee certain aspects of the running of the Province. Secondly, in return, the Irish government for the first time recognised the existence of Northern Ireland and that its legitimacy was based on the will of the majority of the population to remain within the United Kingdom. Thirdly, Britain made a commitment to the gradual redress of Catholic grievances concerning the administration of justice in the Six Counties.

Protestant politicians and the Loyalist community at large were outraged that Dublin had been granted a say in the running of the Province's affairs. Many Ulster politicians, thousands of ordinary God-fearing Protestants and every member of the Loyalist paramilitary organisations believed that they had been sold down the river by the British government. Massive protest demonstrations were held throughout Northern Ireland, a one-day general strike received widespread support, and Loyalists confronted the RUC in pitched street-battles. There were even attacks on the homes of RUC officers. An 'Ulster Says No' campaign was launched; it would last for years, dividing the two communities as never before.

But there were two further aspects of the Anglo-Irish Agreement which caused consternation among the RUC, the security services and the various intelligence-gathering organisations. The surprise agreement had galvanised Ulster Defence Association chiefs into action. They had suddenly realised that in the very near future the ordinary people of Ulster, the Protestant families, might need to defend themselves against all-comers, not just the Provisional IRA but the forces of law and order – the RUC and the British Army – which might be ordered by their political masters in London to crack down on the hardline Loyalist paramilitaries. The more they compared their military capability with that of the Provisional IRA, let alone the RUC and the British Army, the more the UDA realised their military wing was little more than an amateurish, Boy Scout set-up.

The dramatic displays of anger and violence displayed by the Loyalists following the signing of the Anglo-Irish Agreement convinced the security chiefs that the Loyalist backlash which they had always feared was now a serious reality. They believed it was only a matter of time before the Loyalist paramilitaries took the law into their own hands, and that the possible outcome of such action could be civil war.

Sectarian killings by Loyalists had gradually died away by November 1985 and had indeed reached a low point that year, with only four murders that could be linked to the terrorists. The signing of the agreement changed that almost overnight. Both the UDA and the UVF decided to take the law into their own hands and during the following decade the number of sectarian killings by Loyalists rose dramatically until the Protestant paramilitaries were killing more people than the Provisional IRA.

The intelligence and information that had been dribbling into the RUC Special Branch and the Force Research Unit for the last few years came to an abrupt halt. Those few undercover contacts on the ground stopped phoning, refused to take calls or attend meetings. This dramatic turn of events caused immediate concern because, over the years, contacts at all levels had always been maintained between the RUC, the RUC Special Branch and UDA personnel. Many were close friends and drinking partners, on first-name terms; some were family. Information requested by the security services had always been happily supplied by the UDA. But those were the days when the UDA believed the RUC and the army were fighting on their side against the hated IRA. Now, all had changed and the UDA realised they had to adopt totally different tactics. Never again would the Loyalists put their trust in the Westminster government, the RUC or the British Army.

Urgent talks took place at the TCG on how to tackle a situation which appeared to be rapidly escalating out of control. The mood on the streets had deteriorated dramatically and the RUC was taking the brunt of the violent Loyalist reaction to the accord. More worryingly still, the quality of intelligence material being gathered was lamentable, with neither the security services nor the intelligence units receiving any reliable information whatsoever.

It seemed to the RUC and the army that they had become little more than reaction forces, unable to gauge where the next Loyalist violence would occur and unable to warn the security forces. They no longer knew what determined the new Loyalist strategy nor the identity of the men who had taken control of the organisation. But the situation on the streets was becoming increasingly grim and there seemed little that could be done to counter or control the new hardline policy of the Loyalist hierarchy.

As the Protestant backlash gathered pace, demands were made of the security services by the TCG who were now under political pressure from London to get control of the deteriorating situation. Each weekday morning the TCG would hold an intelligence briefing in Lisburn to discuss the current situation and any known forthcoming operations. At any one time the four TCG teams in Northern Ireland might have been involved in thirty or more operations throughout the Province, all of which required first-class organisation among numerous agencies and security services as well as extraordinary attention to planning and detail. And the paucity of intelligence from the Loyalist side was becoming not only highly embarrassing but potentially dangerous as security appeared to be slipping from their grasp.

As a result, the FRU, the RUC Special Branch and the JIS were put under increasing pressure to find good, reliable informants who could keep the authorities abreast of the operations being planned by both the UDA and the UVF as well as any small, wayward Loyalist paramilitary organisations which were also becoming active. At that time the UVF had a hard core of about eighty men and the UFF about sixty. Both hardline groups had access to a few handguns and machine pistols, one or two sub-machineguns and two light machine-guns. The security chiefs were desperate to know the Loyalist potential for causing mayhem. They needed details of the Loyalist organisations, the personnel, finance, planning and, above all, the availability of weapons, ammunition, Semtex and detonators, the four vital elements necessary if they were to become a serious terrorist threat. The intelligence they were receiving from touts on the street was pathetic.

From their previous enquiries over the years the RUC Special Branch had learned that the UDA had never had the capability of causing real trouble in the Province, or of launching a prolonged onslaught, because the organisation had been so open and amateurish. And they knew that the UDA were short of weapons, ammunition, Semtex and detonators. But the fact that the UDA, the UVF and the UFF had closed ranks, and become more secretive, made it imperative for the authorities to find out what was going on behind the scenes. Telephone taps were put on all known UDA phone links and on the homes of high-ranking UDA officers. But this bugging produced little information of any real worth either; the UDA were finally learning.

Someone in the FRU remembered Brian Nelson and wondered if he was still in contact with his old friends back in Belfast. Perhaps the UDA had called on his expertise in their hour of need. In desperation, it was decided to try and contact Nelson to see if he could become the FRU's link to the new, secretive UDA leadership. MI5 asked MI6 to trace Nelson in West Germany and, if possible, supply a phone number. They knew he was living in the Munich area and the request was passed to BND, the West German secret service. Forty-eight hours later, Army Intelligence in Belfast had the correct number.

That initial phone call to Brian Nelson at his home near Munich appeared to be a disaster. Nelson was drunk and spoke incoherently, hardly making any sense at all. The call, of course, was taped in the FRU's Ulster headquarters and even when they listened to the replay it still made little sense. Nelson kept saying that he was still in contact with the UDA but was now also dealing with some unknown organisation called the Grey Wolves. At that time no one in Army Intelligence in Northern Ireland had the slightest inkling of the identity of the murderous Grey Wolves. But MI5 did. As soon as they heard Nelson was involved with both the UDA and the Grey Wolves, they urged FRU officers to fly Nelson secretly to London.

Sean and John, the two intelligence officers who had handled Nelson in Belfast, flew to Heathrow and met their former contact during the last two weeks of September 1986. The three were driven to one of MI5's safe-houses in Knightsbridge, an apartment on the fourth floor of a small block of exclusive flats. Nelson arrived somewhat the worse for drink, which was further exacerbated by the cupboards full of beer, wine and spirits at the safe-house.

In his more sober moments, Nelson explained to Sean and John about his relationship with the Grey Wolves. It appeared that many of the workers at Nelson's West German firm were Turkish and some had a close association with this ultra-right-wing terrorist organisation. The Turkish migrants were constantly being asked to purchase handguns from the thousands of US servicemen living in West Germany. These they would then smuggle to their terrorist friends in Turkey. Nelson also confirmed to Army Intelligence that the UDA were still in contact, phoning him every few weeks. After two days of debriefing in London, Nelson flew back to resume his job in Munich. MI5, of course, had secretly taped Nelson's conversations.

After that meeting, MI5 now became more than interested in the UDA's former intelligence officer, realising he could be of considerable use, hopefully leading them to the politicians and behind-the-scenes leaders who were the real power in the new, streamlined and dangerous UDA. In a desperate bid to prise Nelson from the Force Research Unit's grasp, MI5 surprisingly offered the Belfast floor-layer privileged Agent status, which would mean a handsome salary, a pension and a secure future. MI5 intended to push Nelson into the high reaches of the UDA so that they would know exactly the thinking, the political ambitions and the plans of the main Loyalist paramilitary organisation.

'If you hear from your old friends in the UDA, don't forget to give us a call, will you?' he was asked as his FRU handlers gave him two hundred pounds for his forty-eight-hour stay in London.

'I won't forget you,' Nelson replied, 'if you promise to look after me well.'

'That's a deal,' he was told.

When Nelson flew out of Heathrow, however, British Intelligence was no nearer to discovering who was in charge of the new, secretive UDA. In fact, unknown to British security chiefs, a small band of six diehard Loyalists had taken command of the UDA and were determined to rip apart the entire structure and rebuild the organisation from scratch. But this time there would be professionalism and, more importantly, secrecy. All contact with RUC Special Branch and military personnel was banned and only the six diehards knew exactly what was going on. They would become the Loyalist equivalent of the IRA's Army Council and their commitment would be as unswerving as that of the staunchest Provo officer. Officially, the UDA boasted a membership of 20,000 in

1986 but this was trimmed, almost overnight, to a hard-core of just two hundred dedicated men. And these men were split into cells, self-contained units of six or eight, who were directly answerable only to their commander. No one had any idea of the membership of the cells except the commander. No lists were made; no records were kept; no names were filed on computer.

The British secret services knew that the UDA had access to funds. They believed Loyalist finances were in a healthy state, for over the years revenues had increased from protection scams on building sites, from fruit-mach-ines in Loyalist clubs and pubs, from Post Office robberies and from wealthy Protestant businessmen who wanted no change in the status quo. But the secret services had no idea where the Loyalists were trying to buy arms and ammunition from. MI6, Britain's overseas secret intell-igence service, was alerted to check any leads with right-wing terrorist organisations, particularly in Europe and the United States, which might think of providing Ulster Loyalists with the necessary arms and equipment. But the feedback to the TCG in Belfast was slow while the situation on the streets was deteriorating.

Meanwhile, the UDA High Command was working overtime. They knew their military wing had to be properly equipped with modern arms, reliable information and genuine Semtex if they were to pose a serious threat and answer any challenge they might face. By the spring of 1986 the UDA had access to hundreds of legally held shotguns and legitimate rifle club weapons but only about 150 handguns and sub-machine-guns, the majority of which had been manufactured secretly in the workshops of two of the Province's largest employers, Short Brothers and Harland & Wolff. No one could be sure, however, if those home-made weapons would prove sufficiently reliable on an active service operation. Trusted UDA officers were dispatched to Dublin to make secret telephone contact with various right-wing underground terrorist organ-isations in Europe. They did not dare phone such organisations from anywhere in Northern Ireland for fear of being tracked by the intelligence services, their phones bugged, their plans revealed.

At first, the UDA concentrated on former contacts in various European countries including Turkey, Italy, Portugal and Spain, as well as various right-wing groups in the United States. After months of phone calls, hundreds of faxes, detailed lists of weapons and promises of end-user certificates, the UDA's search for a reliable weapons and ammunition supplier had come to nought. It was then that they turned to right-wing Afrikaners. And, for the first time since the search began, it seemed the South Africans were not only in a position to supply all the UDA's requirements but were more than happy to do so. The Afrikaners believed they were helping their blood brothers in Ulster who, they reasoned, were only defending themselves and their families from the terrorists of the IRA.

The UDA realised that dispatching one of their own trusted officers from Belfast to South Africa on such a secret assignment would probably alert the security services. They were well aware that constant surveillance was kept on everyone travelling between Ulster and the UK mainland, as well as between the north and south of Ireland. The UDA presumed that MI6 kept a close watch on Dublin airport too. They realised that if one person had to make numerous overseas trips to attend various meetings, suspicion would quickly be aroused. They did not underestimate the capability of the British secret services and they envisaged handing over hundreds of thousands of pounds, collecting the weapons and ammunition and then finding an HM Customs reception committee waiting for them back in Ulster.

A senior member of the UDA came up with a possible solution. They could use someone they trusted to represent the UDA and act as an intermediary between Belfast and Johannesburg; someone who need never travel to or from the Province; someone who lived permanently abroad but who would be happy to assist the Loyalist cause. The UDA High Command decided that man would be Brian Nelson.

At the beginning of October 1986, Nelson phoned Army Intelligence headquarters in Northern Ireland and asked to speak to Sean. He had to hold for a couple of minutes before Sean's voice came on the line.

'Nice to hear from you,' said Sean by way of introduction.

'You asked me to stay in touch if I had any news,' Nelson said.

'Yes, that's right,' replied Sean, 'what have you got?'

'I thought you might be interested to know that my friends called me from Belfast last night,' he said. 'They want me to fly to South Africa to arrange an arms deal they've set up.'

The handlers listening into the conversation in their Lisburn headquarters could hardly believe their luck. Outwardly, Sean remained cool. 'That's great,' he said. 'Are you going?'

'Yes,' Nelson replied, 'of course I am. They're sending me the money for my return flight to Jo'burg and the whites down there will look after me when I arrive.'

'Do you know when you're going?' Sean asked.

'Not yet,' Nelson answered, 'but I shall be on my way as soon as everything can be arranged – the money, tickets and accommodation.'

'Thanks for the news,' Sean told him. 'We'll be in touch in a day or so. If you have to leave suddenly, phone us first. Remember, we'll make it worth your while.'

'I know that,' he replied, 'I won't forget.'

Twenty-four hours later Sean phoned Nelson at his Munich apartment. He was calling after Nelson's dramatic news had been passed to senior officers in the FRU, MI5 and the TCG, and a plan of operation had been thrashed out.

Nelson agreed to go along with the plan. Instead of flying directly to Johannesburg as requested by the UDA, he would fly via Heathrow where he would be met and briefed by British Intelligence.

Forty-eight hours later Nelson landed in London to be met by Sean, John and two MI5 officers. He was taken to the Post House Hotel near the airport, handed five hundred pounds in cash and asked to return via London on his flight back from South Africa to Frankfurt. He was then transported back to Heathrow for the overnight flight to Jo'burg. MI6 was ordered to keep an eye on Nelson during his stay in South Africa but not to approach him at any stage without first contacting headquarters in London.

Brian Nelson would spend three weeks in South Africa, meeting the Afrikaner leader Eugene Terre Blanche and staying weekends in the famous Sun City resort, which he loved. He drank heavily, visited the nightclubs and thoroughly enjoyed the South African hospitality. He also discussed the details of the £120,000 arms deal. It was arranged that the shipment would include a variety of weapons: AK47s from neighbouring Mozambique and Zimbabwe, Galliel assault rifles from Israel, as well as handguns, grenade launchers and hand-grenades. The end-user certificates – demanded by customs authorities throughout the world whenever arms were exported to another country – would be arranged by the South Africans and the shipment would go via Holland to Scotland before being transported to Northern Ireland.

Nelson returned to Heathrow and was debriefed by MI5 at the Post House Hotel, giving them all the information he had acquired during his stay in Johannesburg. MI5 gave Nelson a further five hundred pounds and he flew back to Frankfurt a very happy man. He was beginning rather to enjoy the lifestyle of an international intelligence agent, being treated with great respect by powerful leaders in foreign countries, involved in international arms trading and enjoying as much booze, as many loose women and as much casino gambling as he wished during his time off.

It was at this point that the relationship between MI5 and Army Intelligence broke down. MI5 desperately needed Nelson back in Belfast where they believed he would be most useful on the political side, providing inside information not only on the UDA leadership and their plans but also on Ulster's wavering and undecided political leaders. Army Intelligence, on the other hand, were keen to reinstate Nelson on the active-service, operational side of the paramilitary UDA, hoping he could return to his old job as intelligence officer so they would receive a constant flow of vital information on the group's military activities, their planned operations and the gunmen and bombers who carried out their clandestine activities.

Indeed, so desperate was Army Intelligence to recruit Nelson to their cause that two handlers flew secretly to Munich to try and persuade him to return to Belfast and work once more for the FRU. By sending two handlers to Germany on such a mission was totally against Home Office orders, for no FRU personnel were permitted to operate outside Northern Ireland under any circumstances. At that Munich meeting Army Intelligence offered Nelson a deal: three hundred pounds a week cash, a reasonable saloon car, a house in Belfast purchased by Army Intelligence, and a cover – a job as a taxi-driver or whatever Nelson wanted to do. The handlers were surprised that Nelson did not require any arm-twisting. Without a moment's hesitation he said yes and shook hands on the deal.

It was only after Nelson had agreed to join the Force Research Unit that he confessed that officers from MI5 had also visited his Munich apartment offering him a similar deal to work exclusively for them. Apparently, he had been surprised to hear from MI5 that they were offering him a job for life, with full pay and expenses as well as a pension to follow. MI5 had also offered to buy him a family-sized house in Belfast as well as a car.

But Nelson had his doubts about MI5, despite their surprising generosity. As he would say later: 'I feared I would be desk-bound forever and I didn't fancy that. Anyway, I didn't trust MI5; they seemed to me to be a bunch of fucking queers.'

Before flying out to West Germany to see Nelson, the FRU handlers had heard that the UDA, happy and satisfied with the work Nelson had carried out so

professionally in South Africa, had already offered him his
old job back, and with a promotion. Now, he would be the
UDA's intelligence officer, covering the whole of Ireland,
and he would be paid well too. From Army Intelligence's
viewpoint, the outcome was a great success, for not only
had they succeeded in outwitting MI5, but Nelson would
be back inside the very heart of the UDA with access to
every area of the outfit. This time, the FRU believed, the
information they received would be of the highest calibre.

But they needed a cover story to convince Nelson's
former friends and workmates in Belfast of the reasons for
his return to the Province and how he could afford a new
house and a car. At the time he and his family had moved
to Germany, Nelson had vowed never to return to the city.
Military Intelligence approached MI6 for assistance and it
was decided to manufacture a win for Nelson on a weekly
German lottery. MI6 approached their German
counterparts, explained the situation, and they agreed to
announce that £20,000 had been won by Brian Nelson, a
Brit living and working in Germany. No money was
handed over to Nelson, as FRU officers feared he might
blow the lot on a Mercedes. The £20,000 would be used
in fact on a deposit for a house in Belfast and to provide
basic necessities like carpets, beds, a three-piece suite, a
dining table and chairs, kitchen equipment and a washing-
machine. In fact, an FRU officer purchased the house and
equipped the place before Nelson and his family arrived
back in Northern Ireland. With that lottery win Nelson
could tell his mates back home how he had come by the
money to pay for the family's triumphant return to Belfast.
When he arrived there in January 1987, with his family
and their belongings, he was met and handed the keys to
their new home, an end-of-terrace house in West Circular
Crescent off the Springmartin Road.

Nelson arrived back home with his wife and four children in his left-hand drive German-built Ford Granada, a
rather battered-looking vehicle, which he hoped to use as
a taxi. Military Intelligence had decided that on his return
their man would work as a taxi-driver, using his own

vehicle and attached to a Protestant Loyalist taxi firm.

It had been decided that working as a taxi-driver was
the best cover available for Nelson, not only so that he
could drive around the city meeting people and gathering
information but also because it showed that he had a job
and therefore an income. Nelson needed to pretend to do
some work, so that friends and neighbours would never
wonder how he and his family managed to live from week
to week on the dole.

The Ford Granada soon proved unreliable so Military
Intelligence purchased a Mazda 626 for him, as well as a
taxi-driver's licence. From that time on, Nelson was
officially employed as a freelance driver with Woodvale
Taxis. In his vehicle was placed not just an ordinary two-
way radio, used the world over by taxi firms, but a special
one from which Nelson could pick up and listen to many
other frequencies, frequencies given to him by his FRU
handlers. In those first few months, when Nelson worked
quite conscientiously driving his taxi around Belfast, he
would legitimately earn about a hundred pounds a week.
He was also, of course, still earning three hundred pounds
a week from the FRU.

Military Intelligence knew it was important for Nelson
to set up a good cover for his real jobs, working for the
UDA and British Intelligence, and so they were in no
hurry to push him to start producing the material they
needed. They believed they could look forward to gaining
accurate, sound intelligence from the very heart of the
UDA and so, at first, they showed great patience towards
Nelson, who soon dropped back into his old ways of
drinking, talking to everyone and showing off to his
former mates. But FRU officers still believed that their
new agent would eventually become a source of valuable
information vital to their task of finding what the UDA
were planning. They would not be disappointed.

But no one could have foreseen how Nelson's job as the
UDA's intelligence officer, covering the whole of Ireland,
would result in one of the most extraordinary and bizarre
episodes in the history of British Intelligence. Indeed,

Margaret Thatcher, her security chiefs, senior advisers and the men and women responsible for fighting terrorism on the ground in Northern Ireland would all be dragged into a web of murder, deceit and intrigue which would last for two traumatic years. Its repercussions would go on for many more.

## Chapter Five

# Thatcher's Baptism of Fire

The IRA bombing of Brighton's Grand Hotel during the Conservative Party conference in October 1984 caused anger and consternation among the Cabinet and the security services. At 2.54 a.m. on Friday, 12 October, a bomb containing between twenty and thirty pounds of explosives, shook the hotel to its foundations, causing four floors to collapse and the centre of the building to cave in. The act of terrorism infuriated Prime Minister Margaret Thatcher, who herself only narrowly escaped death in the blast. It also resulted in fury and demands for retribution.

The explosion trapped and injured a number of Tory MPs and their wives and killed Sir Anthony Berry MP, Roberta Wakeham (the wife of the government chief whip), Jeanne Shattock, Eric Taylor and Muriel MacLean (the wife of Donald MacLean, a senior figure in the Scottish Conservative Party).

The bomb, hidden behind wall panelling in the bathroom of room 629 – on the floor below the one on which Margaret Thatcher and her husband Denis were staying – had been planted some three weeks earlier. It had been equipped with a timing device of the sort found on video recorders, which allows the recording time of programmes to be pre-set weeks in advance, and heavily wrapped in Cellophane. Search teams with specialist sniffer dogs, which scanned the hotel before the conference, did not detect the explosives.

The IRA's claim for responsibility of the bombing added a chilling rider: 'Today we were unlucky, but remember – we only have to be lucky once; you have to be lucky always.'

Understandably, the very fact that the Provisional IRA had succeeded in planting and exploding a bomb at the Tory Party conference hotel was a severe blow to Thatcher, who had taken a hard line against the IRA from the moment she formed her first government in 1979. Indeed, the IRA's small but potent rival terrorist organisation, the Irish National Liberation Army, had also demonstrated its professionalism in a campaign of direct action against the Tories. They succeeded in planting a bomb under a vehicle in the well-guarded underground carpark of the House of Commons, the epicentre of Britain's democracy. Indeed, that attack, in March 1979, had shocked and deeply saddened Margaret Thatcher for the bombers had killed their target, Airey Neave, the Tory Party spokesman on Northern Ireland. Neave, a right-winger, had not only been a close personal friend of Thatcher, but had also been one of the men primarily responsible for her rise to the leadership of the Tory Party.

Neave, too, had been fiercely anti-IRA. In a celebrated speech in August 1976, in a bid to whip up support for the peace campaign of the mid-'70s, he had said: 'There must be a change in security tactics. The army and the local security forces must be released from their present low profile and go on the offensive . . . the time is ripe to smash the Provisional IRA.'

Eight years later, in her speech to the Tory Party conference the day after the Brighton bomb, Mrs Thatcher echoed Neave's words. She did not dwell for long on the ghastly and dreadful events of that night, but said: 'The bomb attack . . . was an attempt not only to disrupt and terminate our conference. It was an attempt to cripple Her Majesty's democratically elected government. That is the scale of the outrage in which we have all shared. And the fact that we are gathered here now, shocked but composed and determined, is a sign not only that this attack has failed, but that all attempts to destroy democracy by terrorism will fail.'

Those who planted the bomb in Brighton would not escape the investigation that was set up to track them down. The attack had shocked the world, making people realise that the Provisional IRA were not do-gooders demanding civil rights for the Catholic minority of Northern Ireland but, rather, a group of ruthless and determined terrorists using the bomb and the bullet indiscriminately to achieve their political ends. Their goal was the coercion of the majority of the people of Northern Ireland, who had demonstrated their wish to remain part of the United Kingdom, into an all-Ireland state.

Understandably, Thatcher, the Cabinet and members of all political parties were determined that those responsible would be brought to justice. This had been a dastardly and cowardly attack on the British government and it was imperative that the bombers be caught and severely punished. The government and opposition parties were determined to send a strong message to the Provisional IRA: attack our leaders and you will be hunted down, arrested, tried and sentenced to a long period in jail. Every effort was put into the search for the guilty men.

On the ground in Northern Ireland every tout and intelligence agent working for the RUC or the British was told to find out what was being said on the streets and in the pubs, clubs and bars – what were the names of those directly responsible for the outrage which had sent shockwaves through the Thatcher government. Until that moment those in power had believed there was an unwritten agreement not to attack Britain's political élite in exchange for the British not targeting the Sinn Fein/IRA leadership. This attack had ended that cosy little mistaken arrangement.

Prodigious and painstaking forensic work over many months finally led to the discovery of a single fingerprint on one of the Grand Hotel's registration cards. It had been signed by someone naming himself Roy Walsh on 15 September 1984. The fingerprint was identified as belonging to Patrick Magee, a known Provo bomber, who was wanted in connection with an arms discovery in

England in 1983. Following a tip-off and first-rate surveillance, Magee and two other Provos were captured in an armed police raid on a flat in Glasgow in May 1985.

At the time the men were captured, they were planning a bomb blitz on eleven English seaside and holiday resorts – Brighton, Ramsgate, Dover, Southend, Southampton, Margate, Folkestone, Blackpool, Torquay, Great Yarmouth and Eastbourne – as well as an 'IRA spectacular' in the Rubens Hotel, opposite Buckingham Palace. In another Glasgow flat close to where the men were arrested, an arms and explosives hide was discovered, with rifles, booby trap devices, detonators, ammunition, maps, batteries and twenty-five packets of explosives. All three men were later convicted of conspiracy to cause explosions. Magee was also convicted of the murders of the five people who had died in the Grand Hotel bombing.

Following the appalling security blunder of Brighton, Margaret Thatcher, as chairman of the Joint Intelligence Committee, which met weekly at Downing Street, ordered a complete review of the security and intelligence set-up in Northern Ireland to ensure that no such mistake would ever be repeated. She could not understand how the RUC Special Branch or any of the intelligence agencies or their informants had not known that such a attack was being planned. Despite whatever excuses were put forward, the very fact that the IRA were able to penetrate the tight security ring around the Prime Minister and her entire Cabinet, and explode a murderous bomb so successfully, made MI5 and the rest of Britain's security services look like amateurs, if not downright incompetent. Outwardly, this extraordinary lapse was barely reflected in open criticism; but in the Whitehall corridors Thatcher was incandescent with rage that they should have proved themselves so thoroughly incompetent. Internal memos flew hard and fast at all those the Prime Minister felt were to blame for such a breakdown in security, and senior officers were left in no doubt that their performance had to improve significantly if they were to keep their jobs.

From that moment on, Margaret Thatcher decided to

become far more closely involved in what she would call 'the Irish question'. By the mid-1980s she had her new security set-up in operation; the various agency chiefs were in place, their staffing levels were increased and, as a result, she expected there to be no repeat of the Brighton bombing nor of the murder of political allies such as Airey Neave.

Thatcher's own instincts were profoundly Unionist but when she came to office she realised the political realities of Northern Ireland not only prevented a return to majority rule but also meant that the Catholic minority had to be included in any agreement. She would suffer a quick and brutal baptism for only four months after her election victory Earl Mountbatten and three members of his fishing party were blown to pieces when an IRA bomb was detonated within minutes of their fishing smack putting to sea off the Irish coast at Mullaghmore, Co. Sligo. That same day eighteen British soldiers were killed and five others injured in a double explosion triggered by remote control at Narrow Water, Warrenpoint, near Newry, close to the border with the Republic. The Provos had exploded the first bomb and then waited for those who arrived by helicopter to rescue the wounded before they set off the second. Mrs Thatcher was enraged.

In her autobiography The Downing Street Years, Margaret Thatcher wrote that she immediately visited Northern Ireland to show the army, police and civilians that she understood the scale of the tragedy and to demonstrate the determination of the government to resist terrorism. By that time 1,152 civilians and 543 members of the security services had been killed as a result of terrorist action since the troubles began ten years before. She would not forget those two terrible outrages but she was determined that, whatever happened, the IRA would not gain their political aims through terrorism.

Considering that Northern Ireland, a part of the United Kingdom, was on the edge of civil war for much of Thatcher's time at Downing Street, it seems extraordinary that in her autobiography her plans and policies of how she dealt with the men of violence should have received so little attention. She wrote a thirty-five-page chapter entitled 'Shadows of Gunmen' with the subtitle 'The political and security response to IRA terrorism 1979 –1990'; yet virtually no clues were given of any practical policy the Thatcher government introduced to take on the Provo gunmen and bombers.

Mrs Thatcher perceived the IRA to be the core of the terrorist problem and she believed that their counterparts on the Protestant side would probably disappear if the IRA could be beaten. In her book, she explained what she believed was the best chance of beating the IRA: by per- suading the nationalist minority to reject the IRA, to deprive the IRA of international support and to maintain good relations between Britain and the Republic of Ireland. But Thatcher's term in office was peppered with problems and terrible tragedies – the hunger strikers of the early 1980s, the mainland bombings in July 1983 when eleven soldiers were killed, the Christmas bombing of Harrods shoppers in 1983, the Enniskillen cenotaph bombing of 1987, the killing of eight British soldiers in a landmine booby-trap near Omagh in August 1989, the slaughter of ten bandsmen at the Royal Marines School of Music at Deal, Kent, in 1989, bombings in the City of London, Warrington and the Para HQ at Aldershot . . . Thatcher recalled suffering deep personal grief once more when the IRA struck in the heart of London, killing another of her close political friends, the staunch Unionist Ian Gow, when a booby-trap bomb exploded under his car on the morning of Monday, 30 July 1990.

Understandably, of course, Thatcher would not have wanted to detail any of the security or intelligence measures introduced by her government to fight the war of attrition against the IRA for fear of providing free information to the enemy, and yet no mention is made in The Downing Street Years of the vital role she played in co-ordinating the services through the powerful and influential JIC. In fact, no mention of that particular committee is made anywhere in the history of her time in office, though its discussions and decisions would undoubtedly have made fascinating reading. And yet, to many, the foundations of the 1985 peace accord in Northern Ireland were laid by Mrs Thatcher in conjunction with the prime ministers of the Republic during her years in power. There are also those who have been involved in the Good Friday peace accord of 1998 who believe that the foundations of that agreement can be traced to the Anglo-Irish Agreement of 1985, of which Mrs Thatcher was a prime mover.

Yet she would come to rue signing that Agreement. In a review of Simon Heffer's biography of the great orator and political thinker Enoch Powell, Thatcher wrote in November 1998 that Powell was right to oppose the Anglo-Irish Agreement which gave the Dublin government a formal say in the running of Northern Ireland for the first time.

Enoch Powell, who died in February 1998, was then an Ulster Unionist MP, having quit the Tories in 1974 over disagreements on Europe. Powell condemned the accord as a betrayal and considered it the first step towards Irish unification, claiming the agreement resulted in an unprecedented arrangement under which control of part of the United Kingdom had been granted to foreign ministers. During a bitter exchange with Mrs Thatcher in the House of Commons at that time Powell accused the Prime Minister of 'treachery'. According to Heffer, Powell believed that in her heart Thatcher had not wanted the agreement. One 'had only to watch the Prime Minister at the signing at Hillsborough to understand that here was someone doing what she knew was wrong and what she knew was contrary to her instincts and knowledge of the position'. In her review, Lady Thatcher wrote of Powell's objections to the accord: 'I now believe that his assessment was right, though I wish on this as on other occasions he had been less inclined to impugn the motives of those who disagreed with him.'

There were many Ulster Unionists together with the vast majority of Loyalists who in 1985 agreed wholeheartedly with Enoch Powell. And there are numbers of professionals in the security services who believe that the hardline tactics introduced against the IRA during Mrs Thatcher's Downing Street years, when a far more aggressive policy was permitted, was what finally convinced the Sinn Fein/IRA leadership that they should adopt less confrontational policies and go for a political settlement, for they must have realised they could never win the war against the British Army.

In an effort to co-ordinate and streamline intelligence gathered by the RUC and the army, the Thatcher government decided to reconstitute and strengthen the high-level security directorate, the Joint Irish Section, under the command and control of MI5. There had been a fiercely fought battle between MI5 and MI6 over who should control Northern Ireland. In the past MI6 had had the greater say but MI5 forced the issue and finally won the day. They also demanded and won control and management of intelligence-gathering in the Republic; it was logical, they argued, for MI5 to cover the Republic because there was so much cross-border activity by the Provisional IRA. JIS, which was originally formed in the 1970s, was responsible for co-ordinating both the intelligence and security services in Northern Ireland. The head of the JIS was an Assistant Secretary (Political), who had two senior assistants, as well as three other senior MI5 officers who worked out of HQNI in Lisburn. Also assisting them were six MI5 staffers involved with clerical work and administration. At Stormont Castle a further twenty MI5 clerical and admin staff were employed together with five political specialists and advisers. Two MI5 liaison officers worked closely with the RUC at Knock, near Castlereagh, and a single MI5 officer at Castlereagh acted as liaison with the RUC Special Branch. One MI5 officer also sat in the same office as the operations officer of the Force Research Unit.

The Joint Irish Section was supported by an administration staff of between forty and fifty people, mainly civil servants who had volunteered for the two-year tour of duty in Northern Ireland. In effect, the JIS was the British government's eyes and ears in the Province, responsible for collating all high-grade intelligence flowing into various offices in the Province. The JIS was also responsible for passing on all relevant reports to the Joint Intelligence Committee in London, that is, to Mrs Thatcher. She would demand reports on a weekly basis.

The JIS would keep files on all intelligence agents, informants and what the officers and handlers called touts, those people on the ground who, for small sums of money, would often risk their lives providing information for the British government's fight against both the Republican and Loyalist terrorist organisations. The JIS would also keep records of money spent on the fight against terrorism, including the amounts paid secretly to the many informants on the books of the various agencies. And, like any well-ordered civil service, details would be meticulously filed on computers of all past and present covert operations, the handlers and informants, as well as details of those terrorists suspected of being involved. A complicated cross-reference record would also be updated on a weekly basis so that everyone involved in the fight against terrorism, and the suspected gunmen and bombers, could be monitored constantly.

The RUC and the Special Branch did not come directly under the command of the Joint Irish Section, however, though they did of course work very closely together and they were both represented on the Tasking Co-ordination Group, the organisation responsible for co-ordinating police, military and security service operations throughout the Province.

The JIS was also responsible for all covert actions undertaken in the Republic of Ireland and no such actions were permitted by any agency unless approved by the JIS. In reality, however, the JIS never took those decisions. When any action south of the border was suggested or contemplated by any agency, all details of such an operation had to be passed to the JIS in Belfast. In turn, they would immediately give all the relevant information to the JIC in London, who would make the ultimate decision.

In that way there was no possibility of any JIS operational adventures causing political problems between Dublin and London. But the JIS did run agents in Southern Ireland throughout the 1980s and the early 1990s. It is not known whether the Dublin government was aware that MI5 operators, though not based in Southern Ireland during those years, frequently visited the Republic on operational duties, meeting and debriefing informants. However, it is true to say that, in general terms, there were always good relations between senior RUC and Special Branch officers and their counterparts in the Gardai. Much to the IRA's annoyance, the flow of information between Belfast and Dublin was constant and helpful. The close relationship was not simply altruistic, for the two forces needed each other and the information they could exchange in their fight to combat the Provos.

MI5 also had other, more down-to-earth, operations to pursue and command. One vital and important on-going job was to ensure the integrity of the men and women in the British and Army Intelligence agencies and all the personnel who became directly involved with informants. Every so often an MI5 officer would conduct on-the-spot, random checks among handlers, arriving without notice to sit with both Special Branch and Army Intelligence officers while they were debriefing an informant or an agent. The principal reason was to check that the handlers were not becoming involved in any criminal activities or over-stepping their authority when dealing with informants. Understandably, some handlers bridled at such inter-vention, which they believed caused problems for them because their touts would be made to feel ill at ease, and therefore become less communicative. Some would com-plain that the presence of nameless MI5 officers would set back their relationships with touts for weeks and would necessitate a return to the painstaking job of building confidence once again.

Working behind the scenes was also the small army of

MI5 administrators, mainly young, unattached female civil servants, who volunteered to work in the Province not only to earn extra pay but also to experience the surge of adrenaline, the thrill of being a part of an active on-going, undercover operation against a ruthless and determined terrorist organisation; all so very different from their rather boring, mundane lives in London's MI5 headquarters which was often no different from an ordinary clerking job in any big office. All would be volunteers and they would be billeted out singly or in pairs in apartments in and around Belfast.

On arrival in Belfast, all MI5 staff would be taken on 'familiarisation' tours of the Province including trips around Belfast City, Derry, Armagh and even the IRA no-go area of Crossmaglen in South Armagh. The staff would be flown by helicopter into Bessbrook Mill, the heavily fortified base where the British Army battalion guarding the border area was based. There, these young women plucked from a dull civilian life in London would see at first hand how the army lived under the constant threat of a mortar, grenade or small-arms attack from the Provos. It was from Bessbrook Mill that many covert SAS patrols would be organised, the four-man units called 'bricks' sometimes living rough in the countryside for up to two weeks at a time, keeping an eye on the border and checking the identities of those moving back and forth across the unmarked frontier.

In those areas regarded as 'safe', the MI5 operators, accompanied by two FRU handlers, would be taken by car so that they could see for themselves the towns and villages, the districts, the 'tribal' areas of the separated Protestant and Catholic communities and the sectarian areas and streets which they would be reading and writing about over the next two years. During their familiarisation tour they would also see the lovely Irish countryside, the rugged coast, the forests and, in summer, the picture-postcard views of Northern Ireland. But even in these idyllic surroundings the villages would often be divided into their respective sectarian communities. All would be explained so that the new recruits would be left in no doubt about the problems the Province faced. During the ninety-minute tour of killing country, particularly in South Armagh, the MI5 staff would be shown the exact location of fire-fights between the security forces and the Provos, of places bombed by the IRA and of Republican pubs and clubs and places where arms dumps had been discovered.

There were no reports of any of these trips being interrupted by any unwanted attention; because most of the incoming MI5 staff were women, there was little suspicion in two couples driving around both Protestant or Republican areas. All would be dressed in civvies, the cars ordinary saloons and none would be armoured. But the passengers would be in constant radio contact with headquarters.

All such familiarisation exercises in South Armagh would be closely monitored by a quick reaction force of two bricks, eight men, in a Lynx or Puma helicopter. The QRF would comprise men from the battalion on duty, armed with sub-machine-guns. The helicopter and the cars below would be in radio contact with the battalion ops room at Bessbrook Mill and the routes to be taken mapped out beforehand and closely adhered to at all times. No chance would be taken that any of these intelligence service operators might fall into the hands of the local Provos. MI5 were under no illusion that if any of their operatives or back-room staff, no matter how junior or inexperienced, fell into the hands of the Provos, they would end up with a bullet in the back of the head.

But sometimes, of course, there were hiccups. Following the arrest in 1984 of the traitor John Bettany, the MI5 spy who worked for the Soviets, all MI5 personnel in Northern Ireland had to be immediately moved from their lodgings, apartments and hotels and rehoused over a single, hectic weekend, because Bettany had been employed in the Province from 1979 to 1981. No one could be sure that he had not inadvertently or deliberately passed on names or addresses of MI5 personnel. The Special Branch and the FRU were furious when they heard of Bettany's spying activities because when he left Northern Ireland he knew the identities of all IRA informers and agents who were working for the intelligence services at that time. It was further learned that when on remand in London's Wandsworth jail, Bettany had suddenly, rather curiously, decided to embrace the Catholic religion and struck up a close relationship with a known IRA bomber who was also in Wandsworth. The two would meet and talk for an hour or more every week, unguarded and unsupervised, in the prison chapel. Unbelievably, their conversations were not even bugged, so there is no record of the substance or context of their conversations. What passed between them is still a mystery, unknown to the authorities, but such a liaison alarmed the senior officers of the security services when they learned what had been going on. They were far from happy and believed a gross lapse of security had been permitted, maybe putting some of their people at risk.

Senior officers held talks at the highest level, wondering whether any action should or, indeed, could be taken to ensure the safety of those informants and agents whom Bettany might have put in danger. When no action had been taken by the IRA against any agent, the decision was taken to leave well alone and not even warn the the operatives or back-room staff that their identities may have been leaked to the terrorists. In fact, as far as is known, no names were ever leaked.

Also represented on the Joint Irish Section was the Military Intelligence Unit (MIU), an organisation staffed by thirty officers who were responsible for liaison between Military Intelligence and the RUC Special Branch. Its Northern Ireland headquarters were also at Lisburn and officers would work out of main police stations across the Province.

Most important of all the intelligence agencies was the RUC Special Branch, which formed the backbone of the undercover operations principally battling the Provisional IRA but also keeping an eye on the Protestant paramilitaries and any other Republican terrorist groups which were prepared to use violence. Most Special Branch officers were originally recruited from the Northern Ireland crime squads but during the late 1980s and 1990s, between 250 and 300 men and women at any one time were working for the Branch. All were trained, authorised handlers dealing with informants and agents who had infiltrated the IRA network. Without exception, Branch officers worked extraordinarily long hours, week in, week out. One of their more illustrious chiefs was Ronnie Flanagan, who was appointed Chief Constable of the RUC in 1996.

And, of course, there was the aggressive Military Intelligence agency – the Force Research Unit – which was designed and came into force to be the independent eyes and ears of the British Army. When the secret FRU first came into being, nearly all its resources were directed at the Provisional IRA. The FRU handlers, all volunteers, were able to persuade some Republican sympathisers to provide them with information, but it proved an uphill struggle. In those first few years the main task given to FRU officers and handlers by the JIS was to target known Provo gunmen and bombers in and around Belfast as well as near the border, particularly in the hardline Republican areas of South Armagh and Co. Tyrone. The information would be passed to the SAS who would then concentrate their resources on waiting for the Provos to move out on active service operations before hitting them. FRU personnel had been trained to handle informants and agents in exactly the same way as the Special Branch had always dealt with their touts.

There were two further highly important secret organisations involved with undercover surveillance in Northern Ireland: the 14th Intelligence Company and E4A. The fifty members of 14th Int were under the command of an SAS brigadier and were divided into two detatchments, commanded by a major or a captain. Their Northern Ireland headquarters were based near Belfast. E4A was the RUC's surveillance unit, staffed by 120 police

officers of various ranks. Set up in the early 1980s, E4A
was an undercover unit with members always dressed in
civvies. Their headquarters were at Knock near south
Belfast. In operations during the years both organisations
proved their worth time and again, their staff being both
highly professional and remarkably dedicated to some of
the toughest assignments handed out by the authorities.

    With the return to Belfast of Brian Nelson, as the
Ulster Defence Association's chief intelligence officer, and
with extensive undercover and intelligence agencies
securely in place, the British government was ready to
launch one of the most dynamic, aggressive secret campaigns ever undertaken since the troubles began to break
the back of the Provo stranglehold on Northern Ireland.
With Margaret Thatcher in Downing Street there was the
political will to drive home a campaign designed to rattle
the Provo leadership, cause consternation in their midst,
disrupt their bombing campaigns in Ireland and on the
mainland and, if possible, force them to the negotiating
table. But first they had to be taught a lesson, one which
would make them realise that none of their members was
safe wherever they chose to run or to hide. Their only way
out was to agree to talk terms or face the consequences.
What followed was a campaign which would bring fear
and more killings into the communities and even into the
homes of those people prepared to bomb, kill, maim and
injure the people of Northern Ireland for their own
political aims. The Provo terrorists were to be given a taste
of their own medicine. No one could have guessed that
Brian Nelson, an insignificant, streetwise, hardline
Ulsterman, who had been thrown out of the British Army,
would become the linchpin of this remarkable secret
campaign to kill Provo gunmen, Sinn Fein politicians,
Republican sympathisers and, unbelievably, decent,
ordinary Catholics.

## Chapter Six

# *Violence and Murder*

Malachy McIvor was one of those decent, ordinary Catholics. A married man of forty-three with a wife, Rosaleen, his childhood sweetheart, and four children, he lived in the staunchly nationalist village of Stewartstown, Co. Tyrone, an area steeped in the deep-rooted traditions of Irish Republicanism, where the Irish tricolour flew proudly from a number of homes and buildings.

Stewartstown was considered by the British Army to be one of the centres of 'bandit country'. It was a village of a few hundred people who made a living from the land, a little trade, and where, in many cases, dole money kept body and soul together. There were some who also enjoyed a little smuggling, buying goods cheap on one side of the border and selling them for a healthy profit on the other, no questions asked. But Stewartstown was also a place frequented by Provisional IRA activists, gunmen and bombers, as well as their staunch supporters, a place where strangers were never welcome and where Loyalists or Protestants were hardly ever seen – and where members of the forces of law and order only visited carrying guns and wearing flak jackets. Indeed, for many months at a time, Stewartstown would be one of the Province's no-go areas where the the army and the RUC would not set foot without armed support, a helicopter in the sky and their weapons at the ready.

No Brits would find a welcome at the local pubs and clubs; they would be suspected of being a member of the British government's military machine, whether informants, agents, policemen, soldiers or SAS personnel.

In a village like Stewartstown, settled in Victorian times, no stranger could drive or walk down the main street without the inhabitants being aware that an intruder had entered the area, someone to be treated with suspicion if not open hostility.

Malachy McIvor, one of a family of eleven, had lived there all his life. On leaving school at the age of sixteen, he trained as a car and motorcycle mechanic. Indeed, motorcycling became his life and Malachy would travel all over Ireland attending motorcycle race meetings. He would also travel to the Isle of Man for the famous TT races, so keen did he become in the sport. He was skilled as a mechanic and people from far and wide would bring their mechanical problems to the little garage he ran at the junction of Castlefarm Road and North Street in Stewartstown. Nothing was ever too much trouble for the man who simply liked to help his extended family, as well as his friends and neighbours – in fact most of the people who lived in and around the village.

Like many a man from the village, Malachy enjoyed the odd pint at the end of the day; but, apart from his love of motorcycles and racing, he lived for his four children. He was friendly with the young men he had first met at the village school and grown up with in the small, fiercely independent, tight-knit community. Some of them were not simply staunch Republicans but also members of the Provisional IRA, only too happy to go out at night as members of active service units to carry out violent operations against those they looked upon as their enemies. To these Republicans, Stewartstown had become their own fiefdom and they were the unofficial officers of law and order. To many, the only rule of law in the village was that administered by the Provos; if anything went wrong, it was to the commander of the local Provo unit that the villagers would turn for advice and justice and, if necessary, for retribution. Hardly any locals bothered complaining to the RUC, for the residents of Stewartstown realised that the police had little or no jurisdiction in that part of Co. Tyrone.

Unfortunately for Malachy McIvor, he was a well-known man; his reputation as a keen motorcyclist and respected mechanic was recognised far beyond Stewartstown and, as a result, his name was banded about so freely that one day it came to the attention of Brian Nelson and his freelance informants who were targeting Republicans and anyone connected to the Provos or Sinn Fein.

Agent Ten-Thirty-Three knew all about Stewartstown, even though he had never heard of the Republican enclave until he was taken on a tour of the 'no-go' areas by officers of the Force Research Unit. Never for one moment would Brian Nelson of the UDA risk going into such areas unless under the greatest protection. The day he toured Stewartstown, Cookstown, South Armagh and parts of the border he was in the safe custody of three armed FRU officers and in the safety of a car which did not stop once throughout its tour. That day Nelson was being educated, shown the staunch Republican centres, the catchment areas of Provo recruits and some of the nerve centres of IRA activities. He was shown pubs and clubs where, the FRU handlers asserted, the Provos held court. As a result, these places became possible targets for Loyalist gunmen. Nelson would later brief his UDA informants of the areas they should investigate in their search for Provo gunmen so that they could be checked out and, if necessary, targeted. Months later, McIvor's name would be put forward by UDA informants as a man closely connected to the Provos of Co. Tyrone. And, as ever, Nelson asked his FRU contacts about Malachy McIvor.

'Do you have anything on this man?' he asked during one of his routine interviews with his FRU handlers.

A week later the FRU informed Nelson that they had nothing on the mechanic but that they would investigate. As a result, a P-card was established in the name of Malachy McIvor. It included details of known Provo gunmen with whom he had been seen having the occasional drink or a chat – even though his relationship with them may have been entirely innocent, simply the result of living all his life in a Republican village. To Ten-Thirty-

Three and his UDA colleagues, that was evidence enough, and McIvor's friends of many years and his occasional contact with them would seal his fate.

The P-card and all other details of Malachy McIvor were handed over to Nelson at a safe-house meeting with two FRU handlers on the outskirts of Lisburn, including the latest passport-type photo of McIvor. On this occasion, however, Military Intelligence went further, handing over a print-out, taken from the highly classified secret computer operated by the intelligence services. It included details of McIvor's current address, a map reference of his garage, details of the immediate vicinity and up-to-date information of McIvor's current vehicle, including the registration number. Indeed, no one wanting to target McIvor could have asked for more accurate, detailed information.

In October 1987 Brian Nelson reported to his FRU handlers that the UDA had held a meeting with Loyalist sympathisers living in Co. Tyrone and that all the information handed to him by the FRU had been passed on to the local UDA. Nelson's intelligence handlers urged him to keep them informed of exactly what the UDA discovered and to report back. It is understood that plans to target and kill McIvor were drawn up by the local UDA leaders. This attack was not carried out, though McIvor's name and all his details were kept on the UDA file.

It was not until three years later, some months after the arrest of Brian Nelson himself, that Malachy McIvor's fate was decided and, ironically, he only died because of terrorist actions taken by his Republican friends. In November 1990 an IRA active service unit from Co. Tyrone decided to target and kill a part-time Ulster Defence Regiment soldier, Albert Cooper, a man in his thirties who was married with three young children. In many ways Albert Cooper, who was also a mechanic, was the Protestant equivalent of the Catholic Malachy McIvor, two men on opposite sides of the sectarian divide, both steeped in their own traditions but family men of honour who had never been involved in terrorist activity. And yet both would suffer violent deaths and for no good reason whatsoever.

Unknown to McIvor, his life was put at risk when permission was given by the Provo commander in Co. Tyrone for an IRA active service unit to go ahead with the cold-blooded murder of Albert Cooper early on Friday, 2 November 1990. Cooper was targeted solely because he was a part-time serjeant-major with the UDR. According to the Provos of Co. Tyrone, that was good enough reason to murder him. Little did they know that their decision would directly lead to the murder of their friend Malachy McIvor.

Cooper was working in his garage, Mid-Ulster Exhausts, in Station Yard off Union Street, Cookstown, when, shortly after ten in the morning, a woman drove a white Vauxhall Astra estate car into the garage and spoke to him. After a couple of minutes she walked away, never to be seen again. Within minutes the car exploded, killing Albert Cooper instantly and causing people in Cookstown to run to the Yard to see what had happened. Two other mechanics were on the premises at the time but were not injured in the blast. The two men gave descriptions of the woman to the police but to no avail.

Albert Cooper, a quiet family man adored by his children, had been targeted once before by the Provos. Two years earlier he had escaped injury when IRA gunmen opened fire on his car as he drove towards his home three miles from Cookstown. As a result, the family had moved into the town, setting up their new home in Dunmore Close, off the Moneymore Road, where they hoped they would be less conspicuous. But once more the IRA gunmen had found him and this time they were more determined than ever to kill him.

One week later, on the evening of Thursday, 8 November, Malachy McIvor would meet his fate in a tit-for-tat killing. The UDA leadership in Co. Tyrone recalled the P-card handed to them by Brian Nelson three years earlier and selected McIvor to pay the price.

Under cover of darkness, on a cold, wet November evening in 1990, three Loyalist gunman drove from Cookstown to nearby Stewartstown, fully aware of the risks they were taking by entering into what they perceived to be 'enemy territory'. They drove slowly down the main street, checking all the details they had, noting McIvor's small garage at the corner of Castlefarm Road and North Street. They then left the village following the Coagh Road.

Three nights later the same men once again drove into Stewartstown. The man in the front passenger seat was carrying a pistol in his belt; in the back seat was another gunman, holding a sub-machine-gun across his knees. Also on his lap, covering the gun, was an Ordnance Survey map of the area. They were taking no chances.

They parked their car in North Street, got out and quietly closed the doors, not wanting to draw attention to their arrival. They looked around. The place seemed deserted. They pulled masks across their faces and nodded, the sign to walk into McIvor's garage a few yards away.

When they got there they could see that not one but two men were present.

'Malachy McIvor?' shouted one of them, addressing his question to the older of the two men. The other looked not much more than a teenager. As the gunmen stood at the entrance to the garage they were barely visible in the darkness that was lit only by the light in the garage where McIvor was working on his brother-in-law's car.

'Who's that?' McIvor asked, somewhat taken aback, because he wasn't expecting any visitors.

Without another word the gunmen took a few paces towards him and opened fire at point-blank range. McIvor was hit by six rounds, all direct hits, and he immediately slumped to the ground without uttering a word. Before McIvor's body had hit the floor the gunmen had walked quickly out of the garage and away from the scene. Apart from the terrified teenager, no one, it seemed, had witnessed their arrival nor would anyone see them depart.

The killing of Malachy McIvor three years after it was first mooted demonstrates the repercussions that flowed from the recruitment of Brian Nelson by British Military Intelligence. The allegation that the British Army in Northern Ireland colluded with Protestant paramilitary groups in the assassination of suspected Republican terrorists had been made many times during the thirty years of the troubles, but it has always been vehemently denied by both the army and the British government. As a result of the actions of the unique Force Research Unit, evidence has been put forward from a number of corners, including politicians in Northern Ireland, the Republic and the mainland, that the FRU was complicit in a series of murders carried out by the UDA between 1987 and 1990, suggesting that the army unit practised 'assass- ination by proxy'. The facts revealed here, however, show that the army was far more deeply involved than had hitherto been suggested.

Assassinations and killings attributable to Nelson and his UDA friends began within a few weeks of Nelson taking up his job. The first shootings carried out by his UDA gunmen bore all the hallmarks of assassins looking for easy targets on which to hone their skills.

One of the first innocent victims of the UDA's new sectarian campaign designed to cause distress and alarm among the Catholic community was Dermot Hackett, a decent, law-abiding, well-known man who visited both Catholic and Protestant shops and houses every day of his working life as a bread-delivery driver. Shortly before nine o'clock in the morning of 23 May 1987, Dermot Hackett was driving his bread van along the Omagh to Drumquin road in Co. Tyrone when he was forced to slow down as he negotiated a difficult bend outside Drumquin. Waiting around the corner, out of sight of the approaching driver, were two masked gunmen. They opened fire with a sub- machine-gun, firing at least a dozen bullets into the driver's door, shattering the window and hitting Dermot Hackett in the head and body. Shortly afterwards a passing motorist stopped and discovered Hackett slumped over the steering wheel of his van, the engine still running, the driver's door peppered with bullet holes. There was no sign of the gunmen.

Dermot Hackett, a forty-year-old married man, was a well-respected and well-liked local figure known to hundreds of Catholics and Protestants living in and around Omagh, a man who would always have a smile and a cheery word for everyone no matter what their religious beliefs. He had never been a member of the Provisional IRA and had no connection with hardline Republicans. He was, however, a hard-working member of the local St Vincent de Paul charity and the cousin of Stephen McKenna, then the leader of the SDLP group on Omagh Council, although Hackett was not a member of any political party nor had he helped with his cousin's election campaign.

But Hackett, a man of principle, had some months before had an argument with local RUC officers after he was found driving his van in an area close to where a security officer had just been shot by Provo gunmen. Questioned by detectives investigating the shooting, Hackett told police that he was simply on his rounds at the time and knew nothing of the killing. He also told them that he had seen no sign of the gunmen either before or after the incident. Apparently, some RUC officers did not believe Hackett and they began to harass him, stopping him frequently as he made his deliveries and demanding to search his vehicle.

Hackett complained about the constant harassment not only to senior RUC officers in Omagh but, when the campaign against him continued, to his local SDLP constituency representative, Denis Haughey, asking him to take up his case with the RUC. Following Hackett's murder, Mr Haughey commented, 'He had been in touch with me about the harassment he received from the police over a lengthy period of time. He was out working when an incident occurred involving a member of the security forces. He had been questioned and co-operated fully and gave details of his movements that day. From that time on he became an object of harassment from the police. Both I and Joseph McManus, the local chairman of the St Vincent de Paul charity, had made representations to the police on his behalf and after this police pressure had eased off. My fear is that the absolutely unreasonable harassment of this man by the police and the public knowledge of it may have made him a target.'

It had indeed. Nine hours earlier Charles Watson, a former prison warder, had been gunned down by masked Provo hitmen who broke into his home in Co. Down, using a sledgehammer to smash their way through the back door just before midnight as he sat at home with his wife Doreen with their four children asleep upstairs.

Doreen told the RUC, 'As soon as Charlie realised that people were trying to smash their way into our home, he knew they were the Provos out to get him. He had nowhere to run, nowhere to hide and so he ran up the stairs to the bathroom, intending to try and escape through the window and down the pipe. The two masked men broke into the living-room and shouted, "Where is he? Where is he?" I said nothing, I was so shocked and frightened, fearing for Charlie's life. The two men were both carrying guns and I just prayed that Charlie would escape. Then I heard shouting followed by the sound of gunfire coming from upstairs and I knew, I just knew, the worst had happened. Seconds later the two men came racing down the stairs and out the kitchendoor. I ran up the stairs and there was Charlie lying in a pool of blood. I knew when I saw him on the bathroom floor that he was dead. Then suddenly I thought of the kids and I turned round and they were coming out of their room to see what was going on. I didn't want them to see their father lying there and I took them back to their bedrooms and closed the bathroom door before calling the RUC. It was horrible, terrible, and now the children have no father.'

And there was anger in Co. Down over Charlie Watson's murder. Three years earlier he had been involved in a late-night fracas outside a chip shop in Newcastle. He had been found guilty of assault and given a three-month suspended jail sentence which was overturned on appeal. The prison authorities, however, dismissed him from the service. As a result, of course, he was also ordered to give back the handgun – the personal protection weapon – that all prison officers are issued with on joining the prison service;

because so many prison warders had been targeted and killed by the Provos they were permitted, indeed advised, to carry their handguns with them at all times. They were also advised to sleep with the guns under their pillows.

Some blamed Charlie Watson's murder on the prison service for refusing to re-employ him after his successful appeal, as well as the Northern Ireland Office for refusing to allow him to keep the gun for his own personal protection. DUP councillor Ethel Smyth claimed that the prison service and the Northern Ireland Office had left him defenceless. 'They have blood on their hands,' she said. 'As a prominent Loyalist he was always going to be a target. Charlie was a member of the Apprentice Boys and the Orange Order and was well known as a Loyalist. He was very concerned about his safety, especially when his brother in the UDR was shot at by Provo gunmen. Charlie was not even permitted to keep his own shotgun that he used to kill vermin on his farm. I knew Charlie well and I know that he was the sort of man who would not have hesitated to use his gun if he was attacked by armed gunmen. But when they did come to his house to kill him, he was defenceless.'

But Charlie Watson had five brothers, and they all had friends in the Orange Order and acquaintances with contacts in the Loyalist paramilitary organisations. Within hours of Watson's murder, the local hardline Co. Tyrone Loyalist paramilitary activists had been in touch with the UDA in Belfast informing them of what had happened and asking if there was any reason why they should not retaliate by taking out a man they considered to be a hardline Republican. They received the reply they wanted, an affirmative, and Dermot Hackett's fate was sealed. Within hours he too was dead and the Loyalists believed they had taken revenge for Charlie Watson's killing.

During early discussions with his handlers Brian Nelson raised the question of Catholic taxi-drivers. 'Are all those taxi-drivers really Provos?' he asked.

'No, not necessarily,' he was told. 'Why do you ask?'

'Well, we understand that many of the drivers working

for Catholic taxi firms have done time for various offences connected with the Provos,' said Nelson. 'When they come out of jail they have no work and no one will employ them, so the Provos arrange for one or other of the west Belfast taxi firms to give them a part-time job driving taxis. It brings them in some money.'

'Well of course it's true that the Catholic taxi firms will want to employ Catholic taxi-drivers because they spend their times in the Catholic areas,' commented one FRU handler. 'It's also true that some of those drivers have done time for terrorist offences, but not all of them. Some are totally innocent, just doing a job of work.'

Nelson was adamant, however, that his UDA colleagues were convinced that most Catholic taxi firms used known Provo activists and hardline Republicans as drivers. The FRU were aware that pressure was often put on the owners of taxi firms operating in the Catholic part of the city to employ former Maze inmates and, they realised, the taxi firms had no option but to comply. If they had said no to the Provos, they would have found themselves out of business very soon. They put this argument to Nelson forcefully in an effort to persuade him to leave taxi-drivers well alone, but he was never convinced of their argument. Nelson believed he knew better than Military Intelligence.

On Saturday, 3 July 1987, a UDA man walked casually into a pub on the edge of west Belfast which was known to be mainly, though not exclusively, frequented by Catholics from the nearby estates. He was, of course, taking an extraordinary risk, for if anyone in that bar had suspected he was a Protestant his chances of escaping a severe beating, or perhaps a worse fate, would have been nil. He ordered a pint of Guinness and slowly downed it, talking to no one and minding his own business as he watched groups of men, and a few women, enjoying an evening in the pub. He placed his empty glass on the bar and asked the barmaid serving him: 'Could you call me a taxi, love?'

'Aye,' she replied, 'when do you want it for?'

'As soon as possible,' he replied, 'five minutes okay?'

'Here's a card for the taxi,' she said, and handed over a

printed card with the name of the Ardoyne taxi firm on it.
At that moment the UDA gunman knew that the taxi
would almost certainly be driven by a Catholic. The idea
was that passengers would give the card to the driver so he
knew he was picking up the man who had, in fact, ordered
the taxi and not some stranger.

As he waited impatiently for the taxi to arrive, the UDA
gunman didn't want to start a conversation with anyone
for fear of being traced later so, after a couple of minutes,
he walked outside to wait in the summer evening light. A
few yards away another man who had been waiting in a
car, got out of his vehicle, walked over and handed the
UDA man a folded newspaper. They winked at each other
but did not say a word. Wrapped inside the newspaper was
a .9mm handgun.

Minutes later the Ardoyne taxi arrived and the UDA
man waved down the driver, handing him the card from
the pub before getting in the back. He said he wanted to
be taken to Oldpark Road the other side of the Ardoyne.

The driver was forty-year-old Edward Campbell. His
name had never come up during discussions between
Nelson and his handlers. Campbell was totally unknown to
the RUC Special Branch or Military Intelligence, having no
previous convictions and apparently no attachment or
relationship with the Provisional IRA or even its political
wing, Sinn Fein. His only tenuous connection with the
Provos was that the taxi firm for which he worked was
situated in the Catholic Ardoyne area of Belfast and he
therefore may have, from time to time, ferried Provos, Sinn
Fein supporters or Republican sympathisers around the city.

For ten minutes neither man in the taxi said a word as
the driver made his way towards the Ardoyne and on
towards Oldpark Road. When he was not far from his
destination he asked his passenger where exactly he wanted
to be dropped.

'Say nothing,' the gunman said in a threatening voice as
he jammed the barrel of the revolver into the back of
Campbell's neck. 'If you try anything I'll blow your fucking
brains out. Just keep driving till I tell you when to stop.'

During the next couple of minutes the highly agitated Campbell tried desperately to start a conversation in a bid to talk the gunman out of shooting him. But the UDA man would not let him say a word, telling him to 'shut up and keep fucking driving'. As they approached a country lane leading to a quarry the gunman told Campbell that he should stop as he was waiting to meet some friends.

A few seconds later a car that had been following the taxi flashed the headlamps twice. In that instant the gunman fired at point-blank range into the back of Campbell's head. The noise in the car was deafening; the damage to Campbell's head horrifying. He died instantly. The gunman stepped out of the car as his two accomplices drove up. He clambered inside and shut the door as the driver picked up speed and drove away.

'How did it go?' said the man in the passenger seat.

'Perfect,' replied the gunman. 'Went like fuckin' clockwork.'

He handed over the murder weapon. It was one that Nelson had arranged to be imported from South Africa. It was neither the first nor the last time that particular gun would be used to kill someone.

Alliance councillor Mr Tom Campbell (no relation to the dead man) commented the following day, 'This is a horrible murder which bears all the hallmarks of a new sectarian murder campaign. I believe such a campaign has been designed by extremists to stir up community tension in the run up to the marching season and would urge anyone with information about this crime to put it in the hands of the RUC.'

When Nelson met his handlers that day he was in a confident and positive mood, obviously pleased with his success. 'I told you that we were going to take out the Provo taxi firms,' he said. 'Well, I've got news for you, we've decided to declare war on them, all of them. Now you'll see some real action.'

'Why are the UDA targeting taxi-drivers?' one handler asked, shaking his head in disbelief. 'What have you got against the taxi-drivers?'

'They're all in it,' Nelson replied, 'every fucking one of them. They're all running errands for the Provos, giving them lifts, driving them on active service missions around Belfast. We've been watching them and all their drivers are part of the Provo terrorist organisation.'

'That's bullshit,' he was told, 'and you know it.'

'Bollocks,' said Nelson, his arrogance increasing by the minute. 'You tossers think you know everything but you don't. We have far more men on the ground working directly for us and they know what's going on. They've told us that nearly all the Catholic taxis are being driven by Provos or their sympathisers. And we are going to target them.'

'But you can't say that about total strangers,' Nelson was told in no uncertain terms. 'Some of the drivers may be perfectly reasonable, law-abiding citizens who want nothing to do with the Provos. I thought we'd made that clear to you before. They might be taxi-drivers because there's no other work about. You can't go around killing innocent men for no good reason, for God's sake. If the UDA persist in this idea, it is nothing but blatant sectarian warfare, and God knows where that might end. Don't you understand that? Don't your UDA bosses know that?'

But Nelson was adamant and cocky with it. 'That's not the way we see it,' he replied. 'We know they're all in it together, every one of them. It's no good you lot saying we must do this, we mustn't do that, because we know what's going on in Belfast. Our men on the streets tell us what's going on and they say all the fucking Catholic taxi-drivers are in the Provo game up to their fuckin' necks. We know that unless you are, or have been, a Provisional, a member of the IRA, preferably having done time in the Maze, you won't get a job as a taxi-driver in west Belfast. Get it? We know the Provos control all the Catholic taxi firms. It's no good your pissing lot trying to make excuses for them because it won't wash.'

When Nelson had finally stopped talking, one of the handlers said, 'Listen, let me explain this a little further. You must understand that such random killings could easily rebound on Protestant taxi-drivers. It'll be tit-for-tat. You can't think that the Provos will take this lying down. They'll call up a taxi, just like your lot did, and top him. So where's it going to end? Do you envisage this going on for weeks and months? Don't be so fucking stupid and wake up to the reality of what you've done.'

'Listen,' replied Nelson, unfazed by the attack on him, 'I'm one of those taxi-drivers and I'm prepared to take the risk. The Provos have got to be stopped – that's why we're all here. And this is one way of taking them out.'

'Bullshit,' said the No.1 handler. 'Officially you're a taxi-driver but you never go out looking for work. If open warfare breaks out on the streets you won't be risking your neck driving a taxi around the city because you'll stay at home and never venture out. So don't give us any more of your heroic shit.'

'That's as may be,' said Nelson looking downcast at being so easily exposed, 'but you have to understand that the UDA see the Catholic taxi-drivers as easy targets; that's the real reason they want to target them.'

Before Nelson left that day his FRU handlers asked him to take a message to his UDA bosses explaining that attacking Catholic taxi-drivers was a disastrous idea because it could well backfire on the Protestant taxi-drivers and lead to open warfare. The FRU handlers tried to convince him that taxi-drivers weren't anything to do with the conflict on the streets and they should be left out of it altogether. But when Nelson left the safe-house that day his handlers feared that the UDA would, more than likely, continue targeting their easy prey, the wretched taxi-drivers. It seemed to them that Nelson had become more hardline and more anti-Catholic since he began working for them. They recalled their first meeting with him back in 1985 when his overriding reason for wanting to work with Military Intelligence was to get back at the UDA leaders who had refused to take action against one of their own men who had tried to rape Nelson's wife. But the more time he spent in his new job as the UDA's chief intelligence officer the more virulent and bitter he had become towards the Republican movement. It seemed that Nelson had all but forgotten his anger at the UDA leadership. Now all his animosity was focused on those he saw as the enemy: the Republicans, Nationalists, Catholics and, in particular, the Provos.

Edward Campbell was simply shot at random by thugs looking for easy targets. His murder shocked officers of the Force Research Unit because they saw the killing as the opening shot of what could be a new and vicious sectarian feud which would leave many innocent people dead. No matter how aggressive the FRU set out to be, there was never the intention that decent, ordinary Catholics or Protestants should ever be targeted.

Six weeks later another Catholic taxi-driver was shot at the wheel of his vehicle but this was an even more appalling and cowardly attack by the UDA gunmen. Mickey Power, a handsome thirty-two-year-old, was a devout and deeply religious person who attended Mass at his local church every Sunday. He would also attend prayer meetings at Protestant churches in Dunmurry when members of the local community were praying for an end to sectarian violence and the troubles. Mickey Power had never been involved with the Provos, never been involved with politics, never been a member of a political party.

On Sunday, 23 August 1987, he was driving his wife Bernadette and their three young children to Mass from their home in Netherlands Park, Dunmurry. When he stopped at the junction at the top of his street, a white Datsun Cherry drew up beside the Powers' car. Mickey glanced over to see what the driver wanted and found himself looking into the barrel of a revolver.

Not a word was spoken. The gunman, his face masked, just opened fire at point-blank range, hitting Mickey Power in the head and felling him in an instant. But the violent UDA gunman continued to fire his revolver into the head and body of his victim and as a result Power's eight-year-old daughter was blinded, hit in the eye by flying glass. She was later rushed to the Royal Belfast

Hospital for Sick Children and doctors hoped that in time they might be able to save her sight.

When the FRU handlers tackled Nelson about the murder of Mickey Power, a totally innocent man, he was unrepentant.

'It's nothing to do with me,' he claimed. 'I had no idea they were targeting this man Power.'

'But you must have had some idea something was going down?'

'No,' he replied adamantly, 'nothing at all. I hadn't the faintest idea.'

'But you must have discussed the matter,' they argued, 'you are the intelligence officer.'

'Exactly,' Nelson argued, 'I'm just intelligence. I'm nothing to do with the military side and I don't want to know. I tell you I hadn't the faintest idea they were targeting Power. In any case, we heard that he was an operations officer with the Provos.'

'Where did you hear that from?'

'I don't know,' replied Nelson, 'I was told, that's all.'

'Well, we've checked him out too, and he was clean, totally clean. He had never been involved with the Provos or Sinn Fein as far as we know. So we would like to know where you got your facts from.'

'It's true,' Nelson responded, trying to defend his UDA mates.

'That's bullshit and you know it,' he was told.

Nelson was also asked whether any other Catholic taxi-drivers had been targeted but he replied that he hadn't the faintest idea. 'We'll just have to wait and see,' was his answer.

Three weeks after the brutal murder of Mickey Power, the UDA gunmen struck again, this time taking out another totally innocent young man who had no connection with the Provos, Sinn Fein or Republicanism. Jim Meighan was only twenty-two and engaged to be married to his childhood sweetheart, Anita Skillen. The young couple, who had met at school when they were fifteen, had planned to marry the following spring, 1988. A Roman

Catholic, Meighan was an easy target for the UDA gunmen. His girlfriend lived in a Protestant area and each night he would take her back to her home in his Ford Cortina which was easily recognisable because of the custom work he had carried out on the vehicle. Having kissed her goodnight and seen her safely indoors, he would then drive back to his own house.

As usual, on the night of 20 September 1987, the couple had spent the evening watching television and listening to music in Jim's room at his parents' home before setting off in the customised Cortina. Anita would say later, 'We had just arrived outside my house around midnight and were saying goodnight when suddenly someone appeared at the window of the car and started shooting. I couldn't see very much, just the flash of the shots as the gunman fired into the vehicle. I was lucky, I wasn't hit, but Jim was killed instantly with a bullet in the head.'

His mother said later, 'They must have been waiting for Jim and Anita to drive up to her house as he did every night. They would recognise him because of the car. They could not have selected an easier target; an innocent young man without any enemies. I had always worried about Jim driving into a Protestant area every night but he felt confident because he was in his car and believed that he could drive away from any attack. But that confidence was misplaced.'

When Nelson was called to a meeting with his FRU handlers the next morning he appeared nonchalant as if he didn't know why he had been asked to attend the meeting. 'What's up?' he asked cheekily.

'You know what's up,' he was told, 'the shooting of Jimmy Meighan last night.'

'Can't help you, don't know anything about it,' Nelson replied, all but dismissing the matter.

'Did you hear about it?' he was asked.

'Only on the radio this morning,' he said.

'Did you know it was being planned?'

'No, I'd no idea,' he replied.

The two FRU handlers tried to press Nelson, tried to persuade him to tell them what he knew of Meighan's murder but he would not be drawn. He remained adamant that he had no idea the shooting was planned and claimed that news of the killing had been as much of a surprise to him as it had been to the Force Research Unit. Once again, it appeared, the UDA were hellbent on causing as much strife and fear among the Catholic community as they could. They didn't seem to care a damn if they targeted Provos or totally innocent young people, as long as they were Catholics.

But the UDA campaign of the summer and autumn of 1987 did have the effect of galvanising the Provos to hit back at Protestant targets. The Provo gunman, too, did not seem to care whether the people they targeted and killed were members of Protestant paramilitary organisations or ordinary people with no Loyalist connections, going about their daily lives. All that mattered to the IRA was to make sure a Protestant was murdered in this new round of tit-for-tat violence which had been so rife in the 1970s. As Alban Maginness, the SDLP councillor for north Belfast, commented after the murder of Jim Meighan, 'There are two very effective units of the IRA and the UVF now operating in this area. Between them they are obviously trying to create a situation of complete instability and a breakdown of any semblance of law and order.'

It seemed that the UDA leaders and those gunmen of the UVF and the UFF who carried out the killings had achieved one of their aims – to cause strife and mayhem and force the IRA to retaliate, thus creating fear and anarchy. But these weren't the only people responsible for bringing about this dreadful state of affairs; the Force Research Unit, a secret arm of the British Army, could also be held responsible for the rapidly deteriorating situation between the two communities.

# Chapter Seven

## Partners in Crime

●

By late 1987, the Joint Irish Section – sometimes referred to as 'Box' because the postal address of both MI5 and MI6 was simply a box number in London's Curzon Street – were informed that the Provisional IRA and senior Sinn Fein politicians were becoming increasingly concerned about the level of activity on the streets of Belfast by groups of Loyalist paramilitaries. They seemed to be attacking Republicans with impunity, torching clubs and pubs and roaming the streets in their cars, stopping, questioning and then beating up any young Catholic men they came across. IRA intelligence believed that the Loyalists had adopted this new measure of blatant intimidation because the Provo cell network had become so secretive and so successful that neither Loyalists nor the intelligence services had any real idea of the identities of members of Provo active service units.

This interpretation of events was readily accepted by the JIS as the intelligence coming in from agents in the field at that time was increasingly sparse. This meant that the never-ending battle against the Provisionals was even more difficult at a time when their bombers seemed able to strike both in the Province and on the mainland with little fear of their plans being thwarted by the intelligence services. The MI5 officers in the Province felt under pressure to produce results and they were not doing so. The Thatcher government was pushing hard for the intelligence and security forces to do all in their power to frustrate the IRA, keep them under pressure and thus keep down the number of bomb explosions in Belfast and on the mainland. This is why MI5 and Military Intelligence were happy to supply Nelson with all the computer back-up and information he required if such action resulted in a reduction in the Provos' capability to kill and bomb any targets they chose.

Because of the political pressure from Whitehall, the JIS decided that Brian Nelson's unique position inside the UDA headquarters should be put to greater use in an effort to keep the Provos on the defensive. His handlers were ordered to encourage Nelson to continue targeting known Provo activists, Sinn Fein politicians and Republican sympathisers.

One of the most audacious and rash shootings ever organised by the Force Research Unit with the assistance of their agent Brian Nelson was the plot to murder Alex Maskey, one of Belfast's most well-known and well-respected Sinn Fein politicians. Maskey, a well-built man then aged thirty-five, and married with a young family, was at the forefront of politics in west Belfast. He was no fool; he anticipated that he was likely to be targeted by Loyalist gunmen from time to time and, as a result, took sensible precautions in his everyday life, becoming very safety-conscious. Whenever he left his house in the Andersonstown area of west Belfast, for example, he would automatically check for UCBTs (under-car booby-traps). His home, a three-bedroomed house on a large estate, was guarded by infra-red lights at the front and rear and had a spy-hole in the front door. He would never open either the front or back door until he was satisfied he knew the identity of the person visiting him, and he told his wife and children to be just as careful. He was taking no chances for he trusted no one knocking at his door. In the cauldron of hatred between the two communities in the late 1980s, this was the only sensible way to behave, checking everything and trusting no one.

The name Alex Maskey came up during one of Nelson's briefing sessions with his FRU handlers in the summer of 1987 just a few months after Nelson had taken over as the UDA's intelligence officer. Maskey's P-card was produced by the FRU and handed to Nelson along with up-to-date black-and-white photographs of the Sinn Fein councillor. His home address, his telephone number, his car and its registration number were also given to Nelson so that he and his UDA colleagues could check all the details Military Intelligence had on the man they considered to be a troublemaker. Nelson was also provided with a list of the politicians, friends and cronies with whom Maskey mixed in his everyday life. Not surprisingly, many on that list were members of Sinn Fein or the IRA. He was, after all, a Sinn Fein councillor.

Armed with the P-card and details of Alex Maskey on the home computer installed by Military Intelligence IT experts, Brian Nelson set about examining the lifestyle of the man he knew would become not just another target for UDA gunmen but a highly political and high-profile victim of their new campaign.

A couple of weeks later a rather downcast Nelson returned to see his handlers to tell them that he had grave doubts as to whether any of 'his lads' would be able to get close enough to take out Alex Maskey.

'What's the problem?' he was asked.

'He's too tucked up,' Nelson replied. 'It's impossible to get close to him. We could hit him at a distance with a telescopic rifle but that's too risky. We like to get in close, because it gives them no fucking chance.'

'Have you checked out his home?'

'Of course we have,' Nelson replied rather petulantly, annoyed his handlers were treating him like a beginner. 'We know what to do but this one's difficult and highly dangerous. We believe it would be impossible to hit Maskey at his home. His house is situated on an estate surrounded by Republican sympathisers and his constituents. And the place is more difficult to get into than Fort Knox – infra-red lights, cameras all around the fuckin' place and and bulletproof glass on his downstairs windows. The escape route would be difficult to secure – I've taken a long hard look myself. Have you guys any decent ideas?'

Both Nelson and his FRU handlers came to the

conclusion that the only way to get to Alex Maskey was to find a way to lure him out of his fortress home and then shoot him. But because he was so security-conscious they knew that a random caller at his home would receive no reply and there was a serious likelihood that he would immediately phone the RUC to report a suspicious caller. The last thing that handlers and senior officers of the Force Research Unit wanted was any embarrassing interference from the RUC, or the Special Branch asking awkward questions. Nelson reported to his handlers that his hitmen had also looked into the possibility of shooting Maskey when he was being driven around Belfast but that had been shelved because they believed most of the time he was accompanied by armed bodyguards.

Nelson's FRU handlers said they would look into the situation and at a meeting the following week put forward a plan of action which they believed might succeed in luring Maskey out of his home without arousing his suspicion. Their plan, as put to Nelson, was no less than a detailed plot which they were convinced if carried out properly would end in the cold-blooded murder of Alex Maskey, a democratically elected councillor representing the voters of west Belfast.

At that time many Provo activists and Sinn Fein members and politicians used Apollo Taxis, the same west Belfast firm which the UDA were convinced only employed former Provos and Republican activists.

Nelson's handlers knew that Maskey was frequently collected from his home by a car from the Apollo taxi firm. They suggested that one UDA gunman should stay in the car ducking down out of sight of Maskey's house while another gunman should go to Maskey's front door and call for him. To guarantee success, however, they knew they had to find a way of winning Maskey's immediate and absolute confidence. They suggested that a car from a Republican area be hijacked by the UDA and taken to a 'friendly' Loyalist garage where a specially constructed Apollo Taxi sign – an exact replica of the original – would be fitted to the roof of the car. The handlers then advised

Nelson where he should go to have the replica Apollo sign constructed and painted.

Nelson was delighted that British Intelligence were so keen to help the UDA that they would offer such detailed advice, going to such lengths to ensure the murder of a high-profile Sinn Fein politician. Two weeks later the Apollo Taxi sign, expertly fitted to the roof of a stolen vehicle, was handed over to Nelson. The hijacked passenger car looked no different from any of the ordinary, everyday saloons Apollo used to ferry people around Belfast.

At 9.45 a.m. one morning in July 1987, the fake taxi parked directly outside Alex Maskey's home in full view of neighbours, pedestrians or anyone looking out of a window or checking through the spy-hole of Maskey's front door. One UDA gunman stayed in the driver's seat while the other walked to the house and rang the bell.

'Taxi for you, Alex,' shouted the man when someone answered the bell and asked who was calling. But no one opened the front door.

'Give me a couple of minutes,' came the shouted reply. It was Alex Maskey's voice. Though he had not ordered a taxi that morning, the FRU's understanding of the man proved correct. They had been convinced that he would trust the fact that an Apollo taxi had turned up, which often occurred when he was needed to attend an urgent meeting, and a taxi would be sent to pick him up.

A few minutes later, Maskey opened the door and stepped out. In front of him stood the man he believed was the taxi-driver. But this masked man was holding a gun. Before Maskey could react, the gunman opened fire at point-blank range, hitting him in the stomach with three shots. Maskey fell to the ground and his attacker turned and ran to the waiting car. The UDA gunmen drove away unhindered by anyone. It was not surprising that the two men were able to escape without encountering the RUC or any passing army patrol – the Force Research Unit had put an exclusion zone in operation on the estate where Maskey lived. The gunmen's vehicle was found abandoned by the

RUC later that day. There were no fingerprints and no sign of the weapon.

Maskey was rushed by ambulance to the Royal Victoria Hospital where surgeons operated immediately in a bid to save his life. It would be weeks before the Belfast City Councillor had recovered. Doctors proclaimed later that he was very lucky to have survived the shooting.

But the attempt on Maskey's life would have far-reaching repercussions. Maskey was no low-life Provo gunman of little or no consequence to the IRA leadership, but rather a well-respected, well-trusted, well-known Belfast City Councillor who represented the ordinary Catholics of west Belfast. This was no attempted killing that could be investigated superficially by the authorities and then quickly forgotten.

The RUC Special Branch were called in to investigate and their informants were convinced that Maskey's attackers were members of the UDA. Loyalist informers told Special Branch that the man suspected of organising and setting up the attack was Brian Nelson, the UDA's chief intelligence officer. As a result, senior Special Branch officers raised the matter in meetings of both the Joint Irish Section and the Tasking Co-ordination Group, for they were surprised that the UDA had become, almost overnight, more willing to take risks when planning attacks on Provisional IRA men, Sinn Fein councillors or even those Catholics believed to support the Republican cause.

Special Branch were also worried that the UDA appeared to be becoming more imaginative in their plans, going to the trouble of making a taxi sign to gain access to someone they wanted to assassinate. They admitted at the JIS meeting that none of their contacts inside the UDA, of whom there were many, had known anything whatsoever about the attempt on Maskey's life.

Special Branch also told the JIS and the TCG that they were hearing reports from their Loyalist contacts that British Military Intelligence were becoming more closely involved with the UDA. They found this most disturbing because Special Branch had always believed that keeping an eye on the UDA was their prerogative and nothing to do with any other intelligence agency whether military or MI5. At the end of one top-level JIS meeting, Force Research Unit chiefs, as well as senior MI5 officers, were asked to check whether any of their officers were involved with the UDA, and to report back their findings to the JIS.

But no senior officer of British Intelligence was ordered to appear or was asked questions about the shooting of Alex Maskey. And no 'inquest' was ordered into the shooting. Indeed, the FRU handlers were not even spoken to by senior officers and asked to explain what had happened. Their chiefs called in at their officers and, with a wink and a nod and no questions asked, told them, 'You have all heard of the unprovoked attack on the Sinn Fein councillor Alex Maskey and you must have heard that the RUC Special Branch are making allegations that Military Intelligence could well have been involved in some way with the shooting. Now, of course, we all know that is not true and has nothing whatsoever to do with the Force Research Unit. As far as we know this shooting was probably the responsibility of the UDA and this inform- ation has been passed to the RUC for further investigation. We have contacts with the UDA but unfortunately we do not always know when they are planning an operation, nor do we know the name of the targeted person or the location where this might be carried out. However, we must all make sure in future that our contacts with the UDA provide us with more details of operations planned by the UDA so that the forces of law and order can move speedily enough to prevent any killings or injuries of any intended targets, including, of course, any Provo, Sinn Fein or Republican activists, members or sympathisers. We must do all in our power to stop these random killings.'

There was no discussion following this charade of a pep-talk from the FRU's senior officers but a recording was made so that any future investigation could see how the unit's officers had reacted to the shooting of Maskey.

Throughout most of 1987 the keen-minded Nelson

was more involved in organising his computer database of Republican and Sinn Fein targets rather than spending time planning sectarian murders and random killings of Provo activists and political opponents. Nelson would become quite a tidy, conscientious agent in the first few months of starting work for both the UDA and the FRU. Shortly after returning to Belfast he walked into a safe-house meeting one day carrying a bulging briefcase and proceeded to take out a large A4 black book with plastic folders. There were also beige cardboard portfolio files and loose papers, written on in various handwriting styles as though compiled by a number of people. These were sometimes accompanied by black-and-white photographs – mugshots – which looked as though they had originated from official RUC or Ulster Defence Regiment files. These made up the UDA's intelligence material and some had obviously come from either the RUC or Army Intelligence. Files on some people even included the secret P-cards. In all, there must have been details on about two hundred separate people in the portfolio, from all areas of the Province, though mostly from Belfast. Most of the files were of Provo, INLA and Sinn Fein activists, supporters and sympathisers; some were old and useless but others were right up to date.

The FRU handlers were impressed, even taken aback, by the quantity as well as the high quality of some of the material, and offered to sort out the paperwork, put it in some sort of order, and then return it to Nelson at a later date. They also, of course, wanted to copy and check every item.

Two or three times a week throughout the summer and autumn of that year Nelson would meet his FRU handlers, gaining as much information as possible from them about potential targets so that his new toy – his computer system – would be up to date with all the latest highly sensitive intelligence material. He would usually phone to check whether a meeting could be set up. On those occasions he would call the FRU headquarters where the officers and handlers were based. The FRU adopted the same practice as every other intelligence organisation in handling agents and regular informants. The four codes represented different levels of urgency. For example: 'Do you fancy a visit to the chippy?' might be a request to arrange a meeting; 'Do you want to go to the football?' might mean he needed an urgent meeting; 'Do you want to see me for a pint of Guinness?' might mean the agent was in some danger and needed immediate assistance; and 'My mother's been taken sick' might mean some operation, like a shooting or bombing, was due to take place in the immediate future.

The telephonist on duty at the base would have a book with these coded messages and by the side of each the agent's number, which in Nelson's case was Ten-Thirty-Three, though he himself, as was the case with every other agent or informant, would never know that number. Notes in the book by the side of each coded message would alert the telephonist as to how to respond to the message, exactly what he should do and whom he should contact. Included, of course, were the various telephone numbers of the handlers and officers to be contacted. The system had worked most efficiently for decades at least.

Nelson had access to two computers, one which the UDA obtained for him and which he kept in their headquarters, and the other, a more sophisticated model, which was purchased for him by Military Intelligence in May 1987 and installed at his home. It cost nine hundred pounds second-hand. He was also given instruction by computer experts employed by Military Intelligence on how to use the machine. If he ever came across a problem in organising his files or database he only had to phone for help and an expert would be on hand to sort out the problem. He had every confidence that his home computer would never be targeted by the RUC, Special Branch or the army because his home had been put 'out of bounds' by Military Intelligence. He felt totally protected.

'I need all the information you can give me,' Nelson would say regularly, 'so that I can illustrate to my UDA bosses that I have top-secret intelligence about the people they want to target. The greater my credibility with the UDA the more use I can be to Military Intelligence because the UDA will put more faith and trust in me.'

Within a matter of months Brian Nelson had a considerable database of more than one hundred people. By the time his extraordinary career ended, this had grown to between four and five hundred names of potential victims, and he had all the necessary information to target the great majority of them accurately.

Understandably, Nelson was very proud of his computer and of the mass of information he had installed in its database. He kept the computer in his study, a small boxroom upstairs at his home where he kept all his contact files. By the time his infamous career was over Nelson had virtually as many names on file as the IBM computers – with a programme codenamed 'Crucible' – used by the RUC, Special Branch, the army and British Intelligence. Anyone investigating the various databases, including Nelson's, would have come to only one conclusion: that the information contained on all the computers had come from the same, single source. Crucible terminals were in every army base but access by the RUC and the army was only to level 2, whereas Nelson was permitted information to level 5. (The maximum level was 8, reserved for senior intelligence officers and the Political Section, namely MI5.)

Nelson had names and descriptions of Provo, Republican and Sinn Fein targets. He also had their various aliases, their addresses and telephone numbers, the names of their wives and the names and ages of their children. He stored the make, colour, engine capacity and registration numbers of their cars; their employers' names, addresses and telephone numbers as well as any record of arrests, charges faced and sentences and time served. Nelson also collected and logged the various sightings of his targets in meticulous detail, providing himself with a remarkable cross-referenced file. It also contained details of extra-marital affairs, names of mistresses and lovers, houses where top Provo gunmen and bombers spent one or two nights a week in their bid to keep one jump ahead of the law and, more importantly, the UDA gunmen. Nelson also had details of the men's known haunts, particularly the Republican clubs and pubs they frequented.

He was provided with information from another computer, also manufactured by IBM, with a top-secret programme codenamed 'Vengeful', which had been set up for the RUC, the army and British Intelligence. It was fast and accurate, providing a print-out within seven seconds of the information being fed into the computer. Vengeful not only had details of every vehicle registered in Northern Ireland, but also a record of every vehicle that ever visited the Province, including, of course, those from the Irish Republic. This vehicle list – including the names and addresses of the owners – covered not only cars but also all vans, trucks and lorries brought into Ulster by the security forces. The computer stored information tracking the latest sighting of all these vehicles with places, dates and times.

Military Intelligence also supplied Nelson with the all-important 'family trees' of the Belfast Brigade of the Provisional IRA, giving every known detail of the respective commander, second-in-command, intelligence officer, quartermaster and any cell commanders plus details of their addresses and telephone numbers, vehicles and registration plates, their wives, girlfriends, relatives, friends and acquaintances, and the various safe-houses where the Belfast Brigade held their top-level meetings. He was also given details of Provo links with the IRA's Northern Command as well as a breakdown of the seven-man IRA Army Council, including particulars of both Gerry Adams and Martin McGuinness. By the end of 1987 Nelson had details in his computer of about sixty senior Provos, all the known current activists. In addition, he had a full background report on nine activists involved with the smaller, breakaway INLA who were still active in the late 1980s.

As soon as they were available, photographs and montages of everyone on his files, many of them police

photographs taken at the time of arrest, were given to
Nelson. Some of the other pictures taken covertly by 14th
Int or E4A surveillance units. There were sometimes six or
seven photographs of well-known Provo activists and Sinn
Fein leaders, making recognition easy and almost
foolproof.

And that was not all. Military Intelligence gave Nelson
the names and addresses of the firms, companies and
scams that the Provisional IRA were then running in
Belfast, including the names of taxi firms, construction
companies and Republican pubs and clubs. He was also
supplied with information showing how the Provos
laundered their scams, monies earned from fruit-
machines, protection rackets and gambling.

The FRU provided Nelson with a portable radio-
frequency scanner which he would carry around Belfast,
listening in to open RUC and army networks as well as
taxi firms and those frequencies used by Provo leaders. The
hand-held scanner, measuring no more than nine by three
inches, had a small screen which showed whichever radio
frequency the scanner had picked up. In a very short time
Nelson knew precisely whose radio links he was tuned to.
Of course, the scanner could not pick up any secure
frequencies, such as those used by the intelligence services
and some sections of Special Branch, but it nevertheless
proved a very useful tool for Nelson.

The streetwise agent possessed a meticulous mind for
detail which surprised his handlers. They knew that his
education had been sparse, to say the least, and yet he had
a remarkable memory, and this, coupled with his fastidious
attention to detail, meant that he kept immaculate
intelligence files, with no detail missing. When the FRU
handlers visited his home they were somewhat taken aback
by the professional way he had mastered the art of
databasing and cross-referencing so much information.

By the end of 1987 Brian Nelson, the UDA's
intelligence chief, was in an extraordinary position with
access to most of the information about the Provos, Sinn
Fein/IRA and Republican sympathisers, their friends and

relatives, their haunts and their vehicles. His intelligence databases were rivalled only by those held by British Intelligence and the RUC Special Branch. And all had been provided courtesy of Military Intelligence. But the JIS knew precisely what was going on and the extent to which Nelson had been provided with secret data, as well as the level of access he had been granted.

There was another side to Brian Nelson. The highly professional intelligence officer appeared almost childlike in his fascination for handguns. From the very start of his relationship with British Intelligence, he would continually demand that he should be armed, granted a handgun licence and be permitted to carry a weapon at all times for his own personal safety. This was always frowned upon and Nelson was in fact never provided with any type of gun by the intelligence services.

But that didn't deter him from asking endless questions about the various guns his handlers carried with them as well as details of other weapons which they were called on to use from time to time. He would ask to hold their Browning 9mm handguns with extended magazines, capable of firing twenty rounds; their Heckler & Koch S3 assault rifles which held a maximum of thirty .556 calibre rounds; their favourite Heckler & Koch 9mm MP51 submachine-guns which also held thirty rounds; and their tiny Walther .765 pistols which could be hidden inconspicuously inside the wearer's socks. Quite often when attending meetings in safe-houses, Nelson would ask to hold one of the handguns and, after taking out the ammunition, would sit and play with the gun, seemingly mesmerised by the power he realised came from such a weapon.

As the months rolled by, Nelson became so confident of his relationship with Military Intelligence – and the security that it afforded him – that he would turn to his handlers whenever he needed advice, no matter how delicate the subject. Even when his questions involved breaking the law, he would still seek their advice, and, nine times out of ten, it was readily given. Military Intelligence needed Nelson and his freelance Loyalist informants who were starting to provide the type of information necessary for the security services to keep an eye on the Provos. Nelson even turned to his handlers for advice when the UDA chiefs asked him to store weapons which had been used in operations against the Provos. At least one of the weapons, a sub-machine-gun, had been used by the UDA to kill a Provo activist. But Nelson was worried, not sure whether he should risk hiding UDA weapons himself.

At one meeting he tentatively raised the question with his handlers: 'I've been asked to store some weapons by the UDA. I'm not certain, of course, but I suspect they might be hot. Have you any ideas what I should do?'

'Are you asking us to store them for you?' one asked.

'You wouldn't do that, would you?' he asked hopefully.

'No, we couldn't do that.'

'Have you any ideas then?' he asked again.

'Are you prepared to have these weapons at your house?' one asked. 'It wouldn't be too much of a risk; remember, you are officially protected from the authorities.'

'I don't know,' Nelson replied, 'it sounds dangerous, having them at home.'

'Well, have you somewhere on your property where you could hide them or somewhere nearby? Have you a large outside drain, for example?'

'There's a drain with a manhole cover at the end of my garden,' he said, 'would that do?'

'It could be the perfect place,' came the reply, 'but remember, before putting them in a damp environment like that, you must oil the weapons well and roll them in plastic bags so they don't get wet.'

The FRU handlers, however, were taking no chances. They wanted to know what the weapons had been used for because they feared they could well have been employed in any number of killings by UDA gunmen. Nelson was happy to hand over the guns to the FRU for examination by army forensic experts before hiding them away. By comparing marks left by rounds fired during previous attacks, ballistic experts were able to discover for certain that one of the weapons, the sub-machine-gun mentioned above, had been used in at least four previous attacks. There were also two 9mm pistols, one Belgian, one Czech.

All were tested by ballistic experts in the traditional manner, by firing them into a box of sand and then examining and detailing the marks left in the sand by the rounds. By such means, forensic experts knew that if ever any of the weapons Nelson planned to hide were used in any future attack, ballistics would know for sure that they were from Nelson's secret arsenal.

Before they were returned to him, one of his handlers said, 'Make sure we know if you are asked for any of these prior to a UDA attack. We want to know, we must know. And there is one other piece of advice: if any of these weapons are ever used by any UDA gunmen again, never accept them back, otherwise you could be charged with serious offences, including complicity to murder, and that could land you in jail for many years. Under those circumstances, Brian, we would not be able to save you. Do you understand?'

'I'll remember that,' he said. 'Is that right, though – you couldn't save me?'

'That's right,' he was told in no uncertain terms, 'not in those circumstances. Take our advice, and never forget it, okay?'

'Right,' Nelson replied in his thick Belfast accent.

'Never carry those weapons around with you either, no matter how tempted you might be,' he was warned. 'If you're caught holding weapons, we won't be able to save you. Have you got that?'

'Aye,' he replied, as though only half-listening to what was being said.

It seemed, however, that he had taken to heart the advice being offered; but, by the spring of 1988, the cocky, arrogant Nelson was becoming over-confident, almost getting out of control. With his £300 a week cash in hand from Army Intelligence and his expenses from the UDA, he began drinking heavily in Loyalist clubs and pubs, spending money freely and ending up three or more nights a week almost paralytically drunk. He would buy his mates drinks, chat up the young women he fancied and brag about working for the Ulster Defence Association. He found that women responded to his boastful claims of running the UDA. Indeed, he would go out of his way to charm women he fancied, changing almost immediately from a rather uncouth, loudmouth into a far more charming, quietly spoken, even debonair, polite and reassuring man.

At the same time they also had to deal with Nelson's escalating marriage problems. He would call asking that his handlers immediately visit his home to quieten down his wife or ask them to explain to her that his job was so important that he had to be out all hours of the day and night, drinking with important contacts. Understandably, the FRU didn't want to become involved in such domestic problems but on occasion it became a necessity to visit his home to calm the marital situation which sometimes appeared to be careering out of control.

There was also concern that Nelson was using drugs. His handlers were convinced that he was regularly smoking marijuana but they also believed he was taking amphetamines – speed – to keep up his reckless lifestyle.

The drinking and suspected drug-taking worried Military Intelligence. Security is the most important and vital necessity in any intelligence set-up, particularly for agents, informants or those people the security services rather dismissively call touts. And yet Nelson didn't seem to care a damn about his own personal security, or anyone else's either. He began to show off to his mates, not only buying round after round of drinks in the pubs and Loyalist clubs but openly boasting of his privileged position in the UDA.

Despite his outrageous behaviour, Brian Nelson had by now become a valuable intelligence contact. The FRU knew that the man whom they debriefed two or three times a week was in constant touch with the leaders of the UDA, the foremost Loyalist organisation in the Province. More importantly, Nelson knew where and when the next attack against mainstream Republican politicians and IRA gunmen and bombers would be staged.

And yet many times Nelson refused to carry out any of the intelligence tasks requested by his handlers. He would be asked to find out information about the UDA, about the leadership, policies, names and addresses of Loyalist gunmen and bombers, information concerning the UDA's arms, ammunition, explosives dumps and safe-houses. Most of the time he simply ignored such requests and carried out the tasks he wanted to, giving the impression that he believed he had become more important than the officers handling and directing him. He began to use the language of his handlers to describe everything that was going on – a mistake that could have cost him his life had he been overheard talking 'intelligence-speak' by any Provos with the faintest knowledge of the intelligence world.

By the spring of 1988, the FRU became convinced that Nelson knew more, far more, than he was in fact telling them. They believed that he knew precisely when attacks would take place, the intended targets and the method of attack. They conceded that he might not have known the identity of the Loyalist gunmen or the exact timing of the attack, but they were certain he was withholding information.

The primary reason for recruiting Nelson in the first place had been to discover as much as possible about the workings and the plans of the Ulster Defence Association. Until Nelson came on the scene, MI5 and Military Intelligence had little or no idea of the policies, the thinking or the intentions of the UDA leadership. Both intelligence organisations admitted that the RUC Special Branch had excellent contacts with some UDA members and other Loyalist paramilitaries, but they didn't trust the relationship. Both MI5 and Military Intelligence believed in their hearts that on occasions the RUC, the Special Branch and the UDA worked together, all for the benefit of the Protestant cause and all determined to ensure that Ulster remained a part of the United Kingdom. Virtually every RUC officer, Special Branch man and, of course, UDA member was a Protestant, many of them belonging to Orange Lodges and various Orange Orders and, understandably, all implacably against the idea of a united Ireland.

Both MI5 and Military Intelligence, who both knew about Nelson's unique position inside the UDA, were not sure whether the UDA chiefs were aware that he was working for British Intelligence. They had no idea what cock-and-bull story Nelson had told the UDA leadership, and that worried them greatly. They feared that he could well be a double-agent and were under no illusions that at heart Nelson was a proud Protestant, a Loyalist, with no love for a British government which many Loyalists feared were prepared to cut a deal with the Irish government in a bid to bring peace to the troubled Province.

And yet they had no option but to continue supporting Nelson in spite of the fact that he was supplying little intelligence of any note about the goings-on inside the UDA. It seemed to FRU officers and handlers that Nelson appeared to be interested only in targeting 'the enemy' and showed no willingness to provide intelligence about the UDA or any of the Loyalist paramilitary organisations. This turn of events worried senior officers and handlers of the Force Research Unit and reports were submitted to both the JIS and the TCG seeking guidance as to the policy of supporting an agent who appeared to be more concerned with staging sectarian attacks than supplying the intelligence required from his own people.

But they had to remind themselves that Nelson was the only agent working inside the UDA who was in a position to provide vital source material to the intelligence services. Though he was primarily supplying and seeking information about the IRA inside Belfast, he also had files on Provo gunmen and bombers and Republican sympathisers in the Six Counties as well as the few who lived south of the border. And the classified top-secret information he was getting from British Intelligence enabled him to target the IRA, keeping them on their toes, worrying and unnerving them to such a degree that they were unable to concentrate much of their energies on venomous attacks against British forces, RUC personnel or Loyalists.

But, unknown to the IRA leadership, Brian Nelson's reign of terror had only just begun. Equipped with classified top-secret intelligence and protected by the security services, he was about to unleash an extraordinary campaign of sectarian killings.

## Chapter Eight

# The Killing Machine

After some wrangling, a deal was finally struck between the FRU and the incorrigible Brian Nelson who agreed to tell his handlers what plans had been drawn up by UDA operations staff to strike a potential victim, provide the name and address and say where and when the attack was to take place. When he needed advice from his handlers as to tactics, security or information, Nelson would simply ask and the intelligence would be forthcoming at his next meeting. That agreement in itself was extraordinary, for it meant that British Military Intelligence had secretly agreed to an understanding whereby they would have full knowledge of every operation planned by the UDA in which someone would be attacked and, more than likely, murdered.

Immediately after this verbal agreement was made, a Military Intelligence source report was sent to the Force Research Unit's senior officers and passed on to the Joint Irish Section, MI5's political wing working out of Northern Ireland. It would be extraordinary if the JIS had not informed either their MI5 bosses in London or, more importantly, the Joint Intelligence Committee which was effectively chaired by Prime Minister Margaret Thatcher.

Political pressure was being exercised from London, and those senior officers in the British Army, MI5 and Military Intelligence stationed in Northern Ireland felt they had to do everything in their power to keep the situation under control and, if possible, to quell the Provo gunmen and bombers. By the late 1980s the Provos seemed able to strike anywhere in the Province with little fear of their plans being thwarted by the intelligence services.

The security services did occasionally have some success, though these would be few and far between. The slaughter on 8 May 1987 of eight Provo gunmen (and one innocent passer-by) intent on blowing up the police station in the village of Loughgall, a founding centre of Orangemen, devastated the Provo leadership, as did the killing of three unarmed Provisionals by SAS troops on the Rock of Gibraltar in March 1988. Both were the result of exceptional intelligence work, planning and execution (the killing of Danny McCann, Sean Savage and young Mairead Farrell on the Rock of Gibraltar in particular the culmination of constant round-the-clock surveillance over a period of three weeks). Not only was Gibraltar a great success for the security forces, as will be discussed later, but it also, at a stroke, temporarily ended the Provo campaign of targeting British troops posted overseas.

Despite these coups, JIS and MI5 officers in the Province felt under pressure to produce better results but were having great difficulty in doing so. The Thatcher government was pushing hard for the intelligence and security forces to do all in their power to frustrate the Provisionals, to keep them under pressure and thus keep down the number of bombings and shootings. The JIS decided that Brian Nelson's unique position inside the Ulster Defence Association should be put to even greater use and FRU officers were ordered to encourage Nelson to continue targeting known Provo activists, Sinn Fein politicians and Republican supporters.

The decision was taken to encourage Nelson to cast his net further in an effort to bring in more reliable source material. It was known that the UDA had any number of activists who would be only too keen to support the cause and act as freelance intelligence agents, reporting back to UDA headquarters any Provo or Sinn Fein members who they believed could be potential targets for Loyalist paramilitary hit-squads. These Loyalist informants were able to move freely and without suspicion around the

Province whether going about their everyday work, attending sporting events or simply visiting friends and relatives within the Six Counties.

Nelson was urged to recruit forty or fifty of these people, mainly men, who would be happy to provide information about any IRA activists, supplying names, addresses, cars and registration numbers so that the intelligence services could feed the information and sightings into their Crucible and Vengeful computer systems, create accurate and detailed P-cards and thus target IRA and INLA activists. Nelson, realising that he was being given an even more important job than before, happily went along with the new plan. Indeed, he was most enthusiastic to recruit and train others to join his burgeoning intelligence team.

Some weeks later Nelson reported back that he had in place a trusty team of forty agents. 'These fellas are only too happy to help,' he explained enthusiastically. 'They believe the Provos have had it their way for too long and it's about time the Loyalists were allowed to take off the gloves and hit back. I have told them that they are privileged men, that their work must remain secret, and that they can't tell anyone about their new undercover work. In return I've said that I'll provide any necessary intelligence – photos, names, addresses, car numbers – to help them pinpoint Provo gunmen and bombers.'

'What have you told them about the source material?' he was asked.

'Nothing,' replied Nelson.

'Nothing?'

'Well, I did tell them that it was all based on the UDA intelligence network.'

'And where did you say the intelligence came from?'

'Well, I didn't say it came from you lot,' he replied.

'So, these recruits have no idea that any information comes from military sources?'

'No, no idea at all,' replied Nelson.

'Good,' one handler told him, 'make sure it stays that way, okay?'

'Okay,' replied Nelson, 'I understand.'

Surprisingly, one of the first UDA-planned operations under the new arrangement was to send a well-armed hit-squad to gatecrash the Monagh Road club, which was often frequented by known Republicans, open fire with automatic weapons, and kill as many people as possible. The UDA had heard that four top Provos, one of the IRA's most successful and efficient active service units (ASUs), used that club as their headquarters and spent most evenings there drinking and talking.

As Nelson explained the extraordinary UDA plan, the FRU personnel were alarmed that the main Protestant organisation would ever contemplate attacking a Republican club in such a manner, spraying scores of rounds of automatic fire, not caring how many innocent people were killed or wounded, simply in the hope that such wholesale slaughter might also kill Provo gunmen who may have been in the club on that particular evening. But, after consultation, the officers decided that in no way did they want to frighten off Nelson and his crazy plan for fear that he might go ahead with the operation but simply not inform FRU what was going on. They therefore decided to try to put a stop to the plot by pointing out its shortcomings and inherent dangers.

'What happens to any innocent people who might be at the club that night?' he was asked pointedly.

'Well, that's their tough luck,' replied Nelson. 'Serves them right for being in the fucking place.'

'But you can't go around shooting indiscriminately at innocent people; don't you understand that?' asked another FRU man.

'We couldn't care less,' was Nelson's reply. 'We know that three or four Provo fuckers drink there nearly every night and we think this is a golden opportunity to wipe out a Provo ASU. From the photographs you gave us we have been able to identify four men who use the club on a regular basis.'

'And what's your plan?' he was asked by the astounded FRU personnel who were alarmed by such a reckless and ill-thought-out operation.

'Nothing has been finalised yet,' Nelson replied, 'but I've been asked to recce the area and the club. I want to find the best way in and the best escape route for our gunmen. I thought you might be able to help plan the operation, but if you don't want to go along with the idea we'll have to work out something ourselves.'

Three days later Nelson returned with his plan. He seemed eager, indeed proud, to explain the details of the forthcoming mission: 'We will employ a group of our men, perhaps four or five, armed with SMGs, break in through the main entrance and spray the entire place. They will take out as many as possible in the shortest possible time. We will of course aim for the men but if women get in the way that's just bad luck. Three hijacked cars will be used to pick up the group afterwards. Inside the cars will be spare magazines in case anyone gives chase or tries to stop the vehicles leaving. Our men will be driven to other cars parked near by. They will change vehicles, abandon the first cars and drive back to Belfast. Another car will take all the weapons and return them to the quartermaster for safekeeping.'

'Don't you think the club will be guarded?' Nelson was asked. 'No Republican club which entertains known Provo hitmen would be left unguarded. How do you plan to get around that problem?'

'We haven't tackled that yet,' he said, sounding as if the thought hadn't yet crossed his mind.

'Those guards would take out your men before they even got inside the club,' one handler observed.

'I doubt that,' Nelson replied. 'Our guys are shit hot.'

'But how can you be sure?'

'We're looking into that problem; we'll find a way round it, I expect,' Nelson answered, sounding as if he was trying to remain confident.

'What about the innocents who get caught in crossfire?'

'They're none of our business,' he replied, 'they won't be targeted. We're after the Provos.'

A week later, Nelson returned and announced that the attack on the Monagh Road club had been aborted, having

been considered too dangerous. Nelson had discovered
that guards were always stationed outside, a twenty-four-
hour surveillance camera was in operation and that the
UDA had no idea from night to night how many Provos
were in the club at any one time. He seemed undeterred by
the setback, though, stating that the plan would probably
be resurrected at some future date when more accurate
intelligence was available. His handlers had no intention of
supplying him with any further information about the
club if the UDA were planning to machine-gun innocent
men and women. On this occasion the Force Research
Unit were prepared to stop the UDA gunmen at any price
because they could not tolerate the idea of such
indiscriminate slaughter.

A few days later, Nelson requested another meeting
with his FRU handlers, telling them of a new target his
intelligence organisation had pinpointed. While surveying
the Monagh Road club they had identified Gerard Martin
Slane, a twenty-six-year-old married man with three young
children. Photographs of the unemployed Slane, a
suspected Provo activist, had been handed over to Nelson
by Military Intelligence and he had been identified from
those pictures when visiting the club. By checking Slane's
name with the Force Research Unit's secret Crucible
factsheet, Nelson was able to see that the man had been
convicted in September 1985 for possession of a rifle and
a magazine containing twenty rounds of ammunition.
During the court case Slane claimed he had discovered the
brand-new rifle in the outside toilet of his home shortly
before the security forces arrived to search the premises.
Frightened by the troops' arrival at his home, Slane argued
that in a panic he had thrown the rifle and the magazine
over the wall. He was fortunate to be given a two-year
suspended sentence at a time when many other
Republicans were sent to prison for possessing such
weapons.

Thanks to the information passed to Nelson by British
Intelligence, the UDA knew Slane lived in Waterville
Street, in the Clonard area off the Falls Road in west

Belfast. A UDA surveillance team had staked out the
house for some time but had never seen their target visiting
his family home where his wife Teresa and three children
lived. The fact that Slane did not spend much time at the
family home was not surprising – during the previous
twelve months Provo activists had been advised by their
leaders not to stay the night at their home address on a
regular basis for fear of being tracked down by the security
services or UDA gunmen. As a result, many men with
Provo or Republican connections would live out of a hold-
all, moving from address to address, never staying more
than a few nights in one place, so that tracking them down
became almost an impossible task.

But the UDA believed that with luck they now had
Slane in their sights, so they continued to watch the
Monagh Road club. Whenever Slane left the club – usually
in an Apollo taxi – the UDA surveillance team would
follow. Three times in succession in the autumn of 1988
he made the mistake of returning to his home address,
believing he was safe from attack.

On the fourth night he was again followed by a UDA
surveillance team. At 4.15 a.m., neighbours heard the roar
of a car as it came racing down the road.

One neighbour, who asked not to be identified, said, 'I
woke when I heard the car because not many people ever
drive fast in this wee road. Then I heard car doors
slamming and seconds later the sound of wood being
smashed. I looked out of the window and saw masked men
smashing down the door of the Slanes' house. Three men
raced inside and another remained outside. Seconds later I
heard five shots and a woman's screams. Then I saw the
men running out of the house and they drove away.'

Teresa Slane said they were asleep in bed when they
were woken by the crashing, splintering noise from
downstairs. She knew instinctively that someone had come
to get Gerard but she thought it was the army wanting to
search their house again. She told how her husband had
leapt out of bed to confront the men and was standing at
the top of the stairs shouting to those breaking in when the

men below opened fire. He fell down the stairs, killed instantly. The Provisional IRA offered to give Slane a military funeral but the family declined.

This had been a totally successful operation between British Intelligence and the gunmen of the Ulster Defence Association, with Nelson as the go-between. British Intelligence had provided the photographs of Slane and his home address; the UDA intelligence had correctly traced and targeted a man they believed to be a Provo activist. The UDA gunmen had provided the killers and the weapons. And only a handful of people had any idea that Britain's Army Intelligence, working on orders from above to act aggressively, had been responsible for providing the information that led to the killing.

But neither the Force Research Unit officers, Nelson nor the UDA hierarchy appeared to draw any distinction between the young Provo gunmen and bombers – those who were members of current IRA active service units – and the older generation of IRA members or supporters of the Republican cause, even targeting pensioners in their bid to spread alarm and fear amongst the Catholic community.

One such victim was Francisco Notarantino, a sixty-six-year-old pensioner of Italian extraction who had lived in Northern Ireland all his life. Notarantino was one of the old school, a member of the Republican movement going back almost fifty years when he was jailed during the 1940s for involvement in anti-British activities. He had also been one of the Republicans who had been picked up during the internment sweep of the 1970s and spent time in detention with scores of other supporters and sympathisers. Francisco Notarantino had always been a stalwart of the Republican movement, advising the younger generation, and he was still respected though he had played no active part in the new hardline Provo movement which had split from the Official IRA in the 1970s.

Notarantino, the father of six daughters and five sons, was an easy target. He had been forced to give up his part-time job driving a taxi around Belfast some years earlier because of ill health. He spent most of his time at home and always slept in his house in Whitecliff Parade, in the Ballymurphy area of west Belfast.

Shortly after half past seven on the morning of 9 October 1987, he and his wife were sleeping when four hooded gunmen arrived outside in a Vauxhall Cavalier. Two jumped out of the car and kicked down the front door in a matter of seconds. They ran up the stairs and stormed into the old couple's bedroom. The two pensioners were still in bed lying side by side. It made no difference that they were too old to defend themselves or even take any evasive action. The gunmen opened fire with handguns, hitting Notarantino in the chest as he struggled to get out of bed to tackle his attackers. The force of the shots made him turn round and the gunmen fired at him again, this time in the back. It is believed he died instantly. His wife was unharmed though badly shocked.

One of Notarantino's grandsons was asleep in an adjoining bedroom and he ran out onto the landing when the shooting began. The gunmen fired a warning shot at the teenager, slightly injuring him in the hand; he was lucky, for two other shots passed over his head, narrowly missing him. The gunmen fled down the stairs and escaped in the car that was still waiting outside. The killing had taken little more than a minute from the time the Cavalier drew up outside the house to when it sped off down the road. The car, which had been hijacked that morning in the Woodvale area of Belfast, was later found abandoned at Blackmountain Way in the Springmartin area. Police found no clues in the vehicle.

West Belfast MP Gerry Adams said the victim had been a good friend of his father decades before and had been well known in Republican circles all his life. He added, 'When the bedroom door was kicked in, Mrs Notarantino thought it was an army raid. She awoke to see a man in a boilersuit standing in front of her. Her husband struggled to get out of bed and was shot in the chest. Francisco was obviously a soft target for Loyalist gunmen.'

Adams then went on: 'I find it very strange that this area was crawling with Crown forces only yesterday. They swamped the place and the local Sinn Fein councillor, Stan Keenan, was stopped twice. Yet today at half past seven in the morning there was no one around at all, and armed men were able to come in and out of the area with no one around to stop them.'

In that short statement Gerry Adams had highlighted one of the reasons why Nelson's UDA gunmen were able to operate with impunity, somehow never being stopped or caught by either RUC or army patrols while carrying out their murderous evil deeds. On most of those occasions it was obvious that the FRU had put out a restriction order on the area to ensure the UDA gunmen would not be stopped by the forces of law and order.

The murder of Francisco Notarantino in October 1987 forced people to face the fact that the senseless sectarian killings of the 1970s had indeed returned to Belfast. Many local politicians believed the killing was designed to inflict fear and despair into the hearts of both the Catholic and Protestant working-class communities. Gerry Adams said he did not know if the IRA would reply in kind to the killing of one of the Republican movement's senior citizens. 'The IRA has a policy of taking punitive action against the people who carry out these assassinations,' he said, 'though I am totally opposed to random sectarian shootings.'

Workers Party spokesman Mary MacMahon also condemned the murder of Notarantino and said the killers were the enemies of the community: 'Those responsible for such killings must be brought to justice and eliminated from society.'

An SDLP candidate for the Lower Falls, Mrs Gerry Cosgrove, said Notarantino's shooting was a pointless murder: 'This type of killing is prompted by other sectarian killings committed by the paramilitaries on both sides. Both must share the blame for this loss of life.'

This was a vain hope. The targeting and killing of known Provo activists, Republican supporters and sympathisers and even ordinary, decent Catholics with no connection with terrorist activities would continue thanks primarily to the help and assistance given to the UDA gunmen by British Military Intelligence. Most of the attacks were savage, brutal and quick.

One such killing occurred in January 1988 when Billy Kane, a twenty-year-old Roman Catholic and suspected Republican activist, was shot as he lay on the sofa at his home in the New Lodge area of north Belfast at six in the evening. Outside, commuters were making their way home from the city in the dark and wet of a cold January evening, but this did not seem to deter the gunmen from carrying out their murderous operation.

His brother explained in horrific detail what occurred: 'Billy was fast asleep on the sofa and I was in the sitting-room with my sisters Carol and Nicola and our mother Bridget when the door was opened. We always left our front door on the latch so we could all come and go without bothering with keys. There was always someone at home so there seemed no need to lock the door. We thought it was our father returning from work but suddenly these two masked men carrying guns burst into the room, looked around and then walked over to Billy who was still lying on the sofa, and emptied a magazine into his body. They never said a word to him but just opened fire. As the gunmen left, one turned to the other and asked, "Did you shoot him right?" and the man turned back and fired another shot into Billy's body. It was sickening.'

After the murder, the two men went outside, jumped into a car in which two other men were waiting, and drove off towards the Loyalist Duncairn Gardens area. No one stopped the gunmen's car and no one was arrested for the killing. Once again, the UDA had carried out an execution and once again it had been with the help and co-operation of the Force Research Unit and Brian Nelson.

Sometimes months would go by between the time FRU officers alerted Brian Nelson about a suspect Provo or Republican supporter whom they suggested the UDA should target and the actual attack itself. One such target was Declan McDaid, a keen Republican.

It was some time in late 1987 or early 1988 that FRU officers alerted their agent to the fact that he might care to check out Declan McDaid whom they suspected was heavily involved in Republican politics. For weeks at a time Brian Nelson, with the help of a number of his own part-time agents, tracked Declan wherever he went, whether it was to attend meetings or just enjoy a chat and a pint with friends in one of the Republican clubs of west Belfast.

At meetings with his FRU handlers, Nelson would complain that he and his men were having problems tracking McDaid because he constantly changed his everyday movements, almost as though he realised he was being targeted. 'He checks everything he does,' complained Nelson on one occasion. 'Before getting into a car he will check to see whether there is a booby-trap underneath; he will constantly check his car's rear-view mirror to see if he is being followed, and when he walks anywhere at all he will stop and check whether anyone suspicious is following him. He acts as though he knows he is under surveillance but he seems to have no idea precisely who is watching him.'

'Do you put various people onto him?' asked one of his handlers.

'Of course we do,' Nelson replied, as if insulted by the question. 'We sometimes use men and sometimes use women to tail him and we never use the same person too often. But we know he believes he is under surveillance. We hope he thinks it's Special Branch or the army because that gives us a freer rein. We know he won't try anything if he thinks the RUC are tailing him, but if he thought it was us, the UDA, then he might take aggressive action rather than keep running like he does now.'

'Are you sure you have the right man?' Nelson was asked.

'Of course we have the right man,' he replied. 'We have the montages of him that you lot gave us and they match perfectly. Of course we've got the right bastard, there's no doubt about it.'

'Have you got a plan to take him out?' he was asked.

'No, not yet,' Nelson replied. 'We know where he lives but it seems a pretty secure place and difficult to make a quick entry. We've checked it out and it seems his house is well protected with a strong front door with secure locks; not just your run-of-the-mill yale lock which a bloody good kick can force open in seconds.'

'Have you thought about knocking on his front door?'

'Fuck off,' said Nelson. 'If we did that he might come out with a shooter or something. We don't want to take any fucking risks like that.'

Looking pensive, he went on, 'This fucker is a real challenge. He knows we're after him but he doesn't know who we are or what we look like. Nor does he have the faintest idea where or when we plan to hit him. But we will, mark my words. He's got it coming to him.'

Finally, after months of surveillance work, the UDA decided in the spring of 1988 to go ahead and take out Declan McDaid. But this time, before carrying out the operation, Nelson didn't bother to check with his handlers, nor did he go over the plan of attack as he usually did prior to any operation.

On the evening of 10 May 1988, Declan's brother Terence was with his wife Maura, their two daughters and his mother-in-law in their home in Newington Street off the Antrim Road in north Belfast. The two young girls had just gone upstairs to bed and Terence and Maura were watching television when they heard the sound of someone trying to break down the front door.

Terence McDaid had never been involved with the Provos or with hardline Republican politics and he was not even a Sinn Fein activist. It made no difference to those two UDA gunmen who burst into his house that evening. They would ask no questions; they would not check the identity of the man they were about to murder.

Brian Nelson's intelligence personnel had made a mistake, a basic error which resulted in the cold-blooded murder of an innocent man, the husband of a loving wife and the father of two young daughters. They had mistaken Terry McDaid for his brother Declan and their enquiries had led them to the wrong house. The UDA had failed to check whether they had targeted the right man and, as a result, Terence would die in the place of his brother. But not without a fight.

When the two gunmen had smashed down the door they ran into the living-room. Terry and his wife jumped to their feet in a bid to thwart the gunmen. Neither had any idea who was invading their home but they knew that their unwelcome visitors could only mean trouble. Throughout the Catholic areas of Belfast in the spring of 1988 there were grave fears that Loyalist gunmen were on the loose, targeting every Catholic no matter who he was or what he did. It didn't seem to matter whether these people were members of the Provisionals or just ordinary people going about their daily lives who had never for one moment even considered joining a terrorist organisation. Although the targeting and killing of Catholics, orchestrated and masterminded by Military Intelligence, would continue for a further two years, the intention of creating fear and suspicion throughout the community had already been highly successful.

Maura McDaid would say later: 'As soon as I heard the commotion I knew instinctively that whoever had smashed their way into our home would be after Terry. He was the only man in the house and with so many sectarian killings going on, I just knew those breaking in would be after him. I tried to put my leg to the door of the living-room in an effort to stop them but they just pushed it open and two men barged in.

'"Get the fuck out of the way," one shouted.

'"Where the fuck is he?" shouted another.

'They started shooting at the ceiling and at the walls and I picked up the Hoover and tried to hit the one nearest to me across the head but he pushed me aside and continued shooting around the room. He was like some madman and I was convinced we were all going to die.

Instinctively I screamed and ducked down, fearful that he would kill us all.

'In that split second I thought of the girls upstairs and prayed they wouldn't come down to see what was going on. I was convinced that if they had come into the room those bastards would have shot them too. My mother, who was also in the room at the time, threw herself over Terry to protect him because she too was convinced that the gunmen were after him. One gunman shot my mother in the foot and pushed her out of the way so that he could get a clear shot at Terry. Then they blasted him. He didn't stand a chance. Seconds later they ran out of the room and down the hall and away.

'Terry slumped to the floor and I knew the bastards had killed him. I was in tears, desperate that he would survive for me and the girls but I knew in my heart there was little hope. And there was no reason, no reason whatsoever, why they should have killed him. He was a good husband and a wonderful father and he did his best for his family. He wasn't a member of any organisation at all and yet they murdered him, killed him for no reason except that he was Roman Catholic. I hope they rot in hell.'

The cold-blooded murder of Terence McDaid angered the FRU officers and they immediately called in Nelson, asking him to explain exactly what he and his band of gunmen thought they were playing at murdering a totally innocent man.

Nelson was unrepentant. 'We fucked up,' he said, in his cocky manner. 'Got the wrong man, that's all. It was his brother we were after. Anyway, it's one less Mick to worry about; that's the way we look at it.'

One of the senior FRU handlers, fed up with Nelson's cavalier attitude, challenged him: 'You told us that the UDA were a professional outfit and then you go and fuck up something like this. What the hell do you think you're playing at?'

'Don't have a go at me,' Nelson pleaded in a pathetic way. 'That side of it is nothing to do with me. That's operational. I just supply the intelligence, the facts, and they do the rest.'

'But that's precisely the point,' the FRU handler retorted. 'You are the intelligence officer and the information you gave your men was obviously inaccurate. As a result, some poor innocent bastard died and you sit there and tell us that it doesn't matter. Well, it does matter and the sooner you learn that fact, the better for you and for us.'

'It's no good having a go at me,' replied Nelson, 'I'm doing my best. There's hardly ever a fuck-up. It was just a one-off, bad luck on the poor fucker.'

'That's exactly the attitude that you must not have,' replied the FRU man. 'You treat everyone you target as of no importance. Well, innocent people are important. They have a right to live out their lives without you guys storming into their homes and killing them.'

'It was a mistake,' Nelson pleaded. 'These things happen.'

'But don't your men ask questions? Don't they check who's in the house first of all before charging in and spraying the place with bullets? You'd better tell your UDA bosses that they had better check in future operations before targeting and killing people. We can't permit this sort of thing to happen. If ordinary, decent Catholics are taken out for no good reason, you will have been responsible for turning every Catholic in the Province against the Protestants. Do you want that? Where do you think that would lead?'

'Fuck knows,' replied Nelson, showing by his tone of voice that he was bored with the conversation.

'I'll tell you where it will lead. It will bring the Catholics solidly behind the Provos, which is exactly what the IRA want. We don't want that. We want to isolate the Provos from the majority of Catholics, to show that they are not courageous men defending the Catholic minority but just out to kill for killing's safe. By your stupid actions you are helping the Provos – don't you understand that?'

'Maybe, maybe not,' Nelson replied.

'Well, just listen, just listen once more. Always check with us before anything goes down. Do you understand that? You do nothing, nothing whatsoever until you have checked with us, okay?'

'Yeah, all right,' replied Nelson in a defeated tone. 'But I do nearly always check with you anyway, so nothing will change.'

'Well, let's make sure there are no more fuck-ups; no more mistakes, okay?'

'Okay.'

'Right, that's agreed,' said the FRU man, 'now fuck off.'

As well as the 'mistaken-identity' killings, which soon became a regular feature of the UDA under its intelligence officer, there were times when the Loyalist gunmen correctly picked out their target but still had difficulty in achieving their brutal aims.

One of the men at the top of the UDA hit-list was a leading member of Sinn Fein and one of the Provisional IRA's senior officers, Brendan Davidson. He was the Officer Commanding the markets area of Belfast, a small Catholic enclave which apparently contained two or more IRA active service units. A single man, Davidson gave his life to the Republican cause of which he was a passionate and dedicated supporter. He was a well-known figure around the markets area and his authority was undisputed by the people living there. In effect, Brendan Davidson's word was law and no one took any liberties when dealing with him.

In December 1983 Davidson had been arrested on the word of IRA supergrass John Morgan but acquitted when Mr Justice Murray refused to accept the informer's evidence. As a result, Davidson walked free and returned to his role as an active IRA officer. But from the moment of his acquittal, Davidson believed he was a Loyalist target and, sensibly, took great precautions to ensure his safety. It didn't take long, however, before information was gathered which showed that Davidson liked a bet on the horses most days and frequented a bookmaker in Cromac Street where he was well known by many of those who hung around the shop on race days.

Well known to both the RUC Special Branch and

Military Intelligence, Davidson's was also one of the first names the Force Research Unit decided to target shortly after Nelson started working for them. The agent was informed that intelligence reports showed that Davidson spent two or three afternoons a week visiting the betting shop; sometimes he would just a place a bet and leave but, on other occasions, would stand around chatting for an hour or so, listening to the races on the shop's commentary link-up.

All this was fed to Nelson together with a dossier of photographs of Davidson, including police mugshots taken when he was arrested and others taken surreptitiously by undercover officers of the RUC's crack surveillance unit, E4A.

One bright June afternoon, two hooded gunmen walked into the bookmaker's, singled out Davidson and shot him four times. He managed to twist away from the gunmen; his arm took the full force of the shots but he was otherwise uninjured. He was rushed to hospital and, after surgery, was patched up, though he never regained the full use of his arm.

After that attempt on Davidson's life, Nelson reported back to the FRU that his UDA gunmen had panicked rather than taken their time. They recognised Davidson as he turned away from them, he said, but they were confronted by a number of other people in the shop and all they wanted to do was fire off a few rounds and fuck off as quickly as possible in case the other men in the shop turned on them.

A year later, in July 1988, Brendan Davidson was again targeted. The FRU suggested once more that the UDA should check him out to see if it was possible to hit him – more successfully this time. They had learned that one of Davidson's active service units had been heavily involved in a number of shootings and bombings and they believed the only way to stop that unit operating for a while was to take out Davidson and hopefully scare off the members of the ASU. Military Intelligence knew from past experience that by taking out IRA commanders, the whole organisation would take weeks if not months to get back into action because the members feared there might be a tout in their midst who was responsible for betraying the leader. In such circumstances evidence showed that IRA cells would then lie low for a month or two at least, not daring to organise any terrorist operations for fear that they too might be betrayed.

'How are we going to get to him?' enquired Nelson when Davidson's name came up again in the summer of 1988. 'We've checked out the betting shop and he still goes there. Now, though, whenever he visits, he has lookouts standing around outside to make sure he's not surprised again. In fact, Davidson is fucking scared because he sometimes has bodyguards wherever he goes in the markets and we don't know whether they're armed or not.'

'Do you know if Special Branch still watch him?' he was asked.

'The word is the Branch is too fucking scared to watch him since the court case because he would have them for harassment.'

'We'll look into that,' replied the FRU officer. 'We expect he's being kept under surveillance but he wouldn't know about that.'

'Have you got any ideas how we could get access to Davidson?' Nelson asked.

'We'll think about it and let you know,' he was told.

At the next safe-house meeting Nelson returned to the subject of Brendan Davidson and repeated that the UDA were very keen to 'get' him because they were convinced that he was the officer responsible for a lot of the IRA's dirty work, targeting Loyalists and sending out ASUs on killing missions.

'We have an idea,' said one FRU handler. 'If you don't think it's possible to target him at the bookie's or in the streets, he'll have to be attacked at his home.'

'Fucking impossible,' replied Nelson. 'We've checked that out by driving past on lots of occasions and it's well guarded. We believe it has one of those safe doors with three-pronged bolts, making it all but impossible to break down. He's well protected and no fool.'

'So we have to entice him out somehow, right?'

'I fucking know that,' Nelson replied tetchily, 'but how the hell do we do it? He's not just going to open the door when we knock, is he?'

'That's true,' replied the senior FRU officer. 'But he might do so if he thought you were the peelers.'

'And how do we manage that?' Nelson asked, somewhat incredulously.

'By wearing the correct uniforms,' he was told. 'I'm sure that your UDA men with their contacts in the RUC would be able to come up with a couple of uniforms.'

'Fucking right,' said Nelson, a note of glee in his voice, 'yeah, fucking right.'

It was arranged through the FRU that the TCG would be informed that on the morning of Monday, 25 July 1988, an operation would be going ahead some time between 7 a.m. and 11 a.m., and to ensure that no security forces or RUC patrols were in the markets area.

Four men, dressed in the green uniforms of RUC police officers and wearing regulation caps, drove up in a bright orange car which attracted some attention. The driver and the 'peeler' in the front passenger seat stayed in the vehicle after parking a little way from the house in Friendly Way in which Davidson rented the ground-floor flat.

With Davidson that morning was a friend who later told the RUC what happened. The man, who asked not to be named, said, 'We had just finished having some breakfast when there was a knock at the door. Brendan looked at me and I shrugged my shoulders, so presumably he was not expecting any visitors at that time in the morning. He went to the door and looked through the spy hole.

'"Who's there?" he called through the closed door.

'"Peelers," came the reply. "We need to talk to you."

'"Wait a minute," said Davidson and as he opened the front door he told me, "Fucking peelers! I wonder what they want."'

He had only opened the door a little way, his friend continued, when he realised the policemen standing outside were holding sub-machine-guns and pointing them straight at him. At the same time as he tried to slam the door shut the UDA gunmen opened fire, hitting him several times in the head and body. At least nine shots were fired that morning. But the door had in fact taken the majority of the shots and Davidson was still alive when he crumpled to the floor.

The two gunmen turned and ran to the car that was waiting a few yards away, the doors open, the engine revving. But one of the 'peelers' dropped his gun and his police cap as he was running to the car and had to stop to pick them up while his accomplice was shouting at him to get a move on. As the two clambered in, pursued by two men who had heard the gunfire, the car took off. As they watched it disappear down the street, the two men in pursuit reported seeing the men in the back of the car struggling out of their RUC uniforms. One of them, a blond-haired youngster, looked back at his pursuers and roared with laughter. Davidson was taken to Belfast City Hospital but died a short time after being admitted.

Brian Nelson, the UDA hierarchy and the FRU personnel who had helped organise the operation were jubilant that one of their prime targets, whom they believed to be a danger to society in Northern Ireland, had been killed, and could therefore cause no further strife. The FRU also hoped, of course, that his death would halt the activities of the markets ASUs for a while.

Throughout 1988, dozens of other people were targeted by Nelson and the FRU. In most cases, though, Nelson would report back that his intelligence touts had been unable to trace or identify these targets or, if positive identification was proved, that it was impossible to mount a plan of attack that would not only achieve the right result but also allow the UDA gunman to escape. Sometimes, when weeks passed without a hit taking place, Nelson would become agitated, almost as though selecting and taking out a target had become a 'high' for him.

## Chapter Nine

# *Shoot to Kill*

At about the same time as the Force Research Unit was established, 14th Intelligence Company (often called 'Det' because its volunteers were Detached from their regiments for a two-year tour of duty in the Province) was also being set up to carry out dangerous undercover surveillance operations. Originally, the recruits brought in to staff the Det were all SAS personnel but their work became so vital and efficient, as well as highly successful, that the SAS were unable to provide enough personnel so volunteers were recruited from other army units. To this day, however, the Det is still under the control and command of the SAS.

Throughout the thirty years of the troubles, drastic action, euphemistically called 'Executive Action' in official security circles, had resulted in a number of IRA and Sinn Fein personnel being killed by members of the security forces. Secret but officially sanctioned killings of Provisional IRA members, in which the security forces were directly or indirectly involved, had been suspected throughout the on-going war with the Provos. Firstly, there were the MRF 'cowboys' who took the law into their own hands in the 1970s but who were disbanded after protestations from senior RUC officers that MRF personnel risked facing murder charges. Then, in the early 1980s, a series of questionable killings, which became known as the RUC's 'shoot-to-kill' policy, caused serious political repercussions in Northern Ireland and the House of Commons. Allegations were made against members of the RUC's shady Headquarters Mobile Support Unit (HMSU) that young IRA gunmen had been shot dead on occasions when they could just as easily have been arrested.

The series of killings – which Republicans described as 'cold-blooded murders' – began in early October 1982. Officers from E4A – the plain-clothes, surveillance wing of the RUC – had been tipped off that a large consignment of home-made explosives was to be shipped into the North. The lorry, which E4A knew contained the explosives, was tracked from south of the border to a hayshed off the Ballynery road, outside Lurgan. The shed, known as Kitty's Barn, was a ramshackle building made of breeze-blocks and corrugated iron and was owned by Kitty Kearns, a woman in her seventies, who looked after retired greyhounds. The farmhouse and barn lay close to a staunchly Republican housing estate on the outskirts of Lurgan. Kitty Kearns was a local character, the widow of an old-time Republican who had died a few years years earlier.

Some nights later, E4A officers watched from a distance as six men took a total of seven hours to unload the hay lorry. When the men had finished their task and gone home, RUC explosives experts examined the barn and found 1,000lbs of explosives and some old-fashioned guns hidden behind the hay stacks. Officers from MI5, trained in counter-terrorist operations, were called to the scene and installed sophisticated listening devices in the roof of the barn. These were programmed to pick up not only conversations but also any noises suggesting the explosives or arms were being removed.

A standing observation post manned day and night by the Det was set up to keep a close eye on the barn. The RUC hoped to track whoever moved the explosives, discover the Provos' exact target and capture the bomb team red-handed. From sources inside the IRA, the TCG had learned that the explosives had been brought in to launch a specific, planned attack on the security forces, but they had no idea where or when this attack would take place. And they had no clue as to the identity of the bombers.

On 27 October 1982, an anonymous phone call,

supposedly from a member of the public, was received at Lurgan police station informing officers that a motorcycle had been found abandoned on a dirt track called the Kinnego Embankment. Three uniformed officers, Sergeant Sean Quinn and Constables Paul Hamilton and Alan McCloy, were sent to check the motorcycle. No one thought to inform either the HMSU or the TCG. Ten minutes later an explosion rocked the area and the three officers were blown to pieces. Explosives experts discovered that the bombers had planted a booby-trap bomb in a culvert beneath the embankment which had exploded when the officers walked over it. To the horror of the security forces, forensic experts found that the explosives used to kill the three officers were part of the shipment hidden in Kitty's Barn.

The tragedy had been able to occur because of two extraordinary errors. Firstly, the Det patrol detailed to watch the barn had been taken off duty for a twenty-four-hour break, during which a quantity of the explosives had been removed. Secondly, the listening device installed in the barn had been affected by wind and rain and no longer worked. After the tragic deaths of the three officers, a new listening device was fitted to the handle of the barn door where, experts insisted, it would not be affected by adverse weather conditions. And the Det unit was kept in position watching the barn with no breaks.

In November, E4A learned from reliable informants inside the IRA that the two chief suspects believed to be responsible for planting the Kinnego bomb, Sean Burns and Eugene Toman, both aged twenty-one and from Lurgan, had returned secretly to the Province some weeks earlier. Both men had been on the run, taking refuge in the south, for the attempted murder of a police patrol some weeks earlier. Now, after killing three innocent police officers, they were considered to be among the most dangerous IRA activists, a prime target for the security forces. On 11 November E4A traced the two men to the home of a known Provo sympathiser, James Gervaise McKerr, who lived in Avondale Green, near Lurgan. An

HMSU team was immediately dispatched to the area.

The HMSU patrol had only just arrived at the scene – wearing traditional dark-green uniforms and driving an unmarked police car – when E4A radioed that Burns and Toman were leaving the house in a car driven by McKerr. The patrol immediately set up an impromptu vehicle check-point near a T-junction. As the car approached the junction, the HMSU vehicle parked on the left side was blocking half of the narrow road, with one armed officer standing on the right side waving a red light, warning the approaching car to stop. The IRA car, a green Ford Escort, slowed down almost to a halt and then accelerated hard, forcing the officer to leap out of the way. He did, however, manage to fire off five shots from his Ruger mini 14 rifle, shattering the car's rear window and hitting the man sitting in the back. He also managed to puncture a rear tyre. As the terrorists' car sped off, swerving wildly across the road, the HMSU officers gave chase. As they raced along the dark road in pursuit, they grabbed their Stirling machine-guns and opened fire, Chicago gangster-style, leaning out of the windows and firing into the getaway car. When the speeding Provos' car came to a roundabout the driver tried to turn right, lost control, and careered off the road and down an embankment.

The three officers leapt out and opened fire. They poured 117 rounds into the Provos' car. When the firing stopped they gingerly approached the vehicle to find the bodies of the three men shot to pieces. They were virtually unrecognisable. But police called in to investigate and report on the deaths found no weapons in the car.

The deaths of McKerr, Toman and Burns caused a furore. The RUC were accused of having cold-bloodedly murdered three innocent people. Sinn Fein claimed the shooting had been a 'summary execution'. Their families denied that any of them was a member of the Provisional IRA and claimed that, had the police wanted to, all three could have been arrested at home at any time. The men were given paramilitary-style funerals, however, and the North Armagh Brigade of the IRA claimed that all three were members of their organisation. Black berets, gloves and Irish tricolours were placed on their coffins and, at the graveside, a single shot was fired over the coffins by a masked man.

Following the shootings, the TCG decided to remove the rest of the Kitty's Barn explosives but leave behind the rifles to see if any other IRA members knew of their existence. Once again, a twenty-four-hour watch was put on the barn. During the afternoon of 18 November 1982, the listening device in the barn indicated that someone was tampering with the rifles and armed HMSU officers raced to the scene. Wearing flak jackets and carrying sub-machine-guns, they approached the barn quietly and cautiously while others surrounded the immediate area. The officers had no idea of the identity of the men, nor how many were in the barn.

Inside, two teenagers were holding the rifles and examining them closely. The rifles appeared to be antiques. In fact, both were bolt-action weapons from the First World War. Two were German Mausers and the third was of Italian or Spanish origin. Arms experts believed they were all manufactured before 1914. Forensic experts later maintained that all three weapons were in working order but said that ammunition for such weapons would be difficult to find. In fact, no ammunition was ever found at the barn.

When the officers were within ten feet of the barn, one of them opened fire, spraying one side of the barn with bullets, the rounds making a dramatic staccato noise on the corrugated iron. In the barn were Michael Tighe, aged seventeen, and his nineteen-year-old friend Martin McCauley. They fled to the back of the barn to hide in the hay, taking the weapons with them. Then the door was pushed open and in strode three armed officers.

'Right, come on out,' one officer allegedly shouted.

They saw something moving in the hay and opened fire with two bursts from their sub-machine-guns, killing Tighe instantly and seriously wounding McCauley. Both teenagers had been hit by three rounds. Another burst of machine-gunfire followed. Then the three officers walked to the back of the barn, grabbed McCauley and dragged him outside. He would later recover and appear at Belfast Crown Court charged with possession of the three old rifles. Lord Justice Kelly expressed doubts about the police evidence but, nevertheless, gave McCauley a two-year suspended sentence.

But every word that had been spoken in the barn that afternoon had been picked up and recorded by the concealed listening device. That tape-recording would have been crucial to the entire independent investigation that followed the shootings, but no one would ever know what had been said because the tape mysteriously disappeared and could not be produced in the subsequent inquiry.

The shootings caused a wave of anger in Republican circles. There was no evidence that either boy had ever been a member of the IRA. Their parents told the police that their sons had gone to the barn to feed Kitty Kearns's dogs because she had gone away for the day and had asked them to help her.

The third incident which aroused suspicion in the minds of Republicans and in some political circles in Dublin and Westminster that the RUC was indeed operating a shoot-to-kill policy occurred just three weeks later. On 12 December 1982 two leading members of the INLA were shot dead by HMSU officers. The killings of Peter Seamus Grew, aged thirty-one, from Mullacreevie Park, Armagh, and twenty-two-year-old Roderick Martin Carroll from Callanbridge Park, Armagh, became known by Republicans as 'the Mullacreevie Park Massacre'.

Grew had been sentenced to fourteen years in prison in 1975 for attempting to murder a policeman and had only been released eight months before. He was, nevertheless, the chief suspect in a number of murders and attempted murders in the Armagh district. He and Carroll had been visiting friends in the Irish Republic and were driving north across the border in torrential rain when they met their deaths.

Informants south of the border alerted the RUC Special Branch that the two men wanted for questioning would be travelling back home to Armagh. A time and a date were provided. A Det surveillance team as well as a squad of HMSU officers were dispatched south to locate and tail the two men as they travelled north. Three unmarked vehicles – an HMSU car, a Det surveillance team car and a police Ford Cortina – followed them.

During the journey north, however, the HMSU car came to an unexpected halt and, unbelievably, the Det car, skidding on the wet road, crashed into the back of it. The driver of the third police vehicle pulled up, stopped to check his colleagues were not injured and had to watch helplessly as the two Provos in their bright orange Austin Allegro casually drove away, unaware that the three cars by the roadside contained members of the security services who were tailing them. Two of the police vehicles gave chase and caught up with the Allegro just as it was about to turn into the safety of the Republican area of Mullacreevie Park, forcing it to stop. As the armed police clambered out of their vehicles, Peter Grew and Roderick Carroll opened the doors of their car. The police opened fire instantly, killing both men in a hail of bullets.

The following day the INLA vowed to avenge with 'unmerciful ferocity' the deaths of the two men, saying in an official statement, 'These well-paid executioners have now left themselves open to any form of attack and can prepare to suffer the consequences of their actions.' Troops and police were put on full alert as security chiefs prepared for a terrorist onslaught. Three days after the killing of Grew and Carroll, an INLA unit, dressed in the traditional black boilersuits of Republican gunmen at funeral ceremonies, and surrounded by two hundred mourners, fired shots over the coffins with police watching only a hundred yards away. Although such 'military-style' funerals were unlawful, the police made no attempt to intervene.

But this was not the full story. The same day Carroll and Grew would die, a Det surveillance unit working secretly south of the border had seen the INLA activist Dominic 'Mad Dog' McGlinchey get into the car with them. He was carrying a hold-all which they knew contained weapons. This intelligence was supported separately by a reliable source, an FRU agent, who had reported earlier that day that McGlinchey was to be driven into Northern Ireland with a bag of weapons. Those members of the security forces following the orange Allegro that night had been informed that Grew and Carroll, along with McGlinchey and the weapons, were in the car. They would take no chances.

In the autumn of 1982 'Mad Dog' McGlinchey was the most wanted man in Ireland, on either side of the border. He was a fearless man who would take the most extraordinary risks to get close to those he intended to murder, usually shooting them with his favourite weapon, the powerful .44 Ruger revolver. During his reign of terror, which lasted for four years, McGlinchey was said to have killed a total of thirty people, mainly officers of the RUC, the army and the UDR. He also murdered civilians. He had risen through the ranks of the INLA to become 'Double O', the Operations Officer of the General Headquarters Staff, but he would still take part in active service attacks himself.

These three tragic cases formed the basis of the famous Stalker Inquiry. The Deputy Chief Constable of the Greater Manchester Police Force, John Stalker, was asked to undertake an enquiry into the deaths of the six men who were killed within a five-week period in late 1982. He was to investigate allegations that the RUC had a secret but official shoot-to-kill policy against suspected members of the IRA and INLA. As he dug deeper, Stalker complained that he was meeting increasing resistance from members of the RUC at all levels from the Chief Constable, Sir John Hermon, down.

Within days of the investigation starting in May 1984, the trial of the three police officers involved in the killing of Eugene Toman at the embankment outside Lurgan came to an end; the officers were acquitted. The judge,

Lord Justice Gibson, said 'seriously incorrect evidence' was given to a court at a preliminary hearing of the charges and went on to praise the three officers for bringing Toman, Burns and McKerr to 'the final court of justice'. This created an unprecedented uproar. His remarks seemed to remove all doubt that the shoot-to-kill policy existed and was officially endorsed in police and judicial circles of Northern Ireland. From that moment on, there was a generally held belief among Catholics and many others in the Province, as well as on the mainland and in the Republic of Ireland, that some members of the RUC were out of control and had a free rein to kill whoever they suspected of involvement in unlawful Republicanism. Lord Justice Gibson became a marked man, and he and his wife would later be killed by a car bomb at the border in April 1987.

Stalker's investigation should have been completed within nine months but in fact remained open for two years, with Stalker bitterly complaining of 'downright obstructiveness' by RUC officers. In the case of Grew and Carroll, however, he and his team were told by senior officers of the Source report and Det officers confirmed that McGlinchey had also been in the orange Allegro earlier that night but Stalker was refused permission to discuss the sighting with either the FRU source or the Det team. As Stalker investigated the killings he became more convinced that he was possibly looking at murder, or unlawful killing, in all three cases. If that were so, it could only lead to one conclusion: that senior police officers were involved in the formulation of a deliberate policy of shooting to kill.

In May 1986, as he prepared to return to Northern Ireland and finally gain access to the vital missing tape (the one which had recorded the conversations and shootings inside Kitty's Barn), John Stalker was suddenly and dramatically relieved of his duties. In his autobiography, he explained that he was phoned at home by a senior officer of the Greater Manchester Police Authority and told that allegations had been made against him which might indicate he had committed a disciplinary offence. As he wrote later, 'I knew then, as powerfully as it is possible to know, that what was happening to me was rooted firmly in my enquiries in Northern Ireland. It was no secret that I was within a couple of days of obtaining the vital tape and of interviewing the highest policeman in the RUC. I knew that I had nothing to fear from any fair investigation into me, but I had learned enough during the previous years to know that devious and lying policemen do exist, and that they can function without hindrance given the right conditions. In those few seconds after that phone call I fleetingly wondered how much I had to fear from policemen such as those.'

Stalker believed the tape would be highly embarrassing to the RUC and, more particularly, to the officers of the HMSU. The following day he went to Manchester police headquarters and was told that he was being investigated on 'rumour, innuendo and gossip' about his associations with certain people in the city. An official told him, 'I have been authorised by your Police Committee to invite you to take extra leave. You will not be going to London for your conference tomorrow and you can consider yourself off the Northern Ireland investigation for ever.'

Eight days later Stalker was visited by reporters from the Daily Mail after the paper carried a story claiming that he had been 'suspended' because of his 'associations' with a criminal (unnamed) and that he had accepted 'lavish hospitality' from a 'criminal contact'. Stalker wrote later, 'The story was a lie and I was devastated.'

A few days later he was handed an official form under the provisions of the Police Discipline Regulations 1985 that stated: 'Information has been received which indicates that during the past six years you have associated with persons in circumstances that are considered undesirable, and by such association you have placed yourself under an obligation as a police officer to those persons.'

A team of sixteen officers was assigned to investigate the 'rumours' against Stalker, conducting enquiries day and night for five weeks. They failed to find anything of substance against him. No complaints were ever made against Stalker, and yet, after the five-week investigation, he was officially suspended from duty. Three months later, much to his relief, the Police Committee voted by an overwhelming majority – thirty-six to six – not to send the matter to a tribunal and to restore him to his position as Deputy Chief Constable of Greater Manchester Police.

Stalker may have been back at his desk but he was not permitted to continue investigating the shoot-to-kill allegations in Northern Ireland. He always believed – and discussions with certain senior police officers seemed to confirm the fact – that his removal from duty was wholly connected with his far-reaching investigations in Northern Ireland. The spurious questions about his 'criminal links' were contrivances intended to distract attention and to delay further the submission of the final report into what happened in the hay barn.

Eventually, in March 1987, John Stalker chose to resign from the police force and the storm over the alleged shoot-to-kill policy quietly and slowly died down.

It seemed to many FRU officers and senior NCOs that the fact that the Thatcher government had permitted a full-scale inquiry into the three separate killings indicated a worrying trend in the way in which terrorists were being hunted down and killed. The officers believed that the government would be able to hide behind an official inquiry into a possible shoot-to-kill policy, perhaps even pushing all the blame for such a policy onto those responsible for carrying out the operations. FRU officers wondered whether the Stalker Inquiry and all its inherent problems and political ramifications concerning the RUC was the reason why, more and more, the SAS were being brought into action, to take care of missions in which it was likely IRA and INLA gunmen and bombers would end up dead. Two particular high-profile SAS missions against the IRA were frequently discussed and put forward as prime examples of the government's decision to use them rather than the RUC in dangerous situations. And the FRU were convinced that if the two SAS operations in questions had been handled by the RUC instead, there would have been far greater political ructions for the government to contend with. Using the SAS was a brilliant strategy: not only were they feared and respected by the terrorist organisations but they were also accepted by the British electorate as heroes, undertaking 'dirty work' on behalf of the nation who quietly rejoiced whenever they read of SAS missions which ended in the killing of IRA or INLA gunmen or bombers.

The first and most dramatic of these actions, which was mentioned briefly in a previous chapter, occurred on the evening of Friday, 8 May 1987, in the village of Loughgall, a picturesque spot on the back road between Portadown and Armagh. Loughgall was a suitable target for an IRA bombing as the village is known as a founding centre of Orangemen and its 250 inhabitants are almost exclusively Protestant. Twenty SAS troops were tasked to watch the Loughgall RUC station after the FRU had been tipped off that the IRA had begun a campaign of targeting police stations and security bases. The terrorists' aim was to close these stations down, thus allowing IRA activists free access to roam the country with little or no hindrance. The promised attack on the small, insignificant, four-man Loughgall RUC station was the twelfth that year and the seventh in a two-week spell. Most of the earlier attacks had been made with home-made mortars and, though the police stations and bases had been hit, no one had been killed or injured and little structural damage had occurred.

The FRU had been unable to determine the exact time and date of the proposed IRA attack and the SAS had been warned they might have to endure a long stake-out. In fact, the very day after the twenty well-armed SAS men had moved into position in the fields opposite the RUC station, one observation post radioed that a suspect digger was rumbling down the road towards the target.

Because the FRU had learned that the Provos intended to destroy the single-storey building with one huge bomb, orders had been given to vacate the station. The FRU had also learned from their source that because the Provos believed an RUC station in a staunchly Protestant village might be strongly defended, they planned to take a large squad of well-armed men, just in case they ran into heavy arms fire. It was the kind of scenario that the SAS loved – setting a trap for a bunch of unsuspecting killers.

Silently, the SAS men, lying low in heavy camouflage behind the hedgerow across the road from the deserted police station, cocked their weapons – and waited. The yellow digger trundled towards them with a driver and two men in boilersuits standing on either side of the vehicle, their faces hidden with masks. They were carrying AK47s. Twenty yards or so behind the digger a blue van followed as though in convoy. Then it overtook the digger and came to a stop smack opposite the police station, almost in touching range of some members of the SAS patrol. The driver of the digger slowed almost to a halt and turned towards the entrance to the deserted police station and, with the three men still on board, smashed through the barbed-wire perimeter fence and trundled on towards the two-storey white façade. Seconds before the digger crashed into the building, the three men jumped off and ran back towards the road through the gap in the fence. As they ran out, the rear door of the van opened and half a dozen men, also dressed in dark boilersuits and wearing masks, jumped out. All were carrying weapons, some with AK47s, others with handguns.

No warning was given to the Provo gunmen, no effort was made to arrest the bombers. Instead, the SAS opened fire, pouring hundreds of rounds at the men, determined to wipe out the entire IRA unit. Some took refuge behind the van and returned fire but the majority, realising they had been caught in an ambush, simply ran for their lives. Suddenly, the air was rent with the most enormous explosion and the entire roof of the RUC station was lifted off. Thousands of tiles and blocks of masonry were hurled into the air and came crashing down amongst the Provos and the SAS troops. Shielded by the van, five IRA gunmen kept up a sustained defence but as some SAS troops left their positions and circled the van, the gunmen found themselves surrounded and totally exposed. They tried to make a run for it but without success. One by one they were gunned down as they fled, given no chance to surrender. Eight IRA men were killed in total. Not one escaped. And, more importantly, there were no demands for public or police enquiries. A lesson had been learned.

Perhaps the most high-profile operation ever undertaken in the thirty-year battle against the IRA occurred not in Britain or the Province of Northern Ireland but in the British Crown Colony of Gibraltar. The SAS shot dead three unarmed members of the IRA in an operation which caused uproar in Britain, with arguments for and against the operation raging for weeks in the media and, more importantly, in the House of Commons. It quickly became obvious that the killing of Mairead Farrell, Danny McCann and Sean Savage could only be described as unlawful. No attempt had been made to arrest or apprehend them. There were no explosives in their car though the British government had claimed it contained a massive bomb, and none of the dead was armed. It was soon apparent that the entire operation had been planned and ordained by the Thatcher government as an example to the IRA that Britain would use all means at its disposal to attack and kill terrorists whenever and wherever possible.

To the FRU, working in Northern Ireland, the ruthless killings also showed the aggressive methods now being taken by the government in its bid to defeat the IRA. The government had not been slow to learn the lessons from the Stalker affair which had aroused heavy, critical media investigations. That singular experience had shown the politicians that when the RUC took tough, hardline action against the Provos, the political fall-out was far more difficult to contain than when the army became involved in such tactics. Although the Provos had undoubtedly been armed during their attack on the Loughgall police station, no attempt whatsoever had been made by the SAS to arrest them. The soldiers had simply laid an ambush and mowed down the gunmen and bombers with heavy and sustained fire.

Gibraltar, however, was a different matter. The British government argued that the SAS had been forced to kill because it was believed the terrorists were about to detonate a huge car bomb. But this was untrue and the government knew it was untrue. They were trying to defend the indefensible, which is why they received so much criticism both domestically and from international civil-rights organisations.

The members of the Force Research Unit involved with handling Agent Ten-Thirty-Three were also aware of the escalating number of Republicans, IRA activists and Sinn Fein members who were being killed. Senior MI5 political officers in Northern Ireland knew full well that British Military Intelligence was working hand in glove with the UDA whose gunmen carried out these murderous activities. And it seemed that the more the FRU became involved with Brian Nelson and his UDA paramilitary thugs, the greater the number of Catholics that were targeted. It was not only the entire Force Research Unit who was aware of what was going on; the RUC top-brass as well as the RUC Special Branch were becoming increasingly concerned that the killing of Catholics and Republicans, including IRA, INLA and Sinn Fein personnel, was being orchestrated not just by the ineffectual Brian Nelson but by much more powerful forces in the Province, forces which were using Nelson simply as a front man to carry out murder.

## Chapter Ten

# The Murder of Patrick Finucane

The cold-blooded murder of Patrick Finucane in the late 1980s aroused extraordinary anger and passion in Northern Ireland. A leading member of the Province's younger generation of solicitors, he was gunned down in front of his wife and three young children as they ate their Sunday lunch at home in north Belfast.

Patrick Finucane was just thirty-eight. He had fought for the rights of disadvantaged Catholics since the troubles began, and frequently represented Catholics and Republicans who had been arrested and charged with all manner of crimes, including offences under the Prevention of Terrorism Act. He made no pretence of doing otherwise. But Finucane knew his law well and fought tooth and nail for his clients on every occasion, as any good solicitor should. His profile rose significantly during the 1980s as he defended more Republicans, some of them members of the IRA. He even challenged the British government when he figured prominently in the 'shoot-to-kill' inquest held in Craigavon. On that occasion he represented the family of James Gervaise McKerr, a victim of one of the controversial RUC shootings described in the previous chapter, who was gunned down in cold blood by the RUC's HMSU following a car chase near Lurgan in November 1983.

When the RUC officers eventually stopped firing and examined the bodies, McKerr and his companions, Burns and Toman, were found to be shot to pieces, their bodies riddled with bullets, barely recognisable to those relatives who were asked to identify them. The RUC's extraordinary attack on the car seemed even more questionable when the police found no weapons in McKerr's car or anywhere along the road down which the men had driven. There was every possibility that the men had indeed been unarmed, and yet the RUC assault team had responded as though they had been involved in a heavy gun battle.

On that occasion Pat Finucane challenged the Coroner, arguing that the RUC men implicated in the killings of McKerr, Burns and Toman should be brought to the Inquest to give evidence. This demand was refused at first but Finucane's legal argument finally won the day and the officers were forced to give evidence.

As the result of his successful legal challenge, more Provos and Republicans facing charges in the criminal courts asked to be represented by Pat Finucane and he earned a reputation throughout the Province for his skill as a solicitor. Needless to say, this reputation, also meant that the young solicitor was seen as a thorn in the side of the Establishment, the British government and, more importantly, the Protestant Loyalists, many of whom seemed to believe that the Catholic minority were guilty of all terrorist crimes unless proved innocent.

In September 1987 Brian Nelson asked to see his handlers on an important matter. They met, as usual, at one of the safe-houses and sat down for a chat.

'What's up?' he was asked.

'We want information,' he said, 'information on the solicitor Patrick Finucane.'

'Why is that?'

In a belligerent tone, Nelson replied, 'Because we know that he's not just a lawyer but a mouthpiece for the Provos. We believe that Finucane is a fair and legitimate target; he's one of them and we want to target him.'

'Well, what do you want from us?' asked one of the handlers. 'He is a very well-known public figure; his face is known to everyone in Belfast. There's no need for us to supply you with pictures or a montage of the man.'

'We know that,' said Nelson, 'but we wondered if you could help us with his everyday movements, so we could be sure of getting him. After all, he is a legitimate target.'

'We have no reason to believe he is a member of the Provisional IRA,' said one handler. 'Do you have any such evidence?'

'Not exactly,' admitted Nelson, 'but we know he's one of them – he's always in court defending the Provos and hardliners.'

Somewhat exasperated, one handler said, 'But that's his job – he's a lawyer; he's perfectly entitled to defend whoever he wishes. You can't go around killing lawyers because they defend people in court. Everyone is entitled to be represented in court when they are charged with an offence. Just because one lawyer specialises in defending Provos does not necessarily mean that he too is a Provo or even a Republican. He might just want to see fair play.'

The reaction of the Force Research Unit left Nelson looking somewhat down in the mouth. It was obvious that he had hoped for more support and assistance from British Intelligence. He was left in little doubt that targeting Finucane would not be appreciated by his handlers. They told him that if the Ulster Defence Association had any intention of targeting Patrick Finucane then he must inform Military Intelligence before any decisive action was taken. But, when he left them that day, Nelson's handlers weren't sure whether he really would tip them off if the UDA did plan to murder the lawyer.

Nothing more was heard from Nelson on the subject of Patrick Finucane for four months, and the FRU started to believe that their warning had been sufficient to persuade the UDA to abandon their plans to murder him. But then Nelson brought his name up again, reporting that a decision had been taken at the highest level of the UDA to target Finucane.

'What do you mean?' Nelson was asked. 'We told you to steer clear of Finucane.'

'I don't know about that,' replied Nelson, 'but I can tell

you that there is a plan to gun him down when he's driving away from the Crumlin Road court-house.'

'How do you know?'

'Because I was told to carry out the recce,' replied Nelson. 'I've done that and reported back. Every evening after this case in which he is representing a Provo, Finucane leaves the court and drives along the Crumlin Road for a few hundred yards before turning left and heading along a side-road towards north Belfast. That leads to a Protestant area. Along that road he has to slow down and it's there that we plan to ambush him. It'll be a piece of cake. He never has any bodyguards and we have examined his car and found that it isn't even armoured, so there should be no problem.'

'When do you plan to hit him?' he was asked.

'Don't know that,' replied Nelson, 'but very soon. We're ready to go.'

After Nelson had gone, senior FRU officers were immediately informed and the facts were reported 'as a matter of urgency' to the TCG. The TCG officers were of the same opinion as the Force Research Unit – that everything possible must be done to stop the UDA killing Finucane. Orders were immediately issued to the army and the RUC to swamp the Crumlin Road court area and a square mile around it for as long as the current case was being heard. They were not told why they had to do this nor whose life they were there to protect. More importantly, the decision was also taken at TCG level not to inform Patrick Finucane that he had been targeted by the gunmen of the UDA. It was common practice not to inform people who had been targeted because they would then have been entitled to demand police protection. So many people were allegedly targeted by the terrorists that it would have been impossible for the RUC to protect them all. Instead, after evaluation of the circumstances, the RUC, often with the help of the army and the security services, found ways to prevent any action being taken – swamping the area with extra forces, for example, until it was judged that the danger had passed. There were hundreds of occasions when this policy was satisfactorily pursued.

In a bid to ensure Finucane's safety, senior officers of E4A and the Det surveillance units were called to a meeting and told in no uncertain terms that the UDA had targeted Patrick Finucane and were planning to assassinate him as he left the court-house. As a result, both E4A and Det teams were drafted into the area and ordered to keep a close eye on Finucane as he went about his business. MI5 officers, the members of the Tasking Co-ordination Group and the FRU all believed that the UDA were deadly serious in their plan to murder Finucane. As each day passed and no attempt was made, the senior officers began to relax a little.

The day after the court case ended, Nelson returned for another visit, angry that his tip-off had resulted in a decision to prevent the killing of Pat Finucane. 'If you bastards hadn't interfered, he would be dead by now,' Nelson raged. 'You're ruining my credibility, betraying our plans like that. What do you think would happen to me if the UDA thought I was telling you lot all our fucking plans? If you want me to keep operating, back off and let us do what we have to do, okay?'

The FRU officers tried to calm him down, explaining that killing a solicitor of Patrick Finucane's seniority and notoriety was not a good idea and that the UDA bosses should think again before deciding to target him in the future. Nelson's handlers also explained to him that they were duty-bound to pass to higher authority plans to commit murder, especially when the target was in Patrick Finucane's league, a solicitor, a member of the establishment. 'There are limits, Brian, to our work and to your work, and don't you ever forget that,' they told him.

Unknown to Brian Nelson, however, British Intelligence began to watch Patrick Finucane more closely, checking his friends and acquaintances, his meetings and the relationship between senior Provisional IRA officers and the lawyer. Intelligence services continued their surveillance of Finucane throughout 1988 and it appeared to them that he was working more closely than ever with IRA officers as well as Sinn Fein leaders. They discovered that meetings were often held after office hours, and away from Finucane's own Belfast offices, at which he and senior Sinn Fein/IRA activists would discuss a range of topics which were not strictly related to legal matters.

Reports from intelligence agents were passed to the Joint Irish Section showing Finucane's growing closeness, for no apparent good legal reason, to known IRA activists. Suspicions that he was in fact an unofficial member of the Provisional IRA grew stronger, though there was never any proof whatsoever that Finucane was ever involved in advising Provo leaders on targets to be attacked, discussing possible targets or in any way condoning attacks by Provo gunmen, bombers or active service units.

Six months after the abortive attempt to kill Finucane in September 1987 Nelson once again raised the solicitor's name with his handlers.

'We want to target Finucane again,' Nelson said. 'You asked me to tell you and I'm telling you.'

'What's the plan,' he was asked.

'I don't know,' Nelson replied, 'but I'm just letting you know he is a target. Last time you lot stopped us getting him but you won't this time. We know that he is one of them, working with the IRA. We're certain of it.'

'How can you be so certain?'

'Because we've been watching him. Our intelligence tells us that he is making the system look foolish, using every legal loophole to get off these bastards that target innocent Protestants. We're not having it any more. Get it?'

'We understand,' he was told, 'but we know you always do the recces for your mob so you had better tell us what the plans are, Brian. We have to know. This is a two-way relationship between you and us. You have to trust us to take the right decisions. That's not your job. You're the intelligence officer keeping us informed of what's happening on the streets; it's not your job to tell us what we should or should not do. Do you understand?'

'I understand that,' Nelson replied, 'but if I keep you informed on this one, will you promise me that you won't try and stop us?'

'That's not up to us,' replied one of his handlers, 'we don't make the decisions; that's up to senior officers way above our level.'

'All right, then,' Nelson replied, 'but don't let me down, for fuck's sake. I got into enough shit last time you fouled up our attempt to get him. My lot will get pretty sick if you stop us again.'

Nelson confessed that the UDA had planned another ambush, similar to the last one, but that this time Finucane would be attacked shortly after he had left his Belfast office at the end of a day's work. Using a gunman riding pillion on the back of a motorbike, they planned to hit the lawyer between the time he left his office and began the drive home.

'There's only one point,' said Nelson. 'We're not sure which way he will go when he leaves his office. We need his home address. We think he must live in north Belfast but we're not sure.'

'We'll let you know,' replied a handler.

Three days later, after the request for Finucane's home address had been passed to senior FRU officers, Nelson arrived for a scheduled meeting at the prearranged pick-up point. After chatting over a cup of tea he asked: 'Have you got Finucane's address for me?'

'Aye,' came the handler's reply, 'he lives in a detached house in Fortwilliam Drive, off the Antrim Road in north Belfast. You could have got it yourself, you know.'

'How's that?' he asked.

'Because Finucane's home address is in the phonebook,' he was told, 'you only had to look it up.'

'Fuck me,' said Nelson. 'For fuck's sake, keep that to yourselves, otherwise I'll look a right idiot.'

Nothing further was said about Finucane during that meeting, but Nelson now had the vital piece of information which would seal the lawyer's fate. And, phonebook or not, it had been supplied by British Military Intelligence.

Once again the TCG were informed of the UDA's plot to kill Finucane and once again the gunmen's plan was thwarted when the area around his Belfast office was covered each day with RUC officers and army patrols, making any attempt to get close to the Belfast solicitor an impossibility.

And once again Brian Nelson was an angry man when he confronted his handlers. 'I see you bastards managed to stop us again,' he said sarcastically. 'You're not involved with this one. We want to target him and that should be the end of the matter. Now, for fuck's sake, leave him to us. You all know that he's one of them, a fucking Provo, and we have an arrangement. You provide the information and we carry out the killings. Just leave us alone and let us get on with the job.'

'You know that we have to obey orders,' his handlers told him. 'We receive information and pass it on for decisions to be taken. If the officers above decreed an area should be swamped, for whatever reason, it's got nothing to do with us. They give the orders, we carry them out. You've been in the army, Brian, you must understand how it works. Now get off our backs.'

It was at that meeting that Nelson was informed that Patrick Finucane had been persuaded that the time had come for him to have protection. There were fears in the community that he had become so high-profile, defending Provos and Republicans charged with various serious offences, that he should take precautions to ensure his own safety. Although it was the duty of the RUC to defend those believed to be targeted by either the Provos or the Loyalist paramilitaries, some Sinn Fein activists worried that the RUC might turn a blind eye if they heard an attack was planned on someone such as the Republicans' lawyer. As a result, Patrick Finucane finally agreed, after much persuasion, that he should accept a guard, and two Republican hard men were called in to protect him. From that moment on, whenever Finucane left his office, attended court or travelled anywhere by car, he was under constant guard. His two escorts even began accompanying him to and from his home in north Belfast though they did not stand guard outside his home. After dropping him off each evening and ensuring he was safely in the house, they would return the following day to accompany him to his office. But even that strategy would not prove sufficient.

'Shit,' Nelson said on hearing the news, 'we thought he was always on his own.'

'He was,' one handler told him, 'but not any more. Now he's protected whenever he's out of his home. Perhaps he's been tipped off that your lot are after him.'

Nelson immediately rounded on his handlers. 'Have you fuckers told him that he's been targeted? Have you shits gone behind our backs and told him we're after him?'

Nelson would have gone on ranting but the senior officer raised his hand, indicating the agent should calm down and keep quiet. 'No, we haven't done anything of the sort and nor do we think anyone else has warned him. It's not our policy to do that. If we think someone's been targeted then we make sure they are protected and those intending to carry out the attack are stopped in one way or another.'

But Nelson was not happy and when he left the meeting that day the FRU were worried that he now believed Finucane had been tipped off by one of the intelligence agencies. They wondered what course of action he would take.

Incredibly, while the UDA were working out just how to murder Patrick Finucane, and while MI5, the TCG and Military Intelligence knew such an attack was frequently being planned and thwarted by the security forces, an extraordinary speech, provoking a political outcry, was made by a junior Home Office minister, Douglas Hogg. In his speech in January 1989 Hogg suggested that certain Northern Irish solicitors were 'unduly sympathetic' to terrorists. Despite the storm that remark caused in the Province's legal circles, Home Office spokesmen made it clear that Douglas Hogg stood by his controversial statement, despite accusations that his words would put the lives of some lawyers at risk.

There has never been the slightest suggestion that Douglas Hogg's remarks were intended to give the green light to the UDA to proceed with their plan to take out Patrick Finucane, but it is known that plans to target the Belfast solicitor had been forwarded by MI5 in Northern Ireland not only to the Home Office, their political masters in government, but also, of course, to the Joint Intelligence Committee in London. That committee, which met frequently at 10 Downing Street, would, almost certainly, have known of plans to murder Finucane when the issue first came to prominence some eighteen months before Hogg's infamous speech.

On the evening of Sunday, 12 February 1989, Patrick Finucane, his wife Geraldine and their three children had just sat down in the kitchen for their evening meal when there was a knock at the front door. As Patrick Finucane went to see who was there, three masked gunmen simply turned the handle and walked in. Unbelievably, the front door had not been locked; the house was wide open. Before Finucane had even left the kitchen a masked man pointing a handgun appeared and fired twice, hitting Finucane who fell to the floor. Then another masked man came to the kitchen door armed with a sub-machine-gun and riddled the lawyer's body with bullets as Geraldine Finucane and the three children screamed at the men and the horror of what was happening in front of their eyes. One bullet hit Mrs Finucane in the leg; none of the three children was injured in the attack.

The men then turned and ran out of the house to a waiting taxi. The taxi, which had been hijacked earlier that evening, was later found abandoned at the junction of the Loyalist Forthriver and Ballygomartin roads. Within hours of the RUC beginning their investigation, detectives said that the killing bore all the hallmarks of a Loyalist paramilitary group.

Tom King, the Secretary of State for Northern Ireland, immediately expressed his horror at the killing: 'No civilised society can tolerate murder from whichever vicious extreme it comes. The deaths of every one of the seven people murdered so far this year – some by the IRA, some by Loyalist extremists – show the total futility and awfulness of killing. The police and security services will do all they can to bring the perpetrators to justice. Everyone in Northern Ireland must help in ending this awful cycle of violence.'

The day following Patrick Finucane's assassination, the president of the Law Society of Northern Ireland, Colin Haddick, accused Douglas Hogg of having created 'an excuse' for terrorists to carry out murder: 'We are on record at the time Mr Hogg made the statement as having expressed our disbelief at what he said. If Mr Hogg had specific cause for concern about solicitors generally or as individuals, there are well-known channels through which he could have had such matters investigated. Let me add that the Law Society has never once been asked to investigate the conduct of any solicitor. What Mr Hogg has done is to create an excuse for terrorist organisations to carry out murders – something which was not available to them before.'

Anger at Patrick Finucane's killing was shared by many of Northern Ireland's political leaders. Dr Brian Feeney, the SDLP Councillor for north Belfast, who was one of the first to arrive at the murder scene, said, 'This cowardly act was a direct result of Home Office minister Douglas Hogg's remarks some weeks ago. He said then that some Northern Ireland solicitors had links with terrorist organisations. At the time, the Northern Ireland Law Society reacted angrily to the allegation and Mr Hogg's stupid remarks have been used by those who carried out this attack to legitimise murder.'

SDLP chairman Alban McGuinness also condemned the killing and called for Hogg's resignation. At the same time, he appealed to the government to provide protection for solicitors handling terrorist-type cases. Kevin McNamara, the Opposition's chief spokesman, commented, 'I think Mr Hogg should be examining his conscience very carefully.'

And north Belfast solicitor Paschal O'Hare, who had

known Patrick Finucane for twelve years, said that the dead man had never expressed any concern for his own safety. But he added, 'Highly irresponsible remarks about the legal profession were made in the House of Commons in recent weeks. I condemn without reservation the recent remarks of British politicians and those of Mr Douglas Hogg. They were highly irresponsible and have led directly to this horrible and brutal murder.'

Alan Dukes, who was then the leader of the Fine Gael Party in the Republic of Ireland, denounced the killing as 'a savage attempt to discourage people from exercising their legal right to defend themselves in court, which is a fundamental right in any democracy'.

And Belfast's Lord Mayor, Nigel Dodds, condemned the killing of Finucane saying, 'All such murders only serve to heighten tension and fear throughout the community.' Without realising it, Dodds had described perfectly the precise motives behind the aggressive policy of the Force Research Unit's secret operations.

There were demands for Douglas Hogg to resign, but these were firmly rejected by the Home Office. Hogg issued a statement saying, 'This is clearly, like so many others, a tragic and wicked killing. As to its cause, that must be a matter for the RUC. I very much hope those people responsible will be arrested, tried and sentenced to extremely long terms of imprisonment.'

In spite of such statements, there is evidence that certain members of the British government knew exactly what was going on at that time in Northern Ireland because of the constant stream of totally reliable information forwarded to both the Joint Intelligence Committee and the Home Office by their officers working and serving in the intelligence agencies in Northern Ireland. Though the British Army's Force Research Unit may have been more actively involved in directing and aiding Loyalist paramilitary gunmen than any other security force during those three years, an MI5 officer sat in the same office as the FRU's second-in-command, who was known as the Operations Officer, and was privy to everything that was going on. On every single occasion when any one of the FRU's forty handlers had any dealings with Brian Nelson, or any other informant for that matter, the handlers would fill in a Military Intelligence Source Report (MISR). This report, usually between two and five hundred words long, would automatically be passed to the Operations Officer. He would take the decision whether to send it to the FRU's Commanding Officer or even to the TCG. Every report would also be read by the duty MI5 officer who sat in the same room as the Ops Officer. Matters which FRU handlers believed were very important or highly sensitive intelligence material, as was often the case when dealing with Brian Nelson, were written up as MISR Supplements, which could be up to a thousand words long. These would usually be circulated not only to the FRU Ops Officer but also the TCG and the Joint Irish Section.

Handlers were also responsible for passing to the back-room staff the all-important Contact Reports, when details from touts would include sightings of Provo and Loyalist gunmen, their movements, meetings with their friends and acquaintances. These Contact Reports also included as much detail as possible about the sex lives of these Provo and Loyalist activists, containing information of the names and addresses of their lovers. The FRU knew from their touts that many women whose husbands were serving long prison sentences found comfort in taking these dangerous men as their lovers. They also knew that some of the gunmen deliberately boasted about the killings they had been involved in as a way of attracting women who liked such macho behaviour.

All these sightings and contacts would be filed away by the FRU backroom staff of nearly a hundred men and women who would cross-reference the comings and goings of the gunmen on their computer databases. It was by such detailed filing that the FRU were able to keep track of many of the Provo and Loyalist hard men and thus, on occasions, spring traps, make arrests or prevent attacks taking place in both Northern Ireland and the British mainland.

There were, of course, other shootings by UDA gunmen during those years, many ending in the deaths of Provo and Republican diehards, but many others also ending in the murders of totally innocent Catholics. And, of course, the IRA did not just sit around idly waiting for yet another of their men to be targeted and killed. In the early 1980s a British Army analysis of the structure and strength of the Provisional IRA concluded that the Provos had about five hundred full-time activists, including gunmen, bombers, intelligence staff, operatives and back-up staff, with thousands of passive supporters willing to store weapons or hide an activist who might be wanted by the authorities. It was no wonder, therefore, that throughout the three years that Brian Nelson worked with British Military Intelligence, the Provos would hit back whenever one of their men was taken out. And there were times when the Provos would be more ruthless, resorting to the bomb, and seemingly not caring who, or how many, might be killed or wounded in such operations. It was in November 1987 that the IRA killed eleven innocent people and injured scores more in an appalling bombing at the Remembrance Day ceremony at Enniskillen, Co. Fermanagh. A remote-controlled bomb was detonated at 11 a.m., the precise moment the Provos knew the people of Enniskillen would be gathered around the town's cenotaph to show their respect to those local people who gave their lives in the two World Wars. And in August 1988, an IRA landmine killed eight British soldiers near Omagh.

Such callous killings by the IRA had the effect of spurring on the hard men of the Ulster Defence Association, who had no qualms about targeting Provo activists and supporters. Some UDA gunmen saw such IRA atrocities as encouragement to target innocent Catholic civilians themselves. Most of the UDA's attacks were carried out in the name of the Ulster Freedom Fighters (UFF). Others were carried out by the Ulster Volunteer Force (UVF), the other main Loyalist paramilitary organisation. For many years during the 1980s the UDA claimed that they had nothing whatsoever to do with the

UFF, but that was untrue, and was the reason why in 1992 the British government finally outlawed the organisation. Although the UFF and the UVF sometimes resorted to internecine violence, there were occasions when the two worked together, exchanging intelligence and even weapons.

## Chapter Eleven

# *Saving Gerry Adams*

Perhaps the most senior political figure targeted by the UDA during the years when Brian Nelson was the linch-pin of this extraordinary episode was Gerry Adams, the president of Sinn Fein.

Before becoming more politically involved with Sinn Fein, Adams is believed to have been a valued and highly placed commander with the Provisional IRA. Brought up in the tightly packed streets of west Belfast, he claimed that as a teenager he had become actively engaged in direct action on the issues of housing, unemployment and civil rights. Yet in the latest volume of his autobiography, Before the Dawn, Gerry Adams writes nothing whatsoever of his time as an active Provo leader, Adjutant of the Provisional IRA's Northern Command, or of his years as head of the Provos Belfast Brigade during the early 1980s. And, despite his background as the head of an active service unit which was responsible for a number of killings and bombings during the late 1970s and early 1980s, Adams became one of the most important politicians in Northern Ireland, hauling Sinn Fein/IRA away from purely military activities and persuading the hard men of the Provisionals and the seven-man IRA Army Council to look instead at pushing for a political solution which, he maintained, had a greater chance of success. Despite being a member of the Army Council since the late 1980s, Adams earned considerable respectability by shaking the hand of President Bill Clinton in 1996.

Back in June 1987, an excited Brian Nelson asked for an urgent meeting with his handlers and jubilantly proclaimed: 'I've got great news for you. We're going to bump off Gerry Adams and his bodyguard!'

Trying to stay calm, one officer asked, 'Has any date or time or place been fixed for Adams' assassination?'

'Well, I understand he's going to be taken out in two days' time.'

'Where?' said the handler, a note of anxiety in his voice.

'Outside the Belfast Housing Executive offices in the centre of the city,' Nelson told them gleefully, as though everything had been arranged and finalised.

'And who's going to shoot him?' asked the handler, wanting to find out every possible piece of information about the planned killing. He realised that this was one attack that would have to be stopped – the assassination of one of the Republicans' most senior leaders was something that would have to be ordered and agreed at the highest level of government. It was certainly not to be undertaken lightly by some over-eager UDA gunmen who had decided that Gerry Adams should be removed from the scene.

'I don't know the names of the people who will carry out the killing but I think three will be involved,' Nelson replied. 'I've already done one recce and I'll be doing another tomorrow before the go-ahead is given.'

'How's it going to be carried out? What's the plan?'

Nelson's excitement at the prospect of killing the Sinn Fein leader spilled out as he described the plans for the attack. 'This is really good,' he began, 'I've worked out exactly how we will do it. It's brilliant. One bloke will be sitting in a car parked in the square outside the Housing Executive offices. Using his two-way radio, he will notify two other guys who will be waiting round the corner on a motorbike. One will ride the motorbike and the pillion passenger will have a sub-machine-gun.'

He looked to the two officers for approval and, even though none was forthcoming, he continued, still excited at the thought of what lay ahead. 'We know that Gerry Adams arrives between half past ten and eleven o'clock every Thursday morning to attend a housing meeting. He is always driven in his Ford Granada, an armoured vehicle, an ex-police chief's car. We have the colour and the registration number. He is accompanied by an armed bodyguard. As soon as our man sitting in the car sees Adams drive up, he will radio the motorcyclists. They will arrive within seconds, just as Adams and his bodyguard are getting out of the Granada. The pillion passenger will open fire with his sub-machine-gun, killing Adams and the bodyguard. It's all worked out; it can't go wrong. We are certain to get the bastard.'

'How do you know he will be there this Thursday?'

'We don't,' said Nelson sounding cocksure. 'But he turns up at the same time on the same day virtually every week. If he doesn't arrive this week, we'll postpone the attack till next week. One way or another we'll nail him, don't you worry.'

'This is a most serious matter,' stressed the handler who had been asking all the questions, 'why didn't you tell us about it earlier?'

'Because it was only decided a couple of days ago,' replied Nelson, 'I've been busy since doing the recce, planning the operation.'

The officers asked Nelson to sketch the area and explain the plan as accurately as he could. They wanted to make sure that the information he was supplying was correct. They knew that if he had recced the area, as he claimed, he would know every detail of the square, the surrounding streets and the traffic flows. They were concerned and disconcerted to discover that his plan was totally feasible.

'Do you know exactly what weapons will be used?'

'No,' Nelson replied, 'but we anticipate the pillion passenger having an SMG and a handgun. The look-out driver in the car will also be armed in case there's any trouble.'

Nelson's disturbing news made his handlers realise that action would have to be taken immediately to inform all the intelligence agencies and security services of what was going on so that a plan of action could be drawn up to thwart the UDA's plans without anyone being the wiser.

One officer left the room to make a telephone call while the other stayed behind, chatting to Nelson. After talking to a senior officer in Military Intelligence at Castlereagh, the decision was taken to let Nelson go, to allow him to complete his recce the following morning, and ask him to report back immediately to his handlers.

As soon as the officers returned to Castlereagh, the TCG was informed of the murder plot and officers were ordered to devise a suitable plan of action to stop the killing. The TCG debated whether Gerry Adams should be informed that a plot to kill him had been uncovered by British Intelligence, but it was decided not to tell him, primarily because the TCG's senior officers were confident they could stop the assassination taking place without arousing undue suspicion. They also believed that if Adams was informed that he had been targeted by the UDA he might well decide to make a great deal of political capital out of the alleged attempt. But everything possible would be done by the authorities to prevent the attack succeeding.

The Joint Irish Section was immediately informed and, as a result, officers from 14th Int were dispatched to the square to stake out the area, remaining undercover on the scene for the following forty-eight hours, reporting back anything that seemed relevant. They were informed that Brian Nelson was expected to be in the square, checking out the area the following day, Wednesday. As expected, the agent did recce the square the next day and this was reported by 14th Int.

Later the same day, Nelson turned up, as requested, for a meeting with his two FRU handlers.

'Is the operation still on?' he was asked.

'Yes, it's all systems go,' he replied, sounding chirpy and confident.

'And who are the three gunmen?'

'Fuck knows,' he replied, 'I don't fucking know; they don't give me that sort of information.'

The handlers told Nelson to pass on the information he had gathered during his morning recce of the area to the

UDA chiefs and then to make sure that he stayed completely clear of the centre of Belfast the following morning – the time of the attack.

By nine o'clock the following morning the square and the area surrounding the Housing Executive offices was being patrolled by twelve armed E4A officers and men from 14th Int, all in various disguises and all wearing civvies. A strong military and police presence was also ordered in a bid to deter the gunmen. Around the immediate vicinity of the square, fully armed, uniformed British troops were brought in, as well as more than fifty armed RUC officers. The plan was to frighten off the UDA gunmen before they even approached the offices where Adams was expected between 10.30 and 11 a.m.

Officers from E4A and 14th Int were under orders to take out the UDA gunmen – killing them, if necessary – if the terrorists did manage to break through the military cordon and appeared to be in a position to assassinate the Sinn Fein president.

At half past ten Gerry Adams arrived at the offices of the Housing Executive in the back seat of his armoured Ford Granada, totally unaware of the reason for all the police and army activity in the area. Two hours later he left and returned home. There were no incidents.

'What happened?' Nelson was asked when he met the FRU handlers later that evening.

'The hit squad went out as planned,' Nelson told them, 'but when they approached the area they found police and army swarming all over the fucking place. They decided to split up and return to base. It would have been far too risky to go ahead in those circumstances.'

'So what's the plan now?'

'We'll try again in a couple of weeks,' Nelson replied.

Two weeks later Nelson reported to his handlers that the decision to kill Gerry Adams was to go ahead as before, using the same plan. Once again, a tremendous effort to prevent the assassination attempt was ordered by the TCG, the area once again being flooded with troops and police. Officers from E4A and 14th Int were also in position in the square. In spite of this, the UDA driver took an enormous risk, driving through the heavy army and police presence and arriving as planned outside the Housing Executive offices in his car, parking as ordered in the exact spot where he could wait for Gerry Adams to appear. This daring move caused alarm bells to ring at the TCG, army headquarters and among the top brass in Military Intelligence, for there was suddenly a real fear that Gerry Adams could be hit.

Instructions were immediately flashed to the camouflaged 14th Int troops in the square to be on stand-by for the arrival of Adams. They were also told that the 'decoy' car had arrived and parked and the make and registration number were passed to them. They were advised to keep a watch for the arrival of the motorbike which would be carrying two men, and were instructed that, if necessary, they were to shoot the man riding pillion first if Adams should arrive in the square. The troops and RUC officers who had been called in were put on alert but told to do nothing until further orders were given. Everyone in the square, and those at base listening to the army intercom, waited tensely for the arrival of the motorbike and Gerry Adams. Minutes passed and no sign was seen of either. The time of his appointment came and went and still nothing happened. Thirty minutes after Adams should have been shot, the UDA car pulled out of the square and nothing whatsoever had been seen of the motorcyclists or the target. Eventually, the RUC, the British troops, 14th Int and E4A were ordered to stand down. The crisis was over.

The following day, Nelson would report back that the attempted assassination had been aborted because, once again, the area had been flooded with troops, and the motorbike gunmen, having set off for the square and witnessed the extraordinary activity on the ground, had no option but to return to base.

An angry and disappointed Nelson also reported that the UDA had taken the decision to put the mission on hold, to await a better opportunity to target Gerry Adams.

The news brought a sense of relief to the British authorities in Belfast for they feared a vicious backlash of Republican violence across the Province had Gerry Adams indeed been murdered.

At no time was Adams ever informed that the UDA had seriously intended to kill him and that a plan to assassinate him had been worked out, nor did he know that but for Brian Nelson and his close relationship with British Military Intelligence he might well have died in a UDA gun attack in 1987.

But the UDA leaders were in no mood to forget Gerry Adams, the man many believed not only to be a hardline Provo but also the architect of the campaign of the bomb and the bullet which had devastated the lives of the great majority of people in Northern Ireland, both Protestant and Catholic. In Protestant circles Gerry Adams was considered the devil incarnate; because they knew of his background and his well-earned reputation as an IRA brigade commander, they saw him as the mastermind behind many appalling attacks in Northern Ireland and the mainland. They would try to assassinate Adams at a later date. All they had to work out was the surest way of arranging his murder.

Months later Ten-Thirty-Three brought up the question of Gerry Adams at one of his meetings, saying, 'I know your lot are against taking him out but we're adamant and, what's more, we believe we have found the best and the surest way of getting him.'

'What's that, then?' he was asked. The FRU handlers could see that Nelson and the UDA were serious and they needed to find out the plan so they could stop it. The orders from above had not changed: every possible effort had to be made to ensure the safety of Gerry Adams.

'We know that Adams's car is well armoured so there is no way we could stop the vehicle and just open up 'cos we have learned that those windows would stop a grenade attack and maybe even a rocket-launcher hit.'

Nelson paused for effect, watching the reaction his words were having on the handlers.

'Well?' one of them said. 'Go on.'

'Here's the clever part,' Nelson said. 'The top of the car isn't armoured at all. We've checked. And that's how we will hit him.'

'How exactly?'

'With a limpet mine. Get it?' he asked.

'Go on,' he was asked, 'explain yourself.'

'We have planned an attack at a set of traffic lights somewhere in Belfast. We don't know where exactly, but we've been looking at the Broadway traffic lights off the Falls Road. He's always driving around there. We plan to follow his car on a motorbike with the pillion passenger holding the mine. When he stops at the lights our men will pull up alongside and place the magnetic mine on the car roof. Whoosh. Neither Adams nor anyone else in the car will stand a fucking chance; they'll be blown apart.'

'But where are you getting the mine from?' he was asked.

Ten-Thirty-Three replied, 'We've made one already. Our lads in forensic put it together for us. We're almost ready to go. We've stuffed it with gelignite and attached a remote-control detonator. We've already had a dry run on an old banger and it worked brilliantly.'

'When do you plan this?' he was asked.

Nelson gave his customary answer to that question: 'Don't ask me, I don't fucking know. I just come up with the plans. Someone else says when and where. I've explained that a hundred fuckin' times.'

'All right, all right,' he was told, 'keep your hair on.'

'These mines and the detonators are very difficult to handle and the timing has to be spot on,' the senior handler commented casually. 'Why don't you let our lads take a look at it, to make sure it will go off within seconds of placing it on the car roof? You don't want Adams to be driving around with the mine on top of his car, not knowing where the hell it will explode. That could kill others, too.'

Finally it was agreed that Nelson would bring in the limpet mine for the Force Research Unit's forensic team to examine. Two days later he walked in with the mine and the detonator in a hold-all.

'Here it is,' he said. 'Take look if you want to.'

The FRU personnel cast their eye over it and then, after chatting for a while, suggested it would be better if Nelson left it with them so that they could pass on the mine and detonator for examination. In fact, FRU forensic bomb experts were very surprised because the mine had been carefully sculpted with a hollow in the middle so that the full force of the explosion would detonate downwards, into the car. They also confirmed that if indeed the mine did go off when attached to the roof of a car, everyone inside would be blasted into tiny pieces.

One week later the mine and detonator were returned to Nelson. 'It's lucky our men had a look at it,' he was told. 'In the condition they found it there was a real possibility the thing could have gone off at any time – the detonator remote-control device was wrongly set.'

'Great, thanks,' said Nelson. 'Is it okay now?'

'As right as will ever be,' he was told.

Weeks passed and Nelson said nothing about the limpet mine, nor were there any reports of such a device being attached to the roof of Adams's car. Nelson eventually admitted that a decision had been taken not to try to assassinate Adams in that fashion but to wait for a better opportunity.

'So you still intend to target him?' he was asked.

'Fucking right,' was the reply. 'We'll get him one day, you can bet your life on that.'

Military Intelligence chiefs who were on a tour of duty in Northern Ireland at that time were surprised that the authorities, which included the TCG and MI5, had been so determined to prevent any attack on Gerry Adams when they knew him to be one of the most influential members of the Provisional IRA. There had been rumours in intelligence circles some years before that, during the seven months Adams had spent on remand in Crumlin Road jail following his arrest in February 1978, he had been persuaded to work for the British in an effort to bring peace to Northern Ireland. It was noted that after one bail application by his solicitor (which was refused), the judge, for some unknown reason, had asked the prosecution to process the Adams case speedily. Later, in the remand wing of the H-Blocks where Adams enjoyed a cell on his own, he was treated as a special security prisoner, which meant that he was taken on his own whenever he had to go anywhere in the jail, normally for visits from his wife, Colette, but also to attend other meetings. There were not many Provo leaders in Crumlin Road jail who received such special treatment. While these may be nothing more that small titbits of circumstantial evidence, such tenuous scraps can form the basis of an argument in the cauldron of Northern Ireland politics.

## Chapter Twelve

# *Kill, Kill, Kill*

By the spring of 1989, less than two years after Brian Nelson became an integral part of Military Intelligence, all those people in regular contact with the cocky, over-confident, bumptious Nelson were becoming heartily fed up with his posturing, his demands and his arrogance. Agent Ten-Thirty-Three was becoming more and more difficult to control. He had reached the stage in his relationship with his handlers where he saw himself as a Very Important Person – someone who could say or do as he liked, whose every whim should be tolerated and whose every idea be acted upon. He believed that he was God's gift to Military Intelligence and the fact that he was treated with respect, that this handlers were encouraged to listen to his every word and treat him with deference, perhaps persuaded him to see himself as a man of honour engaged in a noble cause. To his handlers he was a nauseating pain, a trumped-up little tout whom, they hoped, would one day have his comeuppance.

In the meantime, however, the intelligence material Ten-Thirty-Three was providing was treated as manna from heaven by those security officers and Intelligence chiefs whose job it was to try contain and, if possible, defeat the Provisional IRA's campaign of violence. Most senior government ministers in the Northern Ireland Office in London believed that if the Provos could be defeated then the Loyalists groups, including the UDA, would end their own military campaign and allow peace to return to Northern Ireland. Consequently, instructions continued to flow from London and the JIS in Belfast that

Ten-Thirty-Three must be encouraged, at all costs, to continue his vital intelligence work. There was a strong belief in 1989 that the new material Nelson was providing, almost on a weekly basis, was having a real effect on the Provos, causing them endless problems, and dividing the Catholic population between those who wanted the bloody conflict to continue and those who would do anything to bring peace to the Province.

Agent Ten-Thirty-Three was almost unique in the annals of Northern Ireland security. Never before had the RUC Special Branch or Army Intelligence had such a good source in such a vital position, throwing down challenges each and every week to the Provos in a way which the forces of law and order could never, for one moment, consider carrying out themselves. This, of course, was recognised by the FRU handlers but they would complain that Brian Nelson had become so arrogant that he had started to take decisions which, rightly, should have been taken by them. Dealing with Nelson was becoming increasingly difficult – at times almost impossible – for he would now accept little advice, believing that he was so knowledgeable about what was going on that he was best-suited to make all decisions.

Nelson had always been known as a heavy drinker but now he appeared to be more addicted to alcohol than ever and this was worried Military Intelligence. Increasingly, he would telephone his contact number and, following the normal procedure, would ask one of four questions which the telephone operator would know from his notes suggested the urgency, or otherwise, of the call. He would be asked to hold a moment while his handler was contacted but would instantly start to be abusive to the telephonist, demanding to be put through immediately, berating the telephonist if there was a delay of more than a few seconds. And this would happen at all hours of the day and night. Handlers would have to be woken and told their informant was on the phone demanding to speak to them. They had to be available to their touts twenty-four hours a day, fully realising that if their contact phoned during the night it must be because vital information was being passed on as a matter of urgency. On such occasions, the handler would take the call and deal with the situation even if it meant clambering out of bed and arranging a rendezvous at four o'clock in the morning.

But when Nelson began phoning in the middle of the night, he was usually the worse for drink, often barely able to speak coherently. And, more often than not, the handlers could tell from the background noise that Nelson was in some club or drinking-den where it must have been possible for people to overhear his conversation. Worse still, Nelson would begin talking about planned operations and past missions or boast about the intelligence work he was carrying out on behalf of the UDA. And he would issue orders over the phone as though talking to some underling. Although most of what he talked about was incomprehensible because he was incapable of stringing a sentence together, his boasts over the telephone sometimes concerned real on-going operations and the targeting of named individuals which he and handlers had been discussing in their safe-house meetings around Belfast. These were highly secret intelligence plans which should never have been discussed outside the confines of the safe-houses, and certainly not blared aloud in a pub or club so that everyone could hear. It was this aspect of Nelson's drinking habits that so deeply concerned his handlers, and they frequently warned their superiors of the danger of continuing to use Ten-Thirty-Three as a high-grade informant. Despite their appeals, no instruction was ever forthcoming from FRU senior officers, or those in the JIS who must have been made aware of the situation, ordering the down-grading of Nelson or cutting off the supply of secret Military Intelligence material that his handlers had been providing him with.

The handlers knew that Nelson was simply showing off to his mates or some woman whom he was trying to impress with his exploits as the chief intelligence officer of the UDA. In such circumstances, which were soon occurring on a weekly basis, they would try to quieten the loquacious, drunken Nelson before he revealed any secrets. But time and time again the same situation would happen and the subject of Ten-Thirty-Three would be raised in discussions at the highest level within the Force Research Unit. Those with experience of drunken touts knew there was a real possibility that the relationship with Nelson would end in severe embarrassment to Military Intelligence and a number of handlers urged their senior officers to dump Nelson before it was too late.

Throughout 1989 the RUC Special Branch, who had dealt with members of the UDA for nearly twenty years, were increasing concerned about the relationship between Nelson and the FRU. Many RUC officers had friends or even relatives who were members of the UDA and knew a great deal about its workings and internal politics. Those Branch colleagues suspected that Brian Nelson was the man primarily responsible for the information supplied to the UDA leadership and they had been led to understand that his source was the Force Research Unit. These Special Branch officers were constantly warning their counterparts in the FRU that they should get rid of Nelson as soon as possible because they feared he would bring Military Intelligence into disrepute. Branch officers also realised that such a close involvement with the UDA gunmen could result in the same sort of political trouble that the infamous 'shoot-to-kill' rumpus had a few years earlier.

The RUC Special Branch had been very worried about the growing number of Loyalist attacks on members of the Catholic community. They had studied in detail many of the killings carried out by UDA gunmen and had come to the conclusion that Brian Nelson, whom they knew to be the UDA's chief intelligence officer, was the linchpin between the UDA and British Military Intelligence. Special Branch investigations had shown that when the Force Research Unit asked the TCG to declare somewhere out of bounds for a particular period, such requests coincided with attacks on Provo, Sinn Fein or Catholic targets. As a result of top-level discussions with senior

RUC officers, unofficial approaches were made to Military Intelligence chiefs alerting them to the fact that their Number One agent was now believed by the authorities, including senior RUC officers, to be a vital link in the on-going campaign of murder.

But the FRU still needed Ten-Thirty-Three as a go-between and as a vital source for gathering information and rumours from street level.

Another problem facing the FRU was the jealousy the Unit inspired in the other security services working in Northern Ireland. They were well aware that the FRU officers were treated as the élite, with higher pay, better conditions and accommodation and more expensive cars. One of the consequences of this jealousy was that personnel attached to other undercover agencies kept a close eye on the Force Research Unit, wondering why they had been handed such privileges and debating among themselves whether there were indeed highly secret activities going on to which they were not privy. That was one of the reasons why the rumours about the activities of Brian Nelson and his UDA gunmen created such interest.

As the death toll of IRA members and Republican supporters grew, the RUC chiefs responsible for tracking down, arresting and bringing Loyalist killers to justice found themselves more and more inclined to believe that Brian Nelson, the UDA's chief intelligence officer, was involved. But there was no proof against Nelson, no proof at all. The RUC also faced a major problem: there was an unwritten agreement between the various intelligence services operating in Northern Ireland that one agency did not steal another service's agents or informants. As a consequence, the very fact that the RUC understood Nelson was working directly with Army Intelligence meant that he was 'off-limits' to their detectives investigating Loyalist killings. By 1988, senior RUC Special Branch officers were certain that Nelson was indeed working for Military Intelligence and they had to presume that he was under the control of the FRU. Before Ten-Thirty-Three's career with Military Intelligence was brought to an abrupt halt, though, there would be more conspiracies and more killings.

The murder of Ian Catney, a twenty-seven-year-old Catholic, was typical of the random killings being carried out by Loyalist gunmen, who seemed hell-bent throughout the late 1980s on causing as much fear and strife as possible in the Catholic community. Not all these killings were the result of intelligence gathered from the Force Research Unit. It was well known that Ian's mother ran a shop in Smithfield Market and that Ian, hard-working and conscientious, also worked there with her. It was also a recognised fact that many Catholics worked in the markets area, a place the RUC Special Branch and Military Intelligence saw as a favourite recruiting ground for Provos and Sinn Fein supporters. To many a staunch UDA member, any young man working in the markets area was automatically assumed to be a Provo activist and, therefore, could be targeted and shot at will.

One such target was Ian Catney. On the morning of Wednesday, 18 January 1989, the young man was sitting in his mother's shop in Belfast's new Smithfield Market complex drinking a cup of coffee. A customer was looking around the shop shortly after 11 a.m. when two men walked in.

Catney looked up to see them standing in front of him, both wearing face masks and combat jackets, and carrying guns. One held a light machine-gun, or machine pistol, while the other appeared to gave a handgun. Before he could move, the gunmen fired six or seven shots at point-blank range into his body. They turned and walked out of the shop. Not a word was spoken and the cold-blooded murder was over in seconds.

But the shots had been heard by other traders near by and they ran out to see what was happening. They saw the two men walk out of the shop and then sprint out of the complex. The traders gave chase but the two killers made good their escape, jumping into a red car and speeding away. Traders managed to take down the registration number but the car was found later that day abandoned in

Boundary Street off the Shankill Road. Police and troops immediately cordoned off the markets area and forensic police examined the shop.

The Ulster Volunteer Force, the hardline Loyalist terrorist group, claimed responsibility for the shooting, but the killers were never traced and no one was ever charged for the murder.

Ian Catney, of Springhill Park, west Belfast, described by other traders as 'a quiet, easy-going young man who troubled nobody', was shot simply because he was a Roman Catholic. He had, in fact, been shot at once before, during the INLA feud of early 1987, when he was targeted because of his family connection with Kevin McQuillan, a leading member of one of the feuding parties, the Irish Republican Socialist Party. On that occasion he was in his car when gunmen approached and fired at him but he suffered only superficial wounds.

Such callous sectarian shootings continued to drive a wedge between the two communities. At the funeral the Revd James Donaghy of the local church said that Catney had been shot 'just because he was a Catholic'.

And there were other murders which were planned and executed by the UDA with the help of Brian Nelson and the knowledge of the Force Research Unit.

The murder of Anthony Fusco was a good example of the relationship between the FRU, Brian Nelson and the UDA. Fusco, a thirty-three-year-old married man, who worked at Smithfield in Belfast and lived in the Lower Falls area, had been born into a staunch Republican family and many of his relations had been associated with the Republican movement. The FRU were aware of his possible links with the IRA. One day Brian Nelson was invited to a meeting and asked if knew anything about Fusco.

'Never heard of him,' was Nelson's reply. 'What does he do? Where does he live?'

One of the handlers showed Nelson a photo of Fusco, telling him that from sight reports Military Intelligence had established that a considerable number of Fusco's associates were members of the Belfast Brigade of the Provisional IRA and some names were mentioned. The officer did not in fact refer to any specific terrorist activities in which Fusco had been involved but it was nevertheless implied that he was guilty simply by association.

'Just the sort of man we're after,' agreed Ten-Thirty-Three, becoming more enthusiastic.

'Good,' replied the officer, 'we'll leave him to you, then.'

'Do you have an address? Do you know where he works?' asked Nelson.

'Yes, he works in Belfast's Smithfield Market every day. You should be able to identify him from the photo we've given you.'

On the morning of Thursday, 9 February 1989, Anthony Fusco set off to as usual to West Street in Smithfield Market. On that cold, rainy morning he had not the slightest idea that two men watched him approach, as they had watched him on numerous other occasions. Twice before, while undertaking surveillance, the two UDA men on a motorcycle had ridden past him, verifying his identity. They wanted to make sure they had the right man and, for several days, they took note of Fusco, checking with the photo provided by the Force Research Unit. Only when they were certain that this was indeed the man they were after did they make arrangements to strike. Handguns were drawn from the UDA secret armoury and it was agreed that it would be better to take out Fusco using a motorbike rather than risk taking a car into the crowded Smithfield Market area.

They decided to hit Fusco when he was on his way to work; they believed he would not be expecting an attack at that time in the morning and would, they hoped, be off his guard. The gunmen circled the area at least three times as they waited for their target to arrive. When they finally saw him walking along the street they followed him at first and then stopped a little way past him at the junction of West Street and Winetavern Street in the centre of the market.

They watched him as he walked down the road towards them and waited until he had gone past. Then the rider, wearing a donkey-jacket and black helmet, turned the bike and followed him. When the riders were only feet away from the unsuspecting Fusco, the pillion passenger, who was wearing a white crash helmet, took a handgun from a shoulder holster and fired five times into Fusco's back. Hardly stopping to see him slump to the ground, the motorcyclists accelerated away along Winetavern Street and within seconds were lost in the crawling traffic. The motorbike used by the killers was later found abandoned in Carlow Street off the Protestant Shankill Road.

That night the BBC newsreader announced the cold-blooded murder of Anthony Fusco, explaining how he had met his death. Market traders interviewed for the programme demanded greater protection and claimed that their pleas for an increased police presence had been ignored by the authorities. Michael King, the chairman of Smithfield Traders Association, said that he had written to the City Council asking for their support for extra police protection in the area but the Council had not even bothered to reply to the letter. Fusco's family protested that he was simply an ordinary Catholic who worked hard and led a good life. They claimed they had no idea why he should have been targeted as he had no connections with any paramilitary organisations. Later, the UVF would claim responsibility for the killing.

The murder of Liam McKee, a thirty-six-year-old devout Catholic, angered not only the Catholic community but also McKee's Protestant neighbours, as well as the officers of the Force Research Unit. Liam McKee was a quiet, gentle man who kept himself to himself. He had never married, preferring to stay at home and care for his elderly widowed mother. There could only have been one reason why McKee was murdered and that was because he was a Catholic living in a Protestant area. His cold-blooded killing was sectarian hatred of the worst kind.

For forty years the McKee family had lived in the same

terraced house in Donard Drive on the Tonagh Estate, Lisburn. Quiet and reserved, they were one of only a few Catholic families on the estate and lived surrounded by Protestants. But they got on very well with nearly all their neighbours, visiting each other's houses, chatting whenever they met on the street, behaving to each other as good neighbours should. But one of Brian Nelson's touts discovered that the McKee family were living in Protestant Lisburn and decided that the UDA should introduce their own brand of ethnic cleansing.

This was really nothing new. Throughout the thirty years of the troubles large numbers of Catholic and Protestant families had been forced to move house if it suited the sectarian bigots. Whole communities were forced to move into their own 'tribal' areas, warned to get out for their own safety. Some were ordered out at gunpoint; others were threatened with a beating unless they moved; still more were advised by friends to pack up their belongings rather than take the risk of living among those of a different religion. Disobeying the orders of the paramilitaries nearly always resulted in a beating or a kneecapping. Since the early 1970s countless numbers of both Catholic and Protestant families who were good, close friends for years have been forced to move away because of the threat of the paramilitaries and the punishment gangs who roamed the streets.

In 1987 the McKees' home had been fire-bombed by Loyalists but Protestant friends of the family had persuaded them to stay. They thought long and hard and decided they did not want to be driven out of the home they had lived in for nearly forty years. Shortly after midnight on Saturday, 24 June 1989, however, a blue Vauxhall Cavalier, which had been hijacked a week before in Donegall Road, Belfast, pulled up outside the McKees' home. Three masked men got out and walked up to the front door. Liam McKee and his mother had both retired to bed and the house was in darkness. Seconds later, neighbours awoke to the sound of wood splintering as the Loyalist thugs broke down the door with a sledgehammer.

Two masked men ran in and up the stairs while a third stood guard outside. Liam McKee woke from his sleep, realised what was happening, leapt out of bed and ran into his mother's room in a desperate attempt to save her. The two of them went back into his room as the gunmen raced up the stairs and Liam tried in vain to barricade the bedroom door. Neighbours heard the sound of a shotgun being fired, then another blast. The gunmen had shot through the bedroom door and hit Liam McKee fully in the chest, killing him outright. The second shot grazed his mother's arm but otherwise she was uninjured. The gunmen forced open the door, saw that Liam was slumped on the floor, turned and ran.

This appalling sectarian killing infuriated the FRU and led to one of the most ferocious rows between Brian Nelson and his handlers. They called him to an urgent meeting that very day.

'What have you got to say about what happened on the Tonagh Estate in Lisburn early today?' he was asked as soon as he arrived at the safe-house.

'Don't know what the fuck you're talking about,' said Nelson.

'You know right enough,' an FRU handler told him.

'I've just told you; I don't know what the fuck you're on about,' he repeated.

'So you've never heard of Liam McKee then?'

'No, never,' he replied.

'Have you not listened to the news today?'

'Oh yeah,' he agreed, 'you mean the lad killed in Lisburn last night. I didn't know his name.'

'Yes, you did,' said one handler, 'because some time ago you asked us if we had anything on him.'

'Did I?' said Nelson. 'Well, I must have forgotten.'

'You know bloody well,' the man continued. 'You asked us for information and we told you that we had nothing on him, that he was clean.'

'So,' said Nelson, shrugging his shoulders as if wanting to end the conversation.

'You're the UDA's intelligence officer and your gunmen

killed this poor bastard,' said the other man, raising his voice. 'And you, Brian, probably set up the whole attack.'

Before Nelson could again deny his involvement, another handler told him, 'Just listen a moment. If you don't tell us the truth and own up to this one then we are all in a lot of trouble. And in your capacity as chief intelligence officer it is quite likely that the RUC will be paying you a call. Do you understand?'

Ten-Thirty-Three knew only too well that with the evidence that the FRU had concerning a range of killings, he would be in trouble. But he was still playing the tough image. 'Don't give me that bollocks,' he said. 'You wouldn't fucking dare. If you dropped me in it then I would just spill the beans and every one of your lot would be in the shit. Now stop trying to give me a hard time; it won't work.'

Nelson was asked what he thought of the killing of Liam McKee.

'Not much,' he replied. 'I just look on it as a bit of ethnic cleansing if you want to know.'

'But a man was shot dead,' a FRU handler told him, exasperated at Nelson's couldn't-care-less attitude.

'Tough,' he replied.

It seemed obvious that Nelson was not about to admit to anything and so one of the chief handlers decided to read him the riot act. 'You carry out another killing like that and you're on your own. We will disown you and, believe me, we have so much on you that we could send you down for twenty years. Now play the game as we want you to or pay the consequences. You do not target innocent Catholics just because you want some "ethnic cleansing" in a Protestant area. We either work together or not at all. Have it your way but remember that of one thing you can be certain: if you don't go along with our plans, you're finished, washed up and totally in the shit. Get it?'

Before Nelson could reply, the man began again: 'Say nothing now. Go away and think. Then let us know. But remember my words of warning. Now fuck off.'

There was disagreement within the Force Research Unit about what should be done about Agent Ten-Thirty-Three's taking the law into his own hands and killing an innocent man. Some handlers believed they should cut their losses and get rid of Nelson, even though they knew that by doing so they would be getting rid of their prime source of information. They also feared that if they gave Nelson his marching orders he would probably take with him the forty or so touts that happily worked for the UDA's intelligence-gathering organisation and obviously provided valuable street-level material. Other handlers saw Nelson was a hero, doing valuable work in an impossible situation, keeping his FRU contacts happy as well as having to provide regular and vital intelligence material to his UDA bosses. Some FRU officers were also convinced that Nelson was working as a double-agent, telling the UDA hierarchy that he had somehow managed to infiltrate British Military Intelligence and that was how he was able to provide hot, up-to-the-minute information on anyone the terrorists wanted to target.

After much discussion it was decided to keep running with Ten-Thirty-Three but somehow try to contain his ambitions, to get him back on side obeying instructions rather than acting as a loose cannon doing whatever he wanted, when he wanted, as though it was he who was controlling the Force Research Unit.

In the summer of 1989 the UDA decided to step up their campaign of murdering Catholics because they weren't having much success in killing their preferred targets – known IRA activists and their supporters or even Sinn Fein members. The UDA were afraid that their killing rate couldn't match that of the Provos, which was far higher at that time. The IRA had killed not only British Army personnel and members of the RUC, but also prison officers and Protestant taxi-drivers, so the Loyalists decided to increase the stakes.

Ten-Thirty-Three took up the matter with his FRU handlers to see if they would approve. At a meeting during that summer Nelson casually asked if there would be any

objection to UDA members on active service using motorbikes as these seemed to have the edge on cars or vans.

'We've discussed it,' he told them, 'and we believe it
would be better to switch to motorbikes when targeting a
man on his own because it is far easier to make a good
escape; far better than a car. It worked well on Fusco.'

'True,' replied a handler, 'motorbikes are always far
better in traffic and escape is easier.'

'Is there anything against motorbikes?' Nelson
enquired.

'Well, protection is almost non-existent,' he was told.
'If someone returns fire there's a good chance the
motorcyclist or his pillion passenger will be hit. You've no
protection whatsoever. In a surprise attack, there's far less
chance of being hit if two of you are in a car. There is
another drawback, too: only one person can fire, unlike in
a car where there can be three armed passengers as well as
a driver. It is true, you know, that there is safety in
numbers.'

'But it's much more manoeuvrable,' Nelson suggested.

'Yes, and brilliant to make a getaway in traffic,' replied
the handler. 'There is also another point. No one can walk
around wearing a balaclava or a mask because it's so
fucking obvious you're up to no good. But no one takes
any notice of someone wearing a helmet and no on can
recognise you.'

Some days later Ten-Thirty-Three returned for a
further chat and he told his handlers that the UDA had
decided to go ahead and use a motorbike on a couple of
hit-and-runs in Belfast city centre.

'But you don't know who you'll be hitting if you just
drive around the centre of Belfast,' they replied.

'We know where the Micks go, don't you worry about
that,' said Nelson, 'we won't make fucking mistakes. In any
case, my fellas can smell a Mick a mile away.' And he
laughed at his joke.

An MISR was immediately sent to the FRU's
operations officer and commander giving details of the
UDA's latest plan. The MISR was passed to the Joint Irish

Section but no guidance was received from above. No instruction came back as to whether the UDA should be permitted to target people using motorbikes or not. As a result, the FRU decided to follow the UDA bikers with two motorcycles of their own and a back-up car, all of which were in constant radio contact.

For three days the UDA motorcyclist and his armed pillion passenger rode around Belfast, mainly in the city centre, looking for likely targets. They knew that they were being followed, that their every move was being watched and, during that time, no offensive action was taken by the UDA bikers.

On the fourth day it was decided to relieve the follow-up team of FRU bikers and personnel and hand over the watch to 14th Int, the famous 'Det', to see if things might hot up somewhat if the UDA bikers thought no one was following them and keeping an eye on their antics. The Det motorcyclists and a back-up car, a blue Vauxhall Astra with two armed men inside, continued riding and driving around the city centre. Then the UDA bikers broke away from their usual tour and headed off away from the city centre and along the Crumlin Road. They believed they had shaken off the bikers who had been tailing them and did not realise they were still being surveyed by the Det motorbike and back-up car.

Shortly after ten o'clock on Saturday morning, 2 September 1989, the UDA bike suddenly stopped outside the shops on the Ardoyne Road. The pillion passenger pulled a revolver out of his shoulder holster and fired four shots at the stranger standing on the kerb. Patrick McKenna, a single, unemployed man in his thirties from nearby Farringdon Court, slumped to the ground. He was dead. He had had no idea that he was being targeted that day and had just walked to the shops from his home. He was given no chance of escape and was shot in the back for no apparent reason.

The soldiers on the pursuing motorbike – officers carrying out a two-year stint with the Det – saw exactly what had happened and immediately swung into action.

They had no intention of letting two thugs who had just gunned down a pedestrian get away with murder.

The UDA bike accelerated away down the Crumlin Road but had not travelled more than a couple of hundred yards before the officers struck, shooting the pillion passenger in the back. Two shots from the soldier's Heckler & Koch machine pistol and the man fell to the ground. Brian Robinson, a member of the UVF, was dead, killed on active service.

The other man decided to make a dash for it but as he tried to accelerate away, the Det back-up car followed, hitting the motorbike broadside, a lesson learned in training. The motorcyclist was catapulted from his bike. Before he had time to pick himself up or use his handgun, the officers had raced to the spot, one soldier throwing himself on the man, pinning him to the ground to prevent him getting his gun.

'Don't move!' another yelled, his gun only a couple of feet from the UDA man's head. 'Don't dare move an inch or I'll blow your head off! Keep still!' he yelled again while his mate took off the man's crash helmet and searched him, taking away his gun and checking if he had any other weapons on him.

The Loyalist rider was injured though not seriously hurt and none of the Det soldiers had sustained any injuries. The shootings had been witnessed by many people, most of whom had been going about their Saturday-morning shopping, some of them accompanied by their children. Within minutes the RUC and ambulances were at the scene. After handing over the UDA man to the RUC and exchanging a few words with the senior RUC officer, the Det team disappeared.

McKenna's killers had known neither his identity nor his religion. Shocked members of his family said they were 'dumbfounded' by the news of his murder. McKenna was quiet and gentle, a man well known and well liked in the area because of his interest in football and his voluntary work for the John Paul Youth Club. Sinn Fein Councillor Gerard McGuigan said that Patrick McKenna had no political connections of any kind. 'It is obvious that he was simply a random victim of what was clearly a sectarian attack by Loyalists.'

Brian Nelson was angry, frustrated and bitter when he next met his handlers. 'Fuck you, fuck you all!' were his opening words. 'You were tailing our men and when they kill some Provo bastard as arranged you fucking shoot our men! What the fuck are you playing at? What's your fucking game?'

'Listen,' one handler said in an effort to calm him down.

But he hadn't finished his tirade. 'I thought we had a deal. You provide the information and we carry out the dirty work. I thought we were in this together. So tell me, why the fuck did you kill our man? I am in deep shit over this and my bosses are fucking fuming. They know he was taken out by your blokes and they want an explanation, otherwise the deal is off. We'll simply piss off and let you bastards stew in your own juice!'

'It wasn't like that,' said one handler. 'If you'll give us a minute, we'll tell you what happened.'

'So it was a cock-up?' asked Nelson.

'In a way, yes.'

'Okay, tell me then,' he said, 'but it had better be no fucking cock-and-bull story 'cos I won't buy it.'

The officer explained exactly what had happened. He said that FRU personnel had been following as arranged and then it had been decided to let the Det team take over the operation so that it didn't look as though the UVF riders were being tracked by the same bikers for long periods of time. The Det team did not, unfortunately, realise that a joint exercise between FRU and the UDA bikers was in progress. When they saw the gunman take a shot at someone walking along the road, they decided to act.

'So you're saying it was just bad luck?' asked Nelson.

'Sort of,' he was told.

'What am I going to tell my bosses?' Nelson pleaded, looking desperate. 'They think its my fault.'

'Tell them the truth. Tell them exactly what happened,' he was told. 'Explain that accidents happen. They'll understand that.'

'I don't know,' said Nelson, looking moody and downcast. 'I could be for the fucking high jump on this one.'

'Don't talk bollocks,' he was told, 'just tell them what happened; they'll understand.'

There would be more conspiracies involving the Force Research Unit and the Ulster Defence Association and most involved Ten-Thirty-Three, the link man who boasted both to his handlers at the FRU and to his UDA bosses that he was the most important person in the campaign to disrupt, wreck and confuse the Provo leadership. But mistakes occurred and innocent men were murdered.

# Chapter Thirteen

## Out of Control

It seemed extraordinary that, despite constant assistance from Military Intelligence, using detailed and accurate information from the most sophisticated computer databases operated by a conscientious and hardworking team of back-room specialists, so many innocent people should have been targeted and killed by Loyalist gunmen during the years when Agent Ten-Thirty-Three was operating. Some might argue that, in the chaotic, crazed cauldron of Northern Ireland, 'accidental losses' would have to be accepted, and that the Loyalists wouldn't have killed anyone had the IRA not tried to bomb and blast their way to power. Most Loyalists would point the finger at the hardline Provos who took over the leadership of the Republican movement in the early 1970s and started their campaign to terrorise the Protestant population in the hope that eventually they would come to accept the principle of a united Ireland.

On a number of occasions during those thirty years Northern Ireland was a hair's-breadth away from all-out civil war and it took the intervention of the British Army, and the heroic discipline of the RUC, to avert open warfare. In the last three years of the 1980s, however, it was the conspiracy between Military Intelligence and the Ulster Defence Association which carried the battle on the streets to the very heart of the Republican movement. And the campaign of intimidation and killing of Sinn Fein/IRA politicians, gunmen, bombers, supporters and sympathisers by the UDA, aided and abetted by British Military Intelligence, was known about by MI5, Prime Minister

Margaret Thatcher and a few senior government ministers and civil servants.

For all the intelligence material and expert free advice that was available to Brian Nelson, it seems extraordinary that the Loyalist gunmen would make such errors as, for example, killing the wrong person and, sometimes, even shooting members of their own side, Protestants that they mistook for Catholics. Whenever such dreadful mistakes occurred, the Force Research Unit officers were at their wits' end to know how they could control Ten-Thirty-Three and his gunmen when the the UDA were allegedly only interested in taking out Provos, hardline Republicans and Sinn Fein activists.

One such killing occurred on a cold, bright January afternoon in 1988, when a young man and his girlfriend were walking along Park Road, near the junction with the Ormeau Road in Belfast. Timothy David Armstrong, aged twenty-nine, was a captain in the Ulster Defence Regiment, a dedicated, keen member of 8 UDR who had served with the regiment since 1978 and was based at Dungannon.

His girlfriend, who was not injured in the shooting, told RUC detectives that no warning whatsoever was given to Armstrong and that neither of the two masked gunmen had bothered to ask his name or what he did for a living. She believed he had been murdered by the Provisional IRA simply because he was a full-time member of the UDR, and that somehow they had tailed him and decided to shoot him at that time on that day, Saturday, 16 January 1988. She had always known that he could be murdered in cold blood by the Provos. She was taken to hospital suffering from shock. When she later discovered that the killers were in fact Protestant UDA gunmen, she was devastated, unable to believe that the organisation would so callously kill someone without having any idea of their identity.

Once again, it seemed, the UDA had stupidly selected the wrong target, revealing how amateurish their set-up had become despite the advice and assistance they received almost on a weekly basis from British Military Intelligence.

The dead man was a well-known, well-liked officer. Ulster Unionist MP Ken Maginnis commented at the time: 'Captain Armstrong served in my constituency and I knew him as someone who was considerate to his men and courteous to the public.'

At Nelson's next meeting with his handlers, he was asked to explain the murder of Armstrong. With a shrug of the soldiers he replied, 'It was a fuck-up, a mistake; there's nothing more I can say. They shot the wrong man.'

'But didn't anyone check first?' he was asked.

'I dunno,' Nelson replied, 'I wasn't there.'

'Why didn't you ask us for advice?' one handler asked him. 'Why didn't you check out the man's name with us? You've asked us about other people before, so why didn't you on this occasion?'

Nelson simply shrugged, unable to offer any explanation.

The killing of Captain Armstrong worried the FRU officers for it showed either that Nelson's advice was not being followed by the UDA leadership or that his authority within that organisation was negligible. And yet, on other occasions, it was obvious that the UDA leadership were taking note of Nelson's information. On this tragic occasion, however, it appeared that a Loyalist hit-squad had simply decided to go out to kill someone that Saturday afternoon and had mistakenly killed one of their own.

One of the killings that alerted the RUC Special Branch to Brian Nelson's possible involvement in the spate of UDA shootings was the murder of Phelim McNally in November 1988. The gunmen had not in fact been interested in Phelim McNally, but were after his brother, Francis, a well-known Sinn Fein member of Cookstown Council in Co. Tyrone. Some weeks before Phelim's murder, Agent Ten-Thirty-Three had informed his handlers that the UDA wanted to check out and perhaps target Francis McNally.

'We understand McNally is as thick as thieves with the Provos,' Nelson told his handlers during one of his bi-weekly chats with them.

'What makes you think that?'

'Our contacts in Cookstown have been keeping an eye on him and they have seen him hanging around with known Provo activists in the area.'

'Are you sure?'

'Well, the people who gave me the information are reliable,' Nelson replied, 'what more do you want?'

'And they're sure the man seen talking to Provos is the Cookstown Councillor Francis McNally?'

'Aye, we're certain, positive,' Nelson replied. 'He's been identified.'

'What do you plan to do?'

'My men are checking out his place now. We have his name and address but no one has yet visited the area to see if it would be possible for one of our teams to get in and out without too much trouble.'

'We haven't been told that this man is in fact working with the Provos,' his handler commented. 'How can you be so sure?'

'You know we have men in Cookstown,' Nelson said, 'and they told me that this fella is one of them. Definite. No doubt.'

Nelson was told to return with any plans that he and his team might draw up before going ahead with any action against McNally. His FRU handlers told him that they would check out the councillor to see if the information Nelson's men had provided could be backed up by any other source.

Nelson didn't like that idea. 'Don't go fucking up my contacts,' he said, raising his voice as if he was in charge of the meeting. 'I know what you fuckers can play at. This one's mine and if we want to get him, we fucking will, okay?'

'Well, we must check first,' he was told as the handler tried to diffuse the situation. He didn't want Nelson raging around, throwing his weight about and setting up operations himself without recourse to advice from his handlers. They knew from experience that such behaviour by a tout – believing in their own arrogant opinions, their own triumphs and their invincibility – was certain to end in disaster.

After that meeting the FRU officers did check out Councillor McNally and discovered that while he was an ardent, enthusiastic Sinn Fein member, there was no hard evidence that he was involved with the IRA. The fact that he was a Sinn Fein councillor simply showed that he was a Republican and possibly a Provo supporter but did not imply he was a Provo activist or a member of the IRA.

This evidence was put before Nelson at their next meeting a few days later.

'I will inform my military wing,' Ten-Thirty-Three told his handlers. 'It will be up to them to make a decision. I've given them my evidence, the word of my contacts on the ground, and they are convinced that Councillor McNally is a Provo.'

'But you have no proof,' one handler protested.

'We have all the fucking proof we need,' replied Nelson. 'He drinks with Provos, he talks to Provos and, for all I know, he probably attends Provo meetings. He's certainly Sinn Fein and that's good enough for us.'

'But you told us that from now on you would only be targeting known Provo activists.'

'I know I did,' Nelson replied, 'but that was then; this is now. In any case, what the fuck's it got to do with you lot? You just keep supplying the information and we'll carry out the jobs. That's the deal we've had from the beginning and there is no reason why it shouldn't continue. You know that we've got loads of info coming in from all over the place, making it easier to target known Provos and their mates. Well, this is just another one, okay?'

It was obvious that Nelson had no intention of backing down. In an effort to ensure that the UDA were not targeting innocent people, the FRU handlers asked Nelson to check Councillor McNally's background once more.

'If it'll make you happy, we'll run another check,' said Nelson, sounding miserable once again, 'but we know we've got the right guy.'

'Have it your way,' he was told, 'but check first, okay?'

'Okay,' he replied and was gone.

The MISR sent forward to senior officers giving details of that meeting with Ten-Thirty-Three included the warning that Francis McNally was, in all probability, to be targeted in the very near future. No instruction came back from senior officers to say that anything should be done by the FRU to stop the attack.

Some weeks later Phelim McNally, aged twenty-eight, was at Francis's home in Derrycrin Road, Coagh, Co. Tyrone, sitting in the kitchen and playing the accordion late into the night. A talented musician and keen trad-itional music enthusiast, Phelim was a married man with five children. On that night, Thursday, 24 November 1988, his wife was in hospital about to give birth to their sixth child.

At 10 p.m. three masked gunmen stopped a car in Mossbank Road, Coagh, and ordered the driver out of the vehicle. They told him that on pain of death he was to say nothing to anyone about what had happened. The men then drove off in the hijacked vehicle.

Twenty-five minutes later the sound of breaking glass was heard at McNally's home by neighbours, followed seconds later by the sharp crack of five shots. The UDA gunmen had walked to the back of the house where, through the kitchen window, they could see the figure of a man playing the accordion. Apparently, there was no conversation between the man and his killers; no identification was checked. As Phelim heard the breaking glass he instinctively looked up and, as he did so, five shots rang out. He died instantly. RUC detectives investigating the murder were convinced that the killing of Phelim McNally was a case of mistaken identity.

When Ten-Thirty-Three was confronted by his handlers later that day he simply shrugged his shoulders as though the matter was of little concern to him. But they pushed him, determined to make him confront the fact that his intelligence work had played an integral part in the murder of a totally innocent man, the father of a young family.

Nelson seemed unrepentant. 'Nothing to do with me,'

he protested, almost in a whisper, giving strong hints that
he had no wish to continue the conversation.

Pressed further, he went on, 'You know all I do is give
the name and the address and, of course, a photograph of
the target. All that was done. We had no idea that his
fucking brother would be in his house that night sitting in
the kitchen playing the fucking accordion. It was just bad
luck.'

'Is that what you call it, "bad luck"?' he was asked.

'What would you call it then?' Nelson retorted. 'What
do you want me to say? That I'm sorry? That I'll send
flowers to his fucking funeral? Well, the answer is no. This
is war we're involved in and we are simply defending the
Loyalist cause. Get it?'

No more was said on the subject because the handlers
realised that their tout was in no mood to give ground or
even admit that a terrible, tragic case of mistaken identity
had robbed a family of their father. Such cases caused
concern and apprehension within the FRU, and not only
because members of the Unit prided themselves on being
a dedicated, efficient and professional outfit which did not
make such basic mistakes.

But the catalogue of mistakes did not end there.
Another extraordinary 'error' was the murder of a
Protestant man by two UDA gunmen who believed their
target was a Catholic. Agent Ten-Thirty-Three had been
informed by one of his streetwise touts that a man believed
to be a Catholic had just been hired to work on a construction site in Lisburn. Most of the other men employed
by the building firm were understood to be Protestants.

In the early-morning darkness of Wednesday, 25
January 1989, twenty-six-year-old David Dornan kissed
his wife and their nine-month-old baby daughter goodbye,
left his home in Carlisle Park, Ballynahinch, and set off for
work at a building site on Knockmore Road, not far from
the Protestant Rathvarna housing estate in Lisburn. He
had been working on the site for just a week, and was glad
of the chance to earn some money.

The Force Research Unit had no idea that an attack was

planned on David Dornan or anyone working on that building site. This was a Loyalist attack which was planned and executed without any reference whatsoever to Military Intelligence. Ten-Thirty-Three had never raised the matter in any of his discussions with his handlers. Not surprisingly, as the FRU knew nothing about it, no arrangements had been made to keep the police and the security forces out of the area surrounding Knockmore Road, and the RUC had arrived on the scene within minutes. As a result, the murder of David Dornan caused a massive and immediate police response and a number of people were arrested and taken in for questioning over the killing.

Dornan had begun work at eight o'clock that morning and was busy driving a mechanical digger, a photograph of his beloved baby daughter pinned inside the cab. He was thrilled to be a father and frequently told his workmates all about the baby and her progress.

Two young men in their late twenties or early thirties casually walked onto the building site and went up to Dornan's vehicle, flagging him down, asking him to stop because they wanted to question him. Not for a moment expecting to be attacked, Dornan stopped the vehicle. As he bent down so that he could hear what the two men wanted, they opened fire, one with a handgun, the other with a sawn-off shotgun. David Dornan slumped forward over the steering wheel, fatally injured. His workmates rushed over when they saw what had happened and gave him emergency first-aid but doctors pronounced him dead shortly after he arrived at hospital.

The two killers were seen running from the scene towards the Loyalist Rathvarna estate. Police and soldiers were drafted in and two army helicopters took to the air in a bid to spot the men. Within thirty minutes of the shooting the housing estate had been sealed off and four men had been arrested and taken to police headquarters for questioning. Other RUC and army personnel conducted house-to-house searches along Ballymacash Road and Knockmore Road, off the main Lisburn-to-Glenavy road.

The local community was shocked and angry at the killing, unable to understand why David Dornan, a family man with no paramilitary connections, had been targeted and killed. Detectives discovered later that Dornan was not in trouble with any terrorist organisation nor was he in debt, and they could not find any motive for the cold-blooded murder. There was in fact no reason. It had simply been a stupid mistake on behalf of the UDA's intelligence section who had misinformed their bosses that the man hired to drive the digger on that building site was a Catholic, and that as such he would be an easy target for Loyalist gunmen.

Sinn Fein Councillor Pat Rice knew what had happened. He said at the time: 'The shooting of David Dornan was purely sectarian. His attackers obviously thought he was a Catholic so they killed him.'

The Workers' Party spokesman, John Lowry, appealed to the public representatives in Lisburn to call for a united stand by all political parties in the area against paramilitary gangs of any sectarian persuasion in an effort to stop the mindless, callous killings and bring peace to the town. But his appeal fell on deaf ears.

Against this, of course, were the IRA bombers who, it was claimed, only targeted Loyalists, RUC members and soldiers but who in reality were happy to risk the lives of women, children and old people in the process. Time and again – like the horrific explosion at the Remembrance Day parade in Enniskillen in November 1987, the Droppin Well Bar, in Co. Derry in December 1982, the bombing of Christmas shoppers at Harrods in 1983, Warrington in March 1993 or Omagh in 1998 – the Provos' bombs killed totally innocent people who had no part in the troubles of Northern Ireland.

But during the late 1980s in particular, the UDA were so eager to destabilise Sinn Fein and the IRA that they seemed prepared to risk killing innocent people who just happened to drink in the wrong pubs or who were simply unlucky enough to be in the wrong place at the wrong time.

One such was Seamus Murray who lived on the Suffolk estate in the Twinbrook area of west Belfast. He was a hard-working Catholic, married with a family, who had never been in trouble with the RUC or involved in petty crime. He had never been interviewed in connection with any criminal offence and had never been arrested. Indeed, at no time had there ever been any suggestion that he was involved with the Provisional IRA, Sinn Fein politics or even the Republican cause. But, unluckily for him, he happened to work on a Housing Executive building site in the protestant Legoniel area of north Belfast. The site was supposedly 'protected' by the Provisional IRA.

In January 1988, UDA men, always on the look out for potential targets, noticed that Murray regularly visited both a known Republican club and a pub frequented by Provo activists. They had no idea if he drank with these activists or with another, non-political, group of men. The UDA traced him to the building site and assumed that Seamus Murray was an IRA activist or, at the very least, a sympathiser and supporter.

For three months one of Brian Nelson's intelligence units stalked Murray, checking his movements and noting where he drank, the friends he met and, of course, finding out his home address. Then, one evening in the early summer of 1988, they struck, smashing their way into his kitchen where he and his wife were eating. His wife screamed at her husband to try and escape and, to her great credit, tackled the armed gunmen, trying in desperation to stop them shooting Seamus. But she was no obstacle to the burly UDA hitmen who pushed her violently out of their way before opening fire on the defenceless Murray.

That unprovoked killing of an innocent man was one of the worst examples of Brian Nelson's reign of power as the UDA's intelligence officer. On that occasion he had not sought information from the FRU, though he had notified his handlers that the UDA were targeting a man named Murray who appeared to have links with the Provos. Worried that another innocent person might be about to die, Military Intelligence checked their files but

could find no one of that name who had any link with the
IRA or the Republican cause. Nelson was informed of this
and advised to leave the man alone. By the summer of
1988, however, Brian Nelson had become almost a law
unto himself, taking little notice of what his handlers told
him, only using them to obtain intelligence, photographs
and information about possible IRA targets.

The following day, the FRU called him to a meeting
and demanded to know why Seamus Murray had been
murdered when Nelson had been advised there was no
evidence to link him with the Provisional IRA.

'I had no idea the killing was to take place,' he told
them. 'My job is simply to target people; I had nothing
whatsoever to do with the murder.'

'But why didn't you ask us for further information on
the man? If you had done so we would have told you that
to the best of our knowledge Murray was an innocent
man.'

'But we had other intelligence,' Nelson argued, 'which
suggested that he was not innocent.'

'What evidence?' he was asked.

'Our own evidence,' was Nelson's weak reply.

'Well, remember this occasion,' one of the handlers told
him, 'and next time ask us? Do you understand?'

'Okay,' he replied but with no great enthusiasm.

At meetings over the next few weeks Nelson's handlers
urged him to keep them informed of exactly who was
being targeted. They could not afford to let any more
innocent people die. Nelson replied that he was now
keeping them 'fully informed' of everything, claiming that
he religiously passed to Military Intelligence every UDA
decision he knew about. His handlers believed he was
lying. They were sure that he knew far more than ever he
declared, but they had no way of checking. In notes to
senior officers, they communicated their fears of the
consequences of their agent's reckless behaviour, and the
matter was discussed at meetings of the Joint Irish Section.
But at no time were they told to stop Nelson's
undisciplined operations or told to curb his apparent

desire to have random killings carried out, even if that meant innocent people died.

But the handlers had no intention of permitting Nelson to dictate to them. They decided the time had come to take firm action if they were to rein in Nelson's headlong dash to open sectarian warfare on the streets of Belfast. That day they warned him to slow down and not to jump to conclusions just because some of his touts on the streets had reached hasty decisions that were probably based on hearsay with little concrete evidence to support them. Nelson was warned that if he persisted in targeting innocent people his arrangement with the FRU, including his three hundred pounds a week, and the information and advice he was given, would end forthwith.

The senior handler advised him, 'If you carry on like this we won't be able to protect you. If UDA gunmen are caught and your name comes up, it will be impossible to save you. In those circumstances you could be done for conspiracy to murder and that would mean twenty years behind bars. So, take note. Do you get the message?'

For a moment Nelson appeared to have accepted what was being said. But a couple of minutes later he had regained his customary bumptious attitude. In fact, he appeared even more cocksure. 'That don't worry me,' he said, 'because I'm doing nothing except passing on information that you lot have given me for months now. I've got all the proof I need in my database. If I'm caught and questioned I'll simply have to tell the truth. Then we'll all be in the shit, won't we? Two can play that fuckin' game.'

'Have it your way,' said the senior handler. 'But you don't frighten us one bit. And don't forget one very important point. We're acting under orders – you're not.'

That seemed to throw Nelson somewhat. 'I'll see what I can do,' he said, but he wasn't convincing. The handlers were sure that Nelson would do nothing to stop the UDA's campaign of targeting ordinary, decent Catholics who were not in any way involved in the clandestine war raging between the Provos and the Loyalists

Behind the scenes, two different schools of thought were being argued by opposing camps in the Force Research Unit and among the MI5 officers of the Joint Irish Section. The political pressure was still on to continue the war of attrition against the Provos, to keep them guessing, to press them as hard as possible and make their attempts to win power by the bomb and the bullet a useless aim, convincing them that such a victory could never be achieved. The other school of thought believed the IRA Army Council may have come to realise that they could not win power by violence alone. Other ways had to be examined, including the political route which some Sinn Fein leaders believed was the best way to achieve the ultimate aim – a united Ireland.

There was a growing feeling within MI5 that the Provos were feeling the squeeze, realising that they were under constant threat, their lives at risk by the British government's heightened campaign against them. Never before had they lost so many activists; never before had the UDA gunmen proved so successful at tracking down and targeting their activists and bombers.

And there was another worry to be considered by the Sinn Fein/IRA leadership. The very fact that ordinary, non-political Catholics were being targeted and killed revealed how impossible it was for the Provos to defend the Catholic minority. One of the proud boasts of Sinn Fein/IRA down the years was that only the Provos could protect their supporters while they were championing the Republican cause for a united Ireland. At weekends in and around Belfast and Derry the clubs and pubs, filled with ordinary people who played no part in the violence, would listen to traditional Republican songs castigating the English reign of terror throughout history and looking forward to the day when Ireland was free of British rule. But the previous three years had revealed a different, more disturbing reality. The Provos' wild claims of protecting their Catholic followers had proved a nonsense, embarrassing the IRA leadership. With the escalating number of Loyalist killings on the streets and in the

Republican housing estates, the Catholics of west Belfast in particular had come to realise that the Provos could not protect their own people from Loyalist attack. Every week, Republicans were being targeted, and every week Catholics funerals were taking place in Belfast and beyond, bringing home to the community that the all-powerful Provisional IRA were losing their grip. Indeed, Sinn Fein/IRA were beginning to lose the confidence of the people they claimed to represent.

And there was another problem rapidly developing which all those who had knowledge of the true role and nefarious activities of Ten-Thirty-Three realised all too well could bring major embarrassment not only to Military Intelligence but also to the politicians at Westminster who knew the precise role of the Force Research Unit. It was recognised that the murderous relationship between the FRU, Ten-Thirty-Three and the UDA terror squads would come to an end sooner or later, because it was very unlikely that all the authorities would continue to turn a blind eye to what was going on. When that moment came, heads would roll, and the intense pressure that was being applied to the IRA's throat would be eased.

# Chapter Fourteen

## The Cover-Up

As the killings continued in Belfast and beyond during the summer of 1989, a phone call from an officer in the RUC Special Branch to a handler of the Force Research Unit heralded the end of Agent Ten-Thirty-Three's reign.

The phone call appeared innocent enough but the conversation that followed over a pint of Murphy's in the pub two nights later started alarm bells ringing that would bring an end not only to Brian Nelson's nefarious career but also lead to the disbanding of the entire Force Research Unit.

After the usual pleasantries, the FRU handler said, 'Well, I doubt that you asked me for a drink just to say hello. What's up? How can I help?'

'You can't,' the Special Branch man replied, 'but I might be able to help you.'

'Go on.'

'The cat's out of the bag,' said the Special Branch man, teasingly.

'What cat? What bag?'

'Brian Nelson,' was the reply.

'What do you mean?'

'We've known each other for some years now,' said the Branch officer, 'and we've always got on with each other. Now, I don't know if you're personally involved or not; you might not even have any idea what I'm talking about for all I know, but I'm here tonight because your name came up and these Branch people believe that you have been one of the men involved in running Nelson.'

'I know about him,' came the reply.

'A lot?'

'Enough.'

'We're on to Nelson,' said the Special Branch man taking a large gulp of his beer and pulling hard on his cigarette.

The FRU man could tell that his friend had not found it easy to broach the subject of Nelson with him, embarrassed that he might be poking his nose into matters that didn't concern him. He understood the professional rivalry between the Branch and Military Intelligence.

'I hear what you're saying,' said the FRU handler. 'Go on. It's all right. Tell me what you know and what they know,' and he lifted his head as if pointing towards the Branch headquarters.

'All right then,' said his mate, taking a deep breath, 'here goes. We understand that Nelson is more than the UDA's intelligence officer. We understand, but we're not yet certain, that Nelson is in fact being run by your lot. That in fact Nelson is one of your main contacts, ferrying info from your lot to the UDA.'

There was a silence for a full minute, both men looking at each other, wondering how to take the conversation forward and contemplating whether anything more should be said. The Branch man knew that if he had not hit the nail on the head he was very close to it in the accusation he had made.

'Anything else?' asked the handler.

'It depends.'

'What on?'

'On your answer.'

'I won't say nothing right now,' said the handler, 'I prefer to hear what else you've got to say. But I get your drift.'

'The Branch noted a year or so ago that UDA gunmen not only became more active but that most of their targets were people we too had been watching. Sometimes, indeed,' and he chuckled at the thought, 'we thought the UDA had been listening in to our frequencies, reading our notes or whatever, because their targeting and hit rate was spot on.'

'Before you continue,' said the man from the FRU, 'I need another pint. Will you have one?'

'Never say no,' said the Special Branch man handing over his glass.

On his return the handler came straight to the point, asking, 'How much is known?'

'Everything.'

'Shit,' said the handler speaking slowly and obviously thinking hard. 'Who knows?'

'Most of those who should know, like the top brass, but not the great majority of Branch men. They've little or no idea. But Nelson has been watched by our lot for some time. We know he works for the FRU and we know he is employed by the UDA. They pay him a regular wage.'

The other man nodded, saying nothing.

'Do you want me to continue?'

'Aye,' came the somewhat disconsolate reply.

'We've listened to Nelson in Loyalist clubs boasting about his role as the UDA's intelligence officer, talking about the contacts who provide him with top-secret material which he acts upon. He's boasted about some of the jobs too, in front of groups of people as though trying to impress them with his knowledge.' He stopped for a moment to let all this sink in. Then he went on: 'Listen to me; I've stood in a bar and heard Nelson boasting in front of some women about his job, his contacts, the fact that he is the man responsible for organising many of the attacks on the Provos. And they lap it up; they love to hear this brilliant, brave man telling them how the UDA are hitting back at the Provos. He gets off on it, I'm sure.'

'Thanks,' said the handler, 'that's very useful to know. Anything else while we're on the subject?'

'Aye,' came the reply, 'I promise you, I'm advising you as a mate, I'm pleading with you to bring this to a halt before the roof comes fucking crashing down on all of you. I don't know the others, but you and I have been mates for some years, and there will be hell to pay for all this. I promise you that the shit is about to hit the fan and when it does you know where the buck will stop.'

The Special Branch officer had now thrown all caution to the wind and was simply trying to persuade his friend to see what would happen if the Force Research Unit continued running Nelson. 'You and I are the fucking worker bees and we are always the ones who get the shit when anything goes wrong. I am telling you all this because I fear what will happen to you and the fellas like you when all this comes crashing around your heads. You know the guys at the top will run for cover and you'll be left holding the fucking baby. You and your lads are the ones who get the shit thrown at them.'

The handler didn't know how he should respond to this warning. His friend was giving him advice which he knew to be true, advice which he knew he would now have to address and take up with FRU senior officers, warning them of what might be about to hit the whole unit. Before the meeting that night the handler had believed that Nelson's work had been contained inside Military Intelligence. Now he realised that the Special Branch knew everything that was necessary if they ever wanted to pull the rug from under them.

He thought it was time to change the subject. He had heard enough to satisfy himself that the FRU would now have to change tack, perhaps get rid of Nelson and move on despite the success that the relationship had brought during the previous two years.

'Thanks,' he said, firmly shaking the Branch man's hand. 'I mean it. I was afraid that one day it might come to this, but now I know the moment has arrived. You've been a real mate.'

'If you want another chat,' volunteered the Special Branch man, 'you know my number.'

'Yeah, thanks,' said the FRU man. And he was gone.

Within a few weeks of that conversation, a murder would take place in Co. Down which would bring to centre stage Nelson's involvement as the link between British Military Intelligence and the UDA.

One of the Provos' intelligence officers in Co. Down, a man by the name of Loughlin Maginn, had been watched

for some time by the Force Research Unit. His name kept
cropping up among contacts of Provo leaders and Sinn
Fein activists, and the FRU, relying on source reports,
became convinced that Maginn, a poultry dealer in his
twenties who was married with four children, was in fact a
man with close ties to the Provisional IRA. The more they
watched him, the more certain they became that Maginn
used his job dealing in poultry as an excuse to reach
contacts, organise Provo active service units and target
potential victims throughout the county.

During one meeting between Ten-Thirty-Three and his
handlers in a safe-house outside Belfast, Nelson was asked
if he knew anything about John Anthony Loughlin
Maginn who lived in Rathfriland, Co. Down.

'Never heard of him,' replied Nelson.

'We suggest you take a closer look,' he was advised by
one of his handlers. 'We believe he is a keen Provo with
responsibility for Co. Down.'

'Do you have a P-Card?'

'Aye, we do,' said the handler. 'And there is a great deal
of evidence suggesting that Maginn, while driving around
the area selling poultry, also uses his time to target UDR
soldiers, RUC men and prison warders in particular.'

'Any photos?' asked Nelson.

'Yes,' said another handler, 'we have a montage of him,
shot from various angles. All black and white, of course.'

'Great,' replied Nelson examining the photographs.
'With that little lot we should have no problem.'

He was also provided with Maginn's home address and
was told that the target was married to a woman who was
also in her twenties. It was understood the couple had a
young family, but the officers weren't sure whether they
had three or four children.

'Don't worry,' commented Nelson, 'this should be a
piece of cake but we'll have to check out the area first. Do
you know if he's got any protection?'

'Not as far as we know,' he was told, 'but he may well
carry a handgun or, as he deals in poultry and moves
around the country, he may have a shotgun.'

'Great,' replied Nelson. 'I'll inform my people and let you know what success we have.'

Shortly after midnight on Friday, 25 August 1989, while watching a late-night movie on television while lying on the sofa in the living-room of his home, Loughlin Maginn heard the sound of breaking glass. As he got to his feet to see what was going on at that ungodly hour he was hit by a burst of fire from two masked men standing in the garden outside the window and firing indiscriminately into the room. In a bid to escape his attackers, the wounded Maginn stumbled upstairs as the men clambered through the window and chased after him. On the landing he turned towards the killers as though inviting them to shoot him, and was hit several times in the chest.

His wife Maureen, woken up by the gunfire, rushed out of her bedroom to see what was happening only to find her husband crumpled on the landing floor, almost motionless, his body covered with blood. The shots had also woken the couple's children. They ran out of their bedrooms to see what was happening and were confronted by the sight of their father's bloodied body lying on the floor. The children became almost hysterical, running around the house screaming and crying, shocked and terrified by the sight of their dying father and shouting 'Daddy, Daddy, Daddy' over and over again.

Neighbours, woken by the shooting and the screaming, ran in their pyjamas to the house after seeing a car with three men inside drive away. They found Maureen Maginn in a state of shock, unable to take in what had happened to her husband and fearful for her screaming, hysterical children whom neighbours had difficulty in calming as they waited for an ambulance.

A woman who went to help said, 'It was a dreadful heart-rending scene with poor Loughlin lying dead on the floor of the landing, his face and body covered in blood and the children screaming for their daddy. I have never seen a family so torn apart like this; it was truly awful. God, may the men who did this rot in hell.'

Other neighbours reported that for three or more years

Maginn and his wife had been subjected to almost constant harassment by the army and the RUC. A friend of the family, who did not wish to give his name, commented, 'Loughlin made official complaints about harassment both to army commanders and senior RUC officers but it didn't stop them. They never left him alone. They would stop him at vehicle check-points and insist on searching his car; they would repeatedly stop him and ask questions about reasons for his journey, the people he was meeting, the places he was visiting, as though trying to catch him out. They deliberately went out of their way to make his life impossible, harassing him at every turn. And Loughlin would tell me that he had no idea why he was constantly being targeted by the army and the RUC. The only possible reason was the fact that he was a Catholic. He was not a Provo and I'm sure he had never been in any sort of trouble. He was a happily married family man who worked hard for his wife and kids. I feel that he was murdered simply because the army and police were always harassing him and the UFF came to hear about it and put two and two together. If that is the case then both the army and the RUC have a heavy responsibility for they would have been directly responsible for his murder. They must be fucking crazy to kill an innocent man like this.'

So thrilled were they at taking out a man they believed to be a Provo liaison officer that the UDA issued a statement not long after Maginn's murder in which the organisation's leadership boasted that its intelligence material was now of such a high calibre that they 'only' murdered Republican terrorists. Their claim was, of course, untrue – they had murdered many an innocent man, including a number of taxi-drivers and some embarrassing 'own-goals'. In a bid to prove their claim of only targeting terrorists, the UDA, incredibly, published a confidential file belonging to the security forces that identified Maginn as an IRA intelligence officer.

The political response was dramatic and immediate. After discussions between the Northern Ireland Office in London and the Joint Irish Section, the RUC top brass announced they were setting up an official inquiry into allegations that the security services were colluding with Protestant paramilitaries to assassinate Republicans. At that time – the autumn of 1989 – no one outside a small nucleus of senior officers in the security and intelligence services knew of the existence of the Force Research Unit because, officially, it did not exist.

On 15 September 1989, John Stevens, then deputy chief constable of Cambridgeshire Police, was appointed to head the inquiry. He would have a far-reaching remit to question and examine every branch of the security and intelligence services in Northern Ireland which he believed might be relevant to his inquiry. Every branch of the security forces, including the army, the RUC, the Special Branch and Military Intelligence, was expected to co-operate fully.

But the initial inquiry by John Stevens and his team (which included a number of lawyers and senior police officers) held no real concern for the officers and handlers of the Force Research Unit because the Ministry of Defence lawyers – who represented the FRU officers – had no reason to discuss with them the work of the aggressive secret organisation nor of their agent in the field, Ten-Thirty-Three. As a result, FRU handlers were ordered to continue their work as usual but to take extra care when dealing with their primary agent. They were also urged to impress on the overconfident Nelson that he should take great care when going about his business with the UDA.

In a conversation with his handlers shortly after the Stevens Inquiry had begun interviewing senior officers within the security forces, Nelson was asked, 'You've read about this inquiry in the papers, haven't you?'

'Aye,' replied Nelson, 'but it's got nothing to do with me, has it?'

'It's got a lot to do with you if you don't keep quiet and play down the fact that you are the UDA's chief intelligence officer,' he was told.

'Why's that?'

'Because you have been supplying information to the

UDA and the Stevens Inquiry is trying to find out their
source for all this accurate intelligence material.'

'Well, we know that,' said Nelson, 'I'm the source.'

'Exactly,' one handler said.

'So there's no problem then,' he retorted.

'Of course there is a problem, because you are probably
the person they want to talk to more than anyone else.'

'But I work for you,' he said, 'I work for the British
Army. I'm your agent in the field – so how can I possibly
get into any trouble?'

'Because this is the world of intelligence where secrets
are of paramount importance.'

'But if I tell the inquiry that I work for you I can't get
into any trouble, can I?' he asked, confused as to why his
handlers appeared so concerned.

'But you're not supposed to be working for us,' one
handler impressed on him. 'No one, not even the Special
Branch or the government knows you work for Military
Intelligence.'

'But why can't I just tell them the truth? I can't possibly
get into any trouble because I'm paid by you and I work
for you. I'll just say what's what – there can't be any harm
in that.'

'There could be great harm for you if you so much as
whisper that you have worked with us,' he was told. 'You
could be in real trouble, I promise you.'

'Why?' Nelson asked, still failing to understand his
vulnerable position.

'Because as a result of what happened, with people
being targeted and killed, you could face a trial and
possible imprisonment.'

'What the fuck for?'

'Because the authorities would see you as the person
providing the information which resulted in people being
killed.'

'Even when I work for Military Intelligence?' he asked.

'Yes.'

'Fuck me,' replied Nelson. 'No one ever said anything
like this to me when I began working with you lot. I

thought that if I worked for Military Intelligence I would be safeguarded, totally protected by the system.'

'It doesn't work like that.'

'Well, I don't like the sound of this,' he said. 'If I'm asked any questions, I'll have to tell the truth; I've got no option.'

'Have it your way, Brian,' said one, treating him more like an equal than he had ever done before. 'But mark my words. Open your mouth and you'll probably end up in jail doing twenty years.'

'Fuck off,' he replied. 'Twenty years for helping Military Intelligence. Bullshit, that's bollocks.'

'It isn't bullshit. I'm telling you what might happen if you ever broke the law. Understand?'

Those last words, spoken slowly and quietly, seemed to impress Nelson and he slumped back in his chair, thinking hard, saying nothing for a few moments. Finally, looking somewhat downcast, he said, 'Is that the truth, the honest truth?'

'I hope it may never come to that,' the officer told him, 'but I'm just giving you the worst-case scenario. However, it's up to you. If you keep stum then all will be well. But if you open your mouth and blab what's being going on we won't be able to save you. The law will step in and, as I've already told you, you could find yourself banged up for twenty years.'

Nelson wiped the back of his hand across his mouth as though that might help him to think more clearly. Then he said, 'I dunno. I'm not sure about all this. I don't believe I could do time for what I've done. I've done nothing wrong; I've just worked with you fellas, that's all. You're British Army, right? Well, working for the army means I'm protected like you guys. I've just passed on intelligence that you lot have given me, nothing else. If I'm in the shit then you're all in the shit, too. Right?'

'Wrong,' he was told adamantly, 'it doesn't work like that. We're officially employed by the army but you're not. You're an agent and that's different.'

'But that's not fair,' replied Nelson.

'We know it isn't,' said the most senior handler, 'we know it isn't fair but that's the way the system works. If there's any trouble, Brian, the odds are that you will take the blame.'

After a couple of minutes and a few gulps of tea, Nelson said, 'Well, I can't believe that's true but if it is I've got just two options, keep quiet or tell the truth.'

'Quite right,' he was told, 'but one way all will be well and nothing whatsoever will happen to you; the other way, speaking out, could end with you doing time. It's your decision.'

Seconds later, Nelson returned to business. 'Well, what have you got for me?' he asked. 'Any new names, any new targets?'

'Good,' said one handler, 'that's the spirit.' And the three men began to discuss the latest intelligence material.

But the Force Research Unit had finally decided to slow down their supply of intelligence material to Ten-Thirty-Three, telling him that a decision had been taken to lie low for a while until the Stevens Inquiry team had completed their investigation, made their report and gone back to the mainland. They didn't want to alarm Nelson that there had been a change in operational circumstances and tried to show him that, officially at least, nothing had altered. They urged him to continue receiving information from his team of amateur agents around the country and to keep them informed of what was going on, but he was advised not to plan any more killings until the air had cleared.

For their part, the UDA leadership were confident that all the information being provided by Brian Nelson was of the highest calibre. They had no intention of stopping their killing machine simply because some chief constable from the mainland, who had little or no idea of how the politics of Northern Ireland really worked, had started an investigation into the possibility of there being a link between the security services and the Protestant paramilitaries. The UDA command also had confidence that officers and handlers in Military Intelligence would keep their mouths shut. The UDA executive had been

convinced for some time that Brian Nelson was receiving
most of his high-grade source material from the British
Army but the matter was never openly discussed with
Nelson. And it is almost certain that members of the UDA
leadership never met or spoke to Force Research Unit
handlers or officers. They were just happy that Nelson was
providing such first-class information, enabling them to
get on with the job of killing Provo terrorists. They also
knew full well that no matter how long the inquiry team
spent interviewing their UDA members they would never
receive any co-operation, assistance or information that
could possibly be used as evidence against them or their
chief intelligence officer. Their men, their killers, they
believed, were too professional, too committed to the
Loyalist cause to breath a word of what had been going on,
week in, week out.

Behind the scenes, Military Intelligence officers were
preparing the defence, making sure that Stevens was kept
well away from the unreliable Brian Nelson. As soon as the
inquiry had been announced, MI5 officers in Northern
Ireland immediately stopped advising their FRU
counterparts how they should deal with the investigation.
Of course, MI5 knew everything that had been going on,
down to the most insignificant detail. They had read all
the Military Intelligence Source Reports from FRU
handlers, all the MISR supplements, and every one of the
all-important Contact Reports – and, of course,
throughout the years of the FRU's existence, MI5 had
always had one of their officers sharing a room with the
FRU's operations officer. Indeed, in their bid to extricate
themselves from what they feared could become a major
problem, MI5 went as far as informing Military
Intelligence officers that they had originally advised the
FRU not to recruit Nelson as an agent because they
believed he was 'a Walter Mitty character'. In their words,
Nelson 'didn't come up to the mark'. Conveniently, MI5
omitted to mention that they had in fact fought hard to
recruit Nelson themselves, even offering him 'Agent
status', a privileged position. But MI5 had neither

forgotten nor forgiven the FRU for beating them to the punch and landing Nelson as their main operational informant. The moment the Stevens Inquiry was announced, MI5 informed the Force Research Unit that they were on their own.

Ironically, the RUC and the RUC Special Branch, who had originally warned the FRU against recruiting Nelson – describing him as a 'head case' and a 'hot potato' – would come to their rescue in more ways than one.

Those staunch Loyalist RUC officers had never forgotten their own experience when being put through the mill during the Stalker Inquiry into the alleged 'shoot-to-kill' policy. They could not forget how they had felt during that time when their every effort to contain the terrorist situation, to root out the Provo activists, to protect the population from IRA gunmen and bombers, often at great personal risk to their own men, had been brought into question and brushed aside. They remembered all too well how they had felt when John Stalker, a senior officer from the mainland, with no experience whatsoever of fighting a ruthless terrorist organisation like the IRA, had come to Belfast and conducted his investigation. They felt such inquiries by senior mainland police officers were unfair, unnecessary and nothing but a waste of valuable time. In their opinion, such officers were trained for policing a normal, ordinary, decent society – like dealing with traffic offences, according to some RUC officers – and totally ill-equipped to comprehend how a force like the RUC should conduct itself when faced with implacable hatred, shootings and bombings, many such attacks directed at the RUC officers themselves.

Many ordinary RUC officers found the situation intolerable: they had to operate on a daily basis with one hand tied behind their backs and now they had to deal with the additional pressure of having official inquiries hanging over their heads if they dared to handle the terrorists with anything but kid gloves. And many deeply resented the strictures placed on their operations. Many RUC officers involved at street level in combating the

Provos were convinced that the politicians of Westminster
and the civil servants of Whitehall had not the slightest
idea of the life and the pressure their men had to survive
week in, week out, not knowing when they left home each
morning whether they would return that night. As a result,
many were prepared to do all they could to help their FRU
counterparts extricate themselves from what they
perceived to be another unjust, partisan, one-sided
government inquiry.

Of course, this was not the view held by the top brass
of the RUC who, understandably, were expected to give
every assistance to any government-backed inquiry,
whether it was investigating alleged misdemeanours by the
RUC or Military Intelligence.

Initially, the Stevens Inquiry team had no interest in the
Force Research Unit for they had been called in to check
the alleged supply of intelligence material from the RUC,
the Special Branch or the Ulster Defence Regiment to
Loyalist paramilitary organisations. The FRU were not in
any way in the frame, nor were they considered a possible
conduit of reliable intelligence to any of the Loyalist
groups. There had been rumours that a young woman
employed by the UDR had been involved in giving
material to a lance-corporal in a British regiment who had
been passing on the material to Loyalist paramilitaries. As
a result, the investigation concentrated on such possible
links to determine whether the supply of intelligence to
the Loyalists was rife within the security services or simply
confined to this one single alleged breach.

Some weeks after John Stevens and his team arrived in
Belfast, they began to hear rumours and bits and pieces of
information from those they were interviewing within the
RUC that much of the source material reaching the
Loyalist paramilitaries had originated from the UDA's
chief intelligence officer, a man by the name of Brian
Nelson. At this stage the Stevens team had no idea that
Nelson worked directly for the Force Research Unit, an
organisation which, in fact, they did not know even
existed. It was in the late autumn of 1989 that they came

to the conclusion that they should bring in Brian Nelson for an interview.

That news sent shockwaves through the Force Research Unit – though they had of course been expecting such a move. At urgent meetings between the officers and handlers, they way they should react to this threat was discussed. Many options were considered and but the question that kept coming up was whether they should put their trust in Brian Nelson, the lad from the Shankill Road whose reputation since the first weeks he was employed by Military Intelligence had been decidedly dodgy.

At one time, Military Intelligence considered resettling Nelson outside Northern Ireland, giving him a completely new identity and settling him a long way from the Province, either in Australia or Canada. They believed that if they took that course of action the investigation would probably take such a long time to trace Nelson and bring him back to Belfast that the political momentum behind the whole investigation would have subsided.

In the end, though, they agreed they had little option but to put their faith in Nelson. They decided to have another candid chat with their man, whom they believed was now in a position to save their jobs and their reputations. More than that, indeed, for there was little doubt that if Nelson confessed there was a real possibility that countless serious charges would be brought against FRU personnel and result in long prison sentences. FRU officers and handlers had to hope and pray that, although MI5 had decided to let them sink or swim, their valuable work in disrupting the Provos and their ASUs had earned them the support of the Thatcher government. They feared that if the government, urged on by the media, also threw their demand for legal action behind the Stevens Inquiry, there would then be the most serious moves to denounce totally and prosecute the FRU officers and disband the unit.

As usual, Nelson was picked up by a car and brought to a safe-house. He was firstly asked whether he was fully aware of the Stevens Inquiry.

'Aye,' he said.

'What exactly have you heard?'

'Well, you told me to watch my step and that's what I'm doing,' he replied.

'You do realise how serious this matter is becoming, don't you?'

'Aye, everyone is talking about it.'

'Have you said anything yourself?'

'Not much.'

'Well, listen, listen very carefully. If you keep quiet and say nothing, everything will go away, understand?'

'Aye.'

'But if you open your mouth and begin talking, the shit will hit the fan and you will be for the high jump.'

'Why? Why me?' he asked.

'Because you would be in the frame, that's why. Because you have given information to the UDA which has resulted in people being killed.'

'But only on your orders,' Nelson protested.

'Not our orders,' the FRU handler said, 'only our advice. What you did with that advice was your responsibility. Get it?'

'No, not really. I thought we were in this together. I thought I was part of your team.'

'You are an agent, an informant, working with us, that's true. But you are still responsible. Do you understand?'

'So who knows what went on?' Nelson asked, confused as to all the fuss.

'No one knows and no one will know if you keep your mouth shut. That's all you've got to do, keep quiet. Okay?'

'But who's going to ask questions?'

The FRU handlers looked at each other in desperation. It was obvious that Ten-Thirty-Three had no idea of what the Stevens Inquiry was all about.

'Members of the Stevens team might want to interview you about what you know, what you did, what your connection was with the UDA and with us.'

'So what do I tell them?' he asked looking from one handler to the other.

'Nothing,' he was told, 'absolutely nothing.'

'But I will have to tell them something.'

'Tell them that you simply gave us information about various people, information that you received from your men in the field, your intelligence agents dotted about the Province.'

'Okay, then,' he replied, 'that's easy.'

'Good,' said an FRU officer, 'anything else?'

'No,' said Nelson, 'that'll be fine. But do you know when they will be questioning me?'

'No idea,' he was told, 'any time during the next week or so, we would imagine. But, remember, as long as you say nothing and just talk about your fellas in the field, everything will be fine.'

'That's okay then,' he said. 'Is that all?'

'That's it, that's all. Okay?'

Nelson was dropped off as usual and the FRU personnel gathered once more, discussing whether Ten-Thirty-Three could be trusted. They concluded that their future was in the lap of the gods; they were not convinced that Nelson understood the seriousness of the inquiry or why he might be questioned and cross-examined. They could only wait and see.

And they didn't have long to wait.

Forearmed with mounting evidence that Nelson was the vital link between the Protestant paramilitaries and the security forces, the RUC were asked to raid the UDA's offices in a bid to determine exactly what evidence could be discovered that might prove this link. Not unsurprisingly, Nelson's fingerprints were discovered on some security-force documents found at the Loyalist headquarters. Stevens let it be known that he would be interviewing Brian Nelson some time shortly after the team returned from Christmas and New Year leave. The arrest was planned for dawn on Thursday, 11 January.

Two days before this date Nelson was asked to attend a safe-house meeting with his FRU handlers and was told that it might be better for him if he was to leave Northern Ireland for a while and spend a period on the mainland.

'Why the fuck should I do that?' he enquired, somewhat puzzled by the turn of events.

'To protect you,' a FRU handler told him.

'Protect me from what?'

'From questions, from the inquiry.'

'But I don't need any protection,' argued Nelson, 'I've got you people to defend me.'

'It's not that simple. It might be better for you to go to England; lie low for a while, just until this blows over.' He was not told during that interview that the Stevens Inquiry had asked the RUC to arrest him at dawn in two days' time.

'What shall I do for money?' asked Nelson. 'Where shall I go?'

He was handed three hundred pounds in cash and a return ferry ticket to the mainland and advised where to go and stay. Later that day an FRU handler visited Nelson's Belfast home and gave his wife a hundred pounds to cover any expenses she might incur while her husband was away. Nelson left home with an overnight bag that evening and, accompanied by a handler, was taken in an FRU car to Larne where he caught the ferry to England.

Hours before Nelson was due to be arrested, four officers from the Stevens Inquiry returned to their Belfast offices in an RUC headquarters complex that was under twenty-four-hour armed guard. As they walked along the passage to their suite of offices they noticed the smell of burning and then saw smoke seeping out from under the door to their offices. When they unlocked the door they discovered a fire raging beneath a table on which many of their files and witness statements were stacked.

One of the officers smashed a nearby fire alarm with the heel of her shoe and pressed the alarm button. Nothing happened. She sprinted up the stairs to the second-floor landing and tried to activate that alarm. Again nothing happened. She ran to a telephone to call 999 but there was no dialling tone. She did manage to get through to the RUC headquarters operator only to be told, inexplicably, that the phone lines were down.

In the meantime, the other three members of the inquiry team tried to tackle the blaze but their efforts were useless against the flames. By the time the fire brigade did arrive, the hoses connected and the blaze put out, most of the witness statements and files had been totally destroyed.

Stevens and his team were convinced that the fire had been started deliberately even though their offices were in an armed RUC complex that was under constant guard. The RUC's own internal investigation concluded that the fire was undoubtedly an inside job. They later briefed journalists that the fire appeared to have been started by someone carelessly discarding a lighted cigarette.

Stevens and his team were beside themselves with rage that the RUC – at some level – had obviously been privy to a conspiracy to set fire to the documents; they were also angered by the RUC's internal investigation, which they described as 'a travesty and a disgrace'. The RUC's report into the blaze neglected to mention that two alarms had failed to work that night, though the report did state that there was 'nothing sinister' about the failure of the telephones because, they claimed, 'it often happened'.

An attempt had been made in the RUC report to explain why the intruder alarms in the inquiry team's offices had failed to go off. The system was connected to the RUC's Belfast Regional Control. It had been switched on at 10 p.m. when the team had left the office to take a much-needed break. When forensic scientists tested the alarm thirteen days after the fire, they found that what was left of it was in good working order.

One senior officer on Stevens' team commented at the time: 'Of all the offices, of all the police stations, of all the nights, the fire starts right next to the fruits of our investigation . . . and it's an accident?'

Nothing was said at the time to Stevens or his team but there were those in the RUC and the Special Branch who recalled that something very similar had occurred in an RUC station during the Stalker investigation. On that occasion a locked safe in the offices used by the Stalker team had been opened, the contents taken out and set alight. Valuable documents, files and statements had been destroyed. And, once again, no one was ever found to have been responsible for these actions.

One week after the fire Brian Nelson returned to Belfast and was duly arrested by the RUC and handed over to the Stevens Inquiry team for questioning. Those at FRU headquarters held their breath, wondering if their agent would keep his part of the bargain and say nothing. Within hours they heard from the RUC that Nelson was 'singing like the proverbial canary'.

Brian Nelson informed the Stevens team that he had been recruited by the Force Research Unit and employed by them, receiving detailed information from them on the names and addresses of Republicans whom the UDA should target and take out. He gave exact details, precise information and names and addresses of IRA terrorists whom the FRU had suggested his UDA colleagues should kill. And he named his FRU handlers.

After debriefing Nelson for weeks, the inquiry's next step was to interview the Force Research Unit handlers whom Nelson had named as his co-conspirators in the many plots to murder Republican activists. It appeared there was little they could do to defend their actions during the previous two years. Fortunately for the FRU, however, there was a way out.

It had been decided at the very outset of Nelson's notorious career that each time he was interviewed, briefed or debriefed at any of the safe-houses, a record should be kept on tape of everything that was said, both by the handlers and by Nelson. Nothing would be destroyed, so, after every interview, the tapes were methodically locked away in a safe for some future occasion when they might be needed as evidence. These tapes were immediately handed over to the investigators. The Stevens team, who spent hour upon hour listening to every recording, taking notes and discussing the questions and answers, were puzzled by what they heard. On a number of the tapes it appeared that Nelson was providing the FRU with intelligence material, not the other way round as Nelson had claimed. And if that was the case, both the FRU and the Stevens team knew full well, there would be no case to answer. It seemed from many of Nelson's conversations that the FRU were trying to obtain information – in other words, simply carrying out a difficult job to the best of their ability.

All was not quite as it seemed. The tapes that the Stevens team had been handed were indeed a complete set of recordings of Nelson's interviews with his handlers, but many of the more delicate matters involving the targeting and killing of Republican activists had been conducted either before the tapes were switched on or after they had been turned off. This was why Nelson's conversations with FRU officers were stilted, affected and sometimes disingenuous. As a result, the team never did discover the precise details of those vital, all-important conversations. It was extremely fortunate for the FRU, as well as MI5 officers serving in Northern Ireland at that time, that the full transcripts of those conversations were never revealed because the Stevens Inquiry might well have tried to force the issue and bring a number of those responsible to court on the most serious of charges.

Some members of the team did smell a rat and decided to push the FRU as hard as possible to hand over all the files relating to Ten-Thirty-Three – including the all-important Contact Reports, laboriously and meticulously written out by the handlers and sent forward to their officers and MI5. Indeed, some of these Contact Reports were even forwarded, usually on request, to the Prime Minister's Joint Intelligence Committee. To all intents and purposes, they contained all the relevant details of the conversations in the safe-house meetings, and they were most detailed.

The Force Research Unit, backed by Military Intelligence, were determined not to hand over these reports – they knew they could be used against them if the authorities considered the Unit had a case to answer. It was recognised throughout Military Intelligence that some of those Contact Reports were extremely damaging.

Detective Chief Superintendent Vincent McFadden, Stevens's deputy, knew all about the intelligence service's famous Contact Reports, and appreciated how valuable such material could be in this particular case. He asked the FRU to hand them over.

This request put senior Military Intelligence officers in an appalling position: if they refused the request it was obvious they wanted to hide the evidence from the inquiry team; if they readily gave up the reports, they would be handing over crucial evidence to the investigators. They decided to play for time. Senior officers and the handlers who had been closely involved with Ten-Thirty-Three knew that the evidence contained in those Contact Reports would be all but conclusive proof of collusion between Nelson and the security services. The fear among Army Intelligence chiefs was that some of the evidence included in those written documents could form the basis of charges of conspiracy to murder against their FRU officers and handlers.

A long and bitter dispute followed with McFadden demanding the documents and Military Intelligence withholding them. That dispute, which went on for weeks, was resolved only when McFadden threatened to arrest senior army officers on a charge of obstruction of justice. Sir John Walters, General Officer Commanding forces in Northern Ireland, was, at one point, summoned back from leave and, as a result, the relevant files were eventually handed over.

After weeks of closely examining the Contact Reports and debating the evidence they revealed, Stevens's team summoned officers and handlers of the Force Research Unit one by one to be interviewed. The Ministry of Defence employs their own band of first-class army officers who are also lawyers and they were immediately drafted in to represent anyone called to give evidence before the inquiry. Every officer and handler who gave evidence was represented by a Legal Officer who sat with them throughout, advising when and when not to answer the questions thrown at them. The interviews would go on for hours at a time, with the Stevens lawyers delving ever deeper and the army officers resisting their attempts to implicate the FRU in any law-breaking.

In May 1990 John Stevens published a preliminary report revealing nothing about the army's Force Research Unit or its dealings with Brian Nelson. At that stage of the inquiry, Stevens's conclusion was that any collusion between the security forces and the Protestant paramilitaries had been 'neither widespread nor institutionalised', involving no more than the leaking to the paramilitaries of standard security-force documents on Republicans suspected of terrorism. These were available to almost every police officer and soldier in the Province.

But Stevens had every intention of pursuing the matter with ever more vigour. He believed that Military Intelligence had been guilty of collusion at the very least and was determined to find out as much as he could.

It appeared to Military Intelligence that John Stevens had turned his investigation into a personal crusade, determined to persuade those in power that the FRU officers and handlers should be charged with certain offences pertaining to Nelson and the paramilitaries and be brought to court.

At this stage of his investigation Stevens was not sure how serious those charges were but he was adamant that those responsible should be charged and made to face the consequences in a court of law.

But John Stevens was never aware that the Force Research Unit was originally set up to undertake aggressive intelligence, carrying the battle on the streets to the Provos, harassing them and disrupting their campaign of terror in Northern Ireland and the mainland. Nor did he have any idea that not only did MI5 know precisely what was going on inside the unit on a day-to-day basis, but that they were also responsible for sending weekly reports on its activities to the Home Office as well as to the Joint Intelligence Committee which usually met weekly at 10 Downing Street. Indeed, in an effort to conceal their involvement in the Nelson affair, MI5 officers gave evidence to the Stevens Inquiry that they had no knowledge of the agent's assassination conspiracies.

Unhappy with that point-blank denial, John Stevens took the matter further, asking to interview MI5's Director and Co-ordinator of Intelligence, who claimed that it had never been MI5's policy to collude with the UDA in killing Provisional IRA activists. Stevens was convinced that MI5 officers and their director were being economical with the truth.

After months of further investigation throughout 1990, John Stevens wrote his second report. It painted a totally different picture from that which appeared in the preliminary document of May 1990. This report pulled no punches. It set out the evidence that the Force Research Unit had colluded with the UDA in targeting members of the Provisional IRA, relying for much of its substance on the inquiry team's long debriefing of Brian Nelson. The file was passed to the Director of Public Prosecutions, Northern Ireland, but, after close consultation with Sir Patrick Mayhew, then the Attorney-General, the decision was taken not to prosecute any officer or handler of the Force Research Unit. Only Nelson would be charged.

John Stevens pushed hard to persuade the government to publish his report. He believed it would create such a furore in the media that the government would be forced to prosecute members of the Force Research Unit. But such a decision could have backfired on the government; they did not know whether the officers charged would have been prepared to carry the can or whether they would have told the court of others who had been aware of exactly what was going during Brian Nelson's three years as an agent. And, of course, the government were obliged to protect their Intelligence operations at all costs, especially as the Provisionals still seemed intent on bombing and shooting their way to power in the Province, regardless of the loss of life that policy entailed. Mrs Thatcher, too, may not have wished to hand Sinn Fein and the IRA such a worldwide propaganda coup where British Military Intelligence officers had to face charges of conspiracy to murder in open court.

During the following year scores of meetings were held involving Military Intelligence, the Director of Public Prosecutions, Chief Constable John Stevens and a host of lawyers, including the all-important army lawyers, in a battle over the charges Nelson would face. Throughout those discussions Nelson pleaded innocent to all the charges. He believed he had done nothing wrong in defending Northern Ireland from the Provo gunmen and bombers. He could not accept that he was to be taken to court on charges which could result in twenty years in jail, when Military Intelligence personnel were being let off the hook, despite advising, encouraging and providing vast amounts of information which permitted the UDA to carry out their attacks.

Finally, after months of legal wrangling, a deal was struck which Nelson reluctantly agreed to. It was agreed that he would not face any murder charges but that he would plead guilty to five charges of conspiracy to murder, fourteen charges of collecting information likely to assist acts of terrorism and one charge of possessing a sub-machine-gun. As a result Nelson would be jailed for a total of ten years but, with remission, and the time he had spent on remand, he would be out in 1994. Military Intelligence persuaded Nelson that after he had completed his prison sentence he would accept a complete change of identity, relocation to anywhere in the world that would take him, a three-bedroomed house worth around £100,000 and a lump sum in excess of £75,000. In return, Nelson agreed never to relate his experiences and never to write a book about his relationship with the UDA and British Military Intelligence.

Despite these arrangements and the assurances that he would only serve a couple of years or so in prison, it was a reluctant Brian Nelson who finally stepped up to the dock at Belfast Crown Court on Wednesday, 22 January 1992. He pleaded guilty to all the charges as arranged and heard the prosecution say that a decision had been taken not to go ahead with fifteen other charges, including two of murder, after a Crown lawyer told the court: 'This decision has been taken after a scrupulous assessment of the

possible evidential difficulties and a rigorous examination
of the interests of justice.'

For the prosecution, Mr Brian Kerr QC told the court
that on Nelson's appointment as senior intelligence officer
with the UDA he gained a considerable volume of UDA
information which was built upon and supplemented by
his own activities. It consisted of information on possible
victims for assassination whom they regarded as legitimate
targets. Kerr argued that it was the Crown's case that in the
collection of information about those individuals – often
carried out with great assiduousness and ingenuity –
Nelson had played a pivotal role.

Later, Kerr would contend that it was evident that
although Nelson was in contact with his army handlers, he
did not relay important information promptly, and on
some occasions not at all. He added that during the period
of the offences, Nelson was in regular contact with his
handlers and in some cases gave quite extensive information about his activities, but there was ample evidence
that there were occasions when the information passed on
was neither as detailed nor as comprehensive as it could
and should have been.

A week later the court case against Nelson was resumed
and an unnamed colonel in Military Intelligence spoke of
the alleged reasons why Nelson had agreed to join the
service. 'Nelson,' the colonel said, 'was motivated by team
spirit and loyalty to the army. I have no doubt it was not
out of loyalty to the UDA. I have no doubt it was to make
up for past misdemeanours, to save lives and eventually to
bring down the terrorist organisation.'

And then the officer claimed in graphic detail what
happened to Nelson when he was suspected of being an
informer. 'He was taken to a house on the outskirts of
Lisburn. Three times an electrified cattle-prod was applied
to the back of his neck, throwing him in convulsions on to
the floor. He was assaulted and brutalised but was
eventually released.' The night Nelson claimed he was
assaulted and tortured he was in fact injured during a
drunken brawl over a young woman.

But accurate statements of his vital work on behalf of Military Intelligence were also discussed in court. Nelson's defence counsel, Desmond Boal QC, explained in some detail: 'Nelson's identity was known to a very small number of people within the security services, such as senior Special Branch officers within the RUC and senior members of the security services. He wasn't, however, an RUC agent . . . In other words, Nelson's information was passed around throughout the intelligence community and at a high level. Because of that he has to be considered a very important agent of some standing.'

But many other statements made to that Belfast Crown Court concerning Nelson and his role were problematic. It was claimed that the agent was a prolific provider of information and that the Army Intelligence unit produced 730 reports concerning threats to 217 individuals as a result of Nelson's information; that large amounts of UDA intelligence material was passed from the UDA to Nelson's home; that army handlers helped Nelson move UDA documents to a new address; and that the army photocopied UDA documents for Nelson.

In mitigation, Desmond Boal said that Nelson had been of enormous service to the community and that many lives had been saved as a result of his activities; that Nelson had not been loyal to the UDA but loyal to the army. He concluded: 'Nelson was a victim of the system, and his was a case that should be regarded as wholly exceptional.'

Jailing Nelson for ten years, Lord Justice Basil Kelly said that the forty-four-year-old UDA intelligence officer had gone beyond what was required of him by the army and involved himself with the murder gangs. The judge believed Nelson had played a 'double game', working with the UDA and as an agent for Army Intelligence, 'that he had with the greatest courage submitted himself to constant danger and intense strain for three years . . . and that he had passed on possibly life-saving information in respect of 217 threatened individuals.'

Ten-Thirty-Three's short period as a double agent

raised many serious issues relating to policing, covert intelligence and the administration of justice in Northern Ireland. In the Brian Nelson affair the facts have revealed that senior government ministers, MI5 and Military Intelligence came to the conclusion that it was justifiable for the authorities to violate the rule of law in fighting a 'dirty war'. It has happened in other democracies faced with similar threats. Those who say such a decision can never be justified will be accused of living in a dream world; those who accept that the means justifies the end will be accused of descending to the level of the terrorists, abandoning the moral high ground which separates the lawful from the lawless.